YOU CAN "DO IT YOURSELF" DIVORCE

THE STEPS TO A SUCCESSFUL DIVORCE

COPYRIGHT 1992 — The Forms Man, Inc.

Preparing Yourself and Your Family
How to make the right decision for you and your family.
Helping the children through it.

Understanding the Law
A simple guide in English not legalese to the terms
and concepts involved.

Making Successful Decisions
A step by step guide showing you how to make the
difficult decisions:
- Custody and visitation
- Property distribution
- Child support
- Maintenance

Writing Your Agreement
A step by step guide to drawing up the agreement you
need. Easy to understand examples and blank forms included.

Filing Your Divorce

Can save anyone money, pain, and emotional
trauma.

Designed for anyone contemplating or seeking a
legal separation or divorce.

A must read book before you pay thousands of dollars for advice.

Can be used by everyone seeking a divorce.

Takes you through the "steps" from start to finish.

VALID IN ALL 50 STATES
Subject to Local Laws

Includes worksheets for collecting data and making decisions.

by **Eric R. Lutker, Ph.D. & Carl F. Wand, Esq.** ISBN #1-879191-06-7

PREFACE

In more than forty five years of combined experience working with divorcing couples and families in distress, we have seen countless examples of the destruction caused by divorce and custody battles which often rage for years and leave devastated couples and children in their wake.

We believe that in most cases, the problems are caused or exacerbated by the very same system that is supposed to help resolve disputes and protect the rights of individuals. Our adversarial legal system does not serve the needs of matrimonial and family disputants.

This belief led us to found The Mediation Center, a comprehensive mediation center dedicated to the resolution of disputes via non-adversarial means.

Mediation has helped many couples to resolve their situations with far less trauma, expense and in less time than previously thought possible with the traditional adversarial system. It has worked!

Now in this book we present an additional alternative means of matrimonial dissolution: self-directed agreement through The Steps to a Successful Divorce. We believe this will work too.

We would like to thank our families, friends and former clients for helping us to formulate the ideas and methods presented here. We also have a special gratitude to Carol Jensen Lutker who spent many hours editing the text.

We also thank you, the readers, for using this book and advancing the cause of alternative dispute resolution techniques which will benefit others in the future.

April, 1992
Eric R. Lutker, Ph.D.
Carl F. Wand, Esq.
The Mediation Center
Long Island, New York

i

INTRODUCTION

Millions of Americans have become the victims of unsuccessful divorces. The unsuccessful divorce is one which devastates the family financially and emotionally. It leads to ongoing conflict because of dissatisfaction with the divorce agreement. It often results in continued harassment, litigation, or unfulfilled obligations such as child support, visitation, or spousal maintenance.

There have been numerous studies documenting the damage done to children, couples, and extended families by the divorce process. Researchers have discovered that not only is the damage wide spread, but that it is also long lasting. Some aspects of the unsuccessful divorce which cause the greatest amount of damage are the anger, the long periods of time living in a state of confusion and uncertainty, the inability of divorced and separated people to maintain communication, the general rage engendered by the process itself, and the financial stress of marital dissolution. With the growing number of divorces the courts have become more crowded, causing additional delays. As a result legal fees have increased significantly. The system seems to be breaking down and is certainly not meeting the needs of the people. Given these conditions, many professionals in the field have hypothesized that the damage wrought by divorce may in fact, be due more to the process than to the fact of divorce itself.

As a result more people seeking divorce or separation are using alternative dispute resolution methods. The object of these alternatives is to create a situation in which neither one spouse nor the children end up losers, but rather, the parties can achieve a successful divorce and feel satisfied with the result.

THE SUCCESSFUL DIVORCE

The successful divorce is one in which both parties feel they have been heard, and had an opportunity to have input in the formulation of the divorce agreement. A sense of fairness and equitability usually predominates even through the pain. The terms of the agreement are adhered to and there is enough communication so that changed circumstances can be dealt with constructively. Children are not as devastated and both spouses can go on with their lives with a minimum of disruption. The successful divorce is one in which both parties win. The win-win techniques which are gaining greater acceptance at this time are mediation and "self planned" divorces.

In mediation, rather than using opposing counsel in the adversarial way, those seeking divorce or separation use the services of an expert neutral mediator who can help them reach agreement on all of the issues so that they can draw up and process a legal separation or divorce agreement. Do-it-yourselfers attempt to do the same thing without utilizing the services of a third party. In the do-it-yourself mode it is obviously very important to do some personal research and study so that you are knowledgeable about what has to be done.

In *The Steps To A Successful Divorce* we have provided a structured approach to completing a successful divorce or separation. The steps are:

1) Preparing Yourself and Your Family
2) Understanding the Law
3) Reaching Agreement
4) Writing Your Agreement, and
5) Filing Your Divorce

This approach allows you to systematically achieve agreement together in a way that promotes mutual satisfaction with the end result. In addition, the steps teach you methods of successfully communicating with each other so that you can deal not only with the issues at hand, but also with post-divorce situations as they arise.

HOW TO USE THIS BOOK

This book is designed to be used by almost anyone considering a separation or divorce, and with it most people can achieve a successful divorce. It is divided into five steps. The first two involve preparing yourself and your family for the process ahead, as well as understanding the law involved in divorce or separation. All of the financial considerations are thoroughly discussed. There are worksheets for your use in assembling the financial information. Proper preparation of the family and an understanding of the law will enable anyone, whether they pursue the adversarial route, use mediation, or do-it-themselves, to understand the process and be better prepared.

The third step, Making The Decisions, is designed primarily for people who are going to use mediation or try to work out their own agreement. Most people utilizing this section of the book will find that many of the decisions which have to be made can be reached on their own. This means that less time will have to be spent with the mediator or legal counsel.

This can save time and energy and might also lead to substantial financial benefits. If you follow the format of the book, you will write your own Memorandum of Agreement.

The fourth step, Drawing Your Agreement, is for people who have opted to do the bulk of the work on their own, and includes samples of legal forms.

The final step, Filing Your Divorce, provides an overview of the kinds of documents that must be filed to achieve a divorce.

With these things in mind the authors wish you the best of luck in getting through the difficult task before you.

DISCLAIMER

This book is presented to help you become knowledgeable and prepare for divorce or separation and to aid you in reaching agreement with your spouse. It is not the province of this book to provide legal advice or to claim to produce specific legal rulings in any jurisdiction where such action might be prohibited by statute. Because of the changing nature of laws in the various states, and the range and complexity of special situations, the authors, publishers and distributors of this book disclaim all responsibility for consequences of actions taken based on information in this book. Users of this book should check with their court system regarding the specific statutes and proceedures in their jurisdiction and obtain competent legal counsel or other expert advice if required. No representations, either express or implied, are made regarding the legal consequences of the use of any information contained in this book.

TABLE OF CONTENTS

PREFACE i

INTRODUCTION v

STEP I PREPARING YOURSELF AND YOUR FAMILY FOR A 1
SUCCESSFUL DIVORCE

CHAPTER 1 MAKING THE DECISION; OR "HAVE I DONE 1
ENOUGH TO SAVE THE MARRIAGE"?
The failed marriage. The decision to separate.
Have I done enough to save my marriage?

CHAPTER 2 WHAT IS A DIVORCE AND HOW WILL IT 5
AFFECT ME AND MY FAMILY?
The effects of divorce. The divorced individual.
Effects on children.

CHAPTER 3 DECIDING HOW TO PROCEED 8
Constructive discussion. The economics of divorce.
Telling the children and family. Talking to others.

CHAPTER 4 THE OPTIONS AVAILABLE 11
Separation vs. divorce. Annulment. Divorce counseling.
How to get there. Using lawyers: the adversarial approach.
Mediation. Doing it yourself. Combined methods. Now what?

STEP II UNDERSTANDING THE LAW 13
CHAPTER 5 GROUNDS FOR DIVORCE 15
No fault divorce. Fault grounds.

CHAPTER 6 CHILD CUSTODY AND VISITATION 18
Joint custody. Joint custody with child's primary physical
residence with one parent. Sole custody. Visitation rights.
When custody is in dispute. Change of custody. Separation of siblings.

CHAPTER 7 CHILD SUPPORT
Medical insurance. Life insurance. Taxes. College.
Collection of Child Support.

CHAPTER 8 MAINTENANCE OR SPOUSAL SUPPORT 22
Considerations in arriving at maintenance. Temporary maintenance
while a case is pending. Maintenance distinguished from child
support. Health and life insurance. Tax considerations.

CHAPTER 9 PROPERTY DISTRIBUTION 25
Marital property. Separate property. Conversion of separate to
marital property. Appreciation of separate property. Marital
liabilities. The marital home.
Pension/retirement benefits.   The license or enhanced earnings
as a marital asset. The business as an asset. The distributive award.

STEP III REACHING AGREEMENT AND MAKING DECISIONS 31

CHAPTER 10 GROUND RULES 32
You don't have to fight. The ground rules for successful agreement.
Professional counseling. Violence.

CHAPTER 11 ORGANIZING YOUR DATA 35
What to collect. The detailed financial statement. Budgeting.

CHAPTER 12 MAKING THE DECISIONS 44
The Memorandum of Agreement. Getting started. Basic data.
Listing of marital assets. Listing marital liabilities.
The asset and liability tables.

CHAPTER 13 PARENTING FOR THE FUTURE 47
General principles. Physical custody. Shared or joint physical custody.
Visitation schedules. Special occasions and emergencies. Extended
vacations. Change of residence. Renegotiation and impasse.
The sharing of information. Decision making or legal custody.
Finalizing your parenting agreement.

CHAPTER 14 CHILD SUPPORT 56
Homework. Who should pay. Pro-rata sharing. Statutory guidelines.
Need based guidelines. What has to be paid for? Modification of support.

CHAPTER 15 DECIDING ON DISTRIBUTION OF 59
MARITAL PROPERTY AND LIABILITIES
Common assets and liabilities. The successful agreement process.
The furniture quandary. The big debt problem. Pension decisions.
The family business. Making it all legal.

CHAPTER 16 DECIDING ON SPOUSAL SUPPORT 63
OR MAINTENANCE.
The factors influencing spousal maintenance.
Preparing for your discussion. Other factors.

CHAPTER 17 INSURANCE DECISIONS 66
Disability insurance. Health insurance. Life insurance.

CHAPTER 18 MAKING TAX DECISIONS 69
Using tax benefits. Moving on.

STEP IV DRAWING YOUR AGREEMENT 71
CHAPTER 19 WHAT IS AN AGREEMENT 71
Preamble. Property distribution . Marital residence. Responsibility
for debts. Custody and visitation. Child support. Life insurance.
College education. Spousal maintenance.

STEP V FILING YOUR DIVORCE 84
Overview of the divorce process.

CHAPTER 20 SAMPLE FORMS 85
The Summons. The Complaint. The Answer. The Judgement of Divorce.
The Qualified Domestic Relations Order (QDRO).

CHAPTER 21 APPEARANCE IN COURT 93
CONCLUSION

APPENDICES:

TABLE 1 DIVORCE DECISION WORKSHEET **95**

TABLE 2 STATE PROVISIONS REGARDING DIVORCE **97**

TABLE 3 LIST OF MARITAL ASSETS **99**

TABLE 4 HOUSEHOLD ITEMS INVENTORY CHECKLIST **101**

TABLE 5 FINANCIAL STATEMENT **103**

TABLE 6 PENSION VALUATION FORM **104**

TABLE 7 MONTHLY EXPENSE BUDGET FORMS A, B, C **105**

TABLE 8 MEMORANDUM OF AGREEMENT **106**

TABLE 9 SCHEDULES OF TIMES & ACTIVITIES **107**

TABLE 10 WANT LIST OF ASSETS AND LIABILITIES **117**

TABLE 11 SAMPLE MATRIMONIAL AGREEMENT **123**
(STIPULATION OF SETTLEMENT)

STEP I
PREPARING YOURSELF AND YOUR FAMILY FOR A SUCCESSFUL DIVORCE

CHAPTER ONE

MAKING THE DECISION; OR "HAVE I DONE ENOUGH TO SAVE THE MARRIAGE?"

Life has its ups and downs, and some rough spots are unavoidable in every marriage. Most of us consider divorce at one time or another, but many years of experience have shown us that the best course is to save a marriage, if possible. There are cases, however, when after all attempts at saving the union have failed, it is necessary to end a marriage, and this may be the only choice available for you and your children.

For almost everyone, divorce represents a failure. There are many reasons for keeping a marriage together, and relationships can change over time in a healthy way. So even a bad situation can improve. In addition, marriage is not just a two party arrangement. Marriages involve children, extended families, complex vocational, financial, and social networks and also provide each member of the couple with a great many conveniences that enable them to live life more easily.

For many years people believed that marriages should always stay together for the benefit of children. During the tumultuous 1960's it became much more acceptable to say that individual needs may supersede the needs of the family. The rationalization supporting this was that a bad marriage is a poor example and damaging to children. This made divorce or separation much more acceptable. In addition, a focus on individual growth and satisfaction made being "tied down" anathema to many. Since then, we've seen a tremendous growth in the divorce rate and less emphasis on keeping the marriage together.

Recent research indicates, however, that the damage done to children by a marital breakup may be much more extreme than previously thought. The indications are that children are almost always harmed and this harm can last for many years creating problems for children of divorce even when they are adults.

More people today are recognizing that there are dangers to health as well as numerous inconveniences involved in divorce. As a result, we see a flattening of the growth rate in divorce and separation, and the rebirth of the idea that it might be better to work on the marriage.

The necessity of earning a living and the difficulties of supporting two households on income that previously supported one, are also very real factors influencing people to keep a marriage together. The need to spend a great deal of time building a career limits the time and energy that one has for building new relationships and finding new social circles.

In summary, there are a number of reasons to keep a marriage together: the welfare of the children, the convenience, the financial benefits, social connections, and others. Given these reasons, one must ask *why do marriages fail?*

THE FAILED MARRIAGE

Marriages fail for many reasons but unmet expectations almost always play a major role. We enter the marriage with very complex and sometimes unrealistic expectations. Whether we were brought up with the "Brady Bunch" or the "Addams Family" we all have an idea of what to expect in our marriage and family. When these expectations are met, we feel that we have been successful. When the relationship does not meet these expectations, we often feel as though we've failed and this can lead to disappointment, depression, or anger. Whether we blame ourselves or our partners for the failure does not seem to be terribly relevant. The bottom line is, that when the failed expectations are great, our disappointment is great. The greater the disappointment the greater the likelihood that a marriage will break apart.

Another source of trouble for marriages is the loss of a job or financial reverses, which can upset even the rosiest of relationships. Often intimate or sexual relationships change because of external pressures, new circumstances, or the maturational process. Our society is exceedingly mobile and this may mean that one partner is required by his or her job responsibilities to move to another part of the country. This kind of move may interfere with family or social relationships to the extent that one or both parties cannot deal with it. One party being away from the home for long periods of time due to job pressures can also cause great stress in a marriage. Unexpected circumstances which put stress on the marriage may ultimately contribute to its failure.

Another leading cause of marital failure is drug or alcohol abuse. More and more people in our society are becoming dependent on alcohol or other substances and this can lead to financial or emotional problems. Many people are unable to deal with these successfully.

Physical problems can appear unexpectedly. An accident, a severe illness, or problems linked to the aging process can create stress for many marriages. Emotional problems are often difficult to deal with and understand. This may be a source of tremendous stress.

Domestic violence is also a cause of marital break up. In fact, violence is often seen as one of the absolute reasons to end a marriage.

In addition to these obvious cataclysmic issues, there are also less dramatic but equally damaging causes of marital deterioration. The slow deterioration of a marriage can occur when couples experience "communication" problems. Often the members of the pair develop at different rates, and find that they are less able to communicate meaningfully with each other. The exuberance and adventure of the youthful marriage gives way to the less exciting routine of the more mature marriage. If this natural process is not recognized and dealt with in a constructive manner, then fighting, arguing, and a gradual loss of affection can take place. This slow deterioration is often unnoticed for many years and only when the fighting or loss of affection reaches crisis proportions does the decision to end the marriage occur.

Another major cause of marital break-up is the inability to deal with crises. The loss of a job, a physical crisis or disability, the birth of a handicapped child, or, sometimes, the birth of any child can trigger feelings and emotions that people were unaware of previously. The inability to deal with crisis may lead to the deterioration of a marital relationship and may prompt people to seek separation or divorce.

When circumstances lead to the deterioration of marriage, whether it occurs gradually or suddenly, the decision must be made whether to separate or to stay together and try to improve the situation.

THE DECISION TO SEPARATE

The decision to separate or divorce is seldom an easy one. In most cases people experience a great deal of conflict and must wrestle with the idea over a period of time. It is interesting that breaking up is usually seen only from the point of view of making the decision to separate. Many don't consider that there can also be a decision to stay together. The real issue is whether separating or staying together is most desirable. I believe that if people brought a more active approach to the decision to stay together, fewer marriages would end up in divorce. Unfortunately, this is not the case. Very often one member of the couple thinks about separating or divorce for a long time without discussing it with their spouse. This obviously lessens the opportunity for shared concern and commitment to improve the marriage.

It often amazes me to see how many couples come into my office seeking a divorce with one person claiming that they had no idea that there was a major problem. By not sharing their concern, the unhappy spouse has lost the opportunity for constructive change, and for the assistance and support of others who might have helped deal with the situation in a rational way.

When contemplating a divorce or separation, as with any major decision, it is very important to look carefully at the pros and cons of each option. We've already discussed some of the reasons to keep a marriage together as well as some of the reasons why marriages break up. However, each marriage is so complex and so individualized that no simple formula can be devised to decide whether or not it is best to break up or continue.

In making your decision, you must consider many issues. You may find it helpful to make some lists, as given in Table 1 in the Appendix. Write down the good points and the bad points of the marriage. Consider why you ever got married in the first place. What is it that drew you to your spouse when you originally met? What qualities of your spouse did you admire, respect, or love when you decided to get married? What does your spouse do for you now? What are the conveniences that are afforded by your marriage? How do your children feel living within the household? What aspects of your marriage are enjoyable to you and what are the best times that you spend together? These are some of the positive qualities that should be considered.

You should also list the negatives. What aspects of your marriage are dissatisfying to you? What qualities of your spouse do you find difficult to take? What do you fight about? What important things are missing from the relationship? What causes the most anger, fighting, or disruption? Look at the things you and your spouse have in common and what you each appreciate separately. We often feel that the "grass is greener". In order to evaluate this, list your realistic expectations for living singly or in a new marriage and evaluate what you really think can happen for you. Table 1 in the Appendix will help you go through this process.

In considering Table 1 and all the things that you've listed, it is very important to understand that in almost all cases there are hurt and guilty feelings involved. There are always negative consequences especially if there are children. These negatives must carefully be weighed against the positives before it is too late to make an active decision to save the marriage.

The decision to end the marriage can be balanced by a decision to save the marriage. Both possibilities involve effort, commitment and time as well as risk and both may either succeed or fail. However, in my more than twenty years of experience dealing with couples in conflict it has always seemed that the "prime rule" is that *except in extraordinary circumstances it is better to save a marriage than to end it.* This is especially true in long term marriages and when there are children involved. Therefore the question must be asked: "Have I done enough to save my marriage"?

HAVE I DONE ENOUGH TO SAVE MY MARRIAGE?

Up to now we have been concentrating on the internal processes of the individual in deciding whether or not a marriage is to be ended or whether it is better to attempt to save it. Once the individual has reached a fairly good level of confidence regarding what direction to take, it is time to examine what the appropriate actions are.

Obviously, if the individual decides that he or she wants to save the marriage, then it is a relatively easy matter to move into a problem solving mode. The ideal problem solving situation would be one in which the problem is identified early, discussed with the spouse, and worked through, to resolution.

All marriages have ups and downs and go through cycles. It is very important not to mistake a down cycle as a reason to end the relationship but rather to take it in stride as a normal part of every relationship.

IDEAL PROBLEM SOLVING METHOD

1. EARLY IDENTIFICATION OF PROBLEM
2. DISCUSSION AND WORKING THROUGH PROCESS
3. PROBLEM RESOLUTION

Usually people don't deal with problems in the ideal way. This is especially true in the troubled marriage because the very fact that the marriage is experiencing difficulty means that the people involved don't communicate very well and probably have difficulty bringing up issues in a constructive way. However, before a decision to end the marriage is made, some attempt at resolving the problems should take place.

The first step is to identify the problem in your own mind, then discuss your feelings and problems with your spouse. Try to do it in a non-provocative and constructive way. It is often advisable to involve friends or trusted advisors, possibly family members, in the initial discussions if you feel unable to open discussion without provoking serious dissention.

Frequently it is necessary to seek help from outside sources when trying to discuss and work through marital problems. Usually friends and family are the first line of help. Religious leaders or counselors are usually trained and willing to help people to discuss the possibility of resolving difficulties and trying to save a marriage. There are also peer support groups available, such as "marriage encounter" groups. They are often sponsored by churches or synagogues and can be helpful in dealing with marital problems. When non-professional levels of help are not adequate, couples may seek professional marital counseling. This service may be offered by religious leaders trained in the process or professional mental health practitioners trained in marital and family counseling.

By using the resources available in the community to attempt to resolve marital problems, most people can take comfort in knowing they have done the best that they can do to try to save the marriage.

```
┌─────────────────────────────────────┐
│        COMMUNITY RESOURCES          │
│            AVAILABLE                │
│                                     │
│  1. FRIENDS AND TRUSTED ADVISORS    │
│  2. RELIGIOUS LEADERS               │
│  3. SUPPORT GROUPS AND PEER SUPPORT │
│     GROUPS                          │
│  4. PROFESSIONAL MARITAL COUNSELING:│
│     EITHER RELIGIOUSLY ORIENTED OR  │
│     MENTAL HEALTH ORIENTED          │
└─────────────────────────────────────┘
```

Remember if the decision to divorce comes as a complete surprise to your spouse, this means that you did not do enough to adequately prepare, nor did you go through the Problem Solving Method to try to save your marriage.

If you took an active role in deciding whether to end or save your marriage, discussed this decision with your spouse and interacted in a constructive way regarding it, and if you sought outside help to resolve the issues and problems of the marriage, and you still find yourself leaning strongly toward ending your marriage, then you should proceed to the next chapter of this book.

CHAPTER TWO

WHAT IS A DIVORCE AND HOW WILL IT AFFECT ME AND MY FAMILY?

In years of working with people who have gone through divorce I've heard many different descriptions of the process. One gentleman came into my office and said "Doc, I just got a divorce and it was great. I've never felt so good in my life. I know that this was the right thing for me to do and I'm confident in the future." This fellow had just received his divorce decree in the mail and was clearly in second heaven. After discussing the situation with him for some time and learning more about what had led up to this feeling of elation, it became evident that this man had gone through three and half years of war and chaos. He had been involved in an ongoing court battle. His children had been devastated. He had lost his job and had experienced numerous physical and emotional difficulties. How then, you might ask, could a person who had endured such a torturous process say that he "just got a divorce and it was great"?

The answer is that this gentleman was viewing divorce as a concrete event that takes place at a specific time. This event was represented by the passing of the divorce decree and the legal end of his marriage.

Most people when asked to define divorce say that divorce is the end of a marriage. **A divorce is a legal decree usually signed by a judge which ends the legal union between two people.** While this is true, a divorce is a legal event that ends the marriage, divorce is also a process which takes place over a long period of time. If the gentleman who had come to my office in such an elated state had arrived several months sooner and had been asked how he was feeling he probably would have said that he was going through a divorce and was absolutely miserable.

The process of divorce includes the gradual unfolding of both legal issues and emotional issues. (See Figure 1, THE DIVORCE LADDER). There are really two separate and parallel processes which culminate in the final legal event, the divorce decree. The legal process of divorce usually starts when one party makes it clear to the other that they want to "start an action". There is usually some discussion between the two parties, directly or through counsel, complaints are generally set forth, and a process of negotiating the end of the marriage proceeds.

Whether couples choose an adversarial, mediated, or self-directed procedure determines many of the specifics of the process, but in general, negotiation and the setting out of terms take place over a period of time and eventually the two individuals reach some agreement on how they are going to handle all of the issues that must be dealt with in any legal separation or divorce. Once the individuals reach an agreement a formal document is prepared delineating each of the points agreed upon. The document is then finalized either through a formal signing or through application to the courts for a final decree. This legal process culminates in the legal event, the dissolution of the marital union.

At the same time that the legal process takes place, there is a parallel emotional process. At the beginning there is the decision-making process which has already been described. There is usually a good deal of soul searching. With discussion of the divorce comes family disruption, worry, anxiety, and depression. As fighting takes place there are the beginnings of separation and differentiation between the two parties.

As the negotiating process proceeds, the separation and differentiation continue as the parties try to find a comfort zone in which they can function. There is give and take on both sides. There are many occasions when anxiety, worry and anger flare up. Finally, as agreement is reached there is a sense of resignation. With agreement comes resolution and once the resolution becomes an emotional reality people start to get on with their lives. They learn to live with the new realities of the divorce.

The legal event takes place with the issuing of the divorce decree but the emotional process usually continues for some time after that. In the aftermath of the legal event individuals may feel sorrow, relief, or confusion. Some of these issues will be discussed later.

The emotional process of the divorce continues for many years after the legal event. Divorced couples must deal with each other on a number of issues, especially when there are children. A new interpersonal entity, "the divorced couple", develops and changes over time.

FIGURE 1

THE DIVORCE LADDER

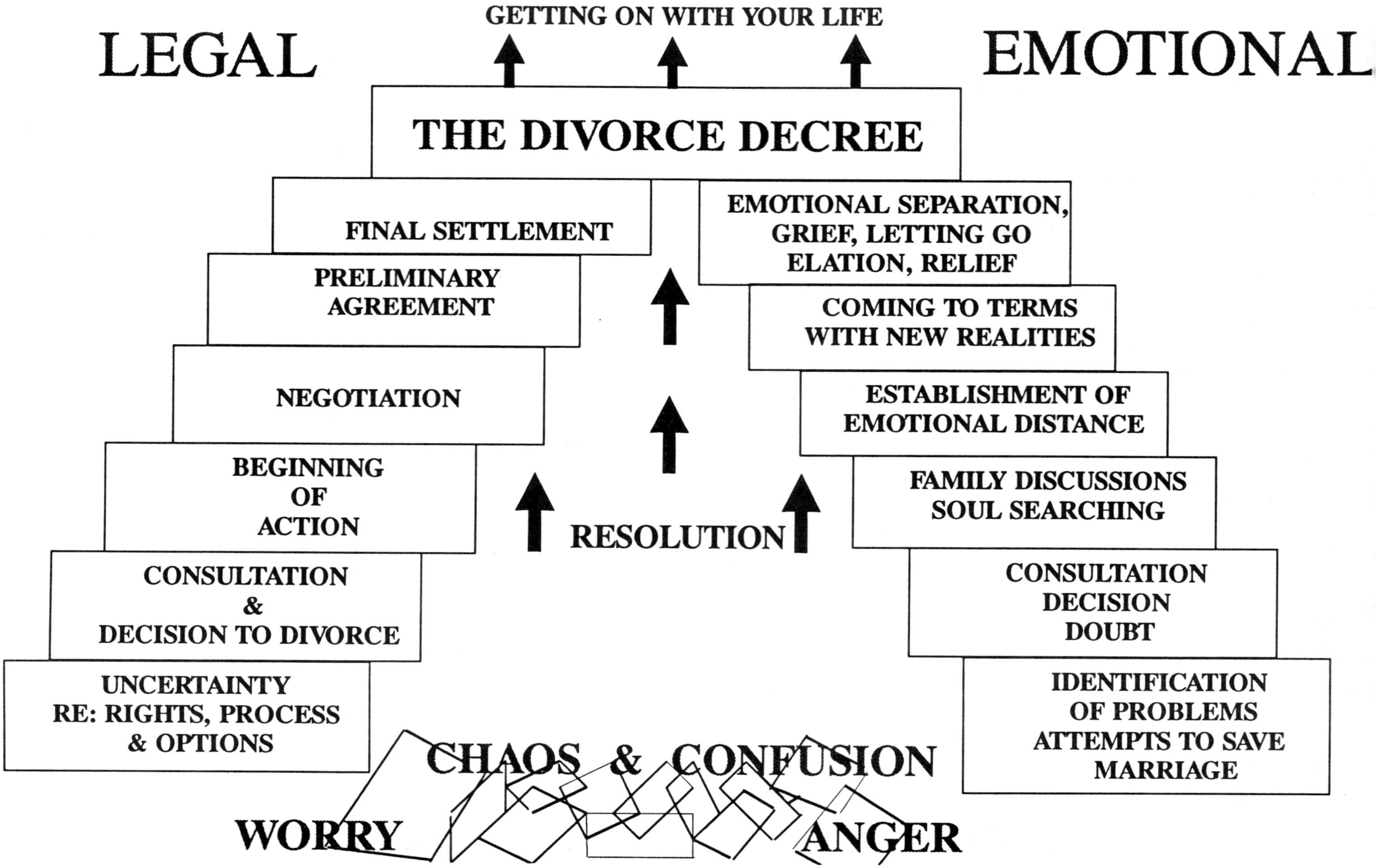

GETTING ON WITH YOUR LIFE

EMOTIONAL

LEGAL

THE DIVORCE DECREE

EMOTIONAL SEPARATION, GRIEF, LETTING GO ELATION, RELIEF

COMING TO TERMS WITH NEW REALITIES

ESTABLISHMENT OF EMOTIONAL DISTANCE

FAMILY DISCUSSIONS SOUL SEARCHING

CONSULTATION DECISION DOUBT

IDENTIFICATION OF PROBLEMS ATTEMPTS TO SAVE MARRIAGE

FINAL SETTLEMENT

PRELIMINARY AGREEMENT

NEGOTIATION

BEGINNING OF ACTION

CONSULTATION & DECISION TO DIVORCE

UNCERTAINTY RE: RIGHTS, PROCESS & OPTIONS

RESOLUTION

CHAOS & CONFUSION

ANGER

WORRY

6

THE EFFECTS OF DIVORCE

Most people entering into the divorce or separation process understand that there will be an end to the marriage, a change in the relationship between each parent and his/her children, a change in finances, and a change in relationships with extended family and friends. However, it is often not understood that divorce also takes its toll in many other ways.

EFFECTS ON DIVORCED INDIVIDUALS

Some of the most prominent effects on an individual going through divorce involve feelings of guilt and having second thoughts about the divorce. It sometimes takes a considerable amount of time before an adjustment can be made and you can expect to have times when you are unsure of the rightness of decisions.

During this period of adjustment there may be a confusing roller-coaster of feelings regarding the former spouse. These can include the full gamut of emotions such as anger, despair, affection, or love.

Sometimes people go through a phase known as "Post traumatic shock syndrome" during which time you can experience depression, anxiety, confusion or an inability to think clearly. During this shock syndrome many people experience difficulties on the job as well as in interpersonal relationships. This can last for weeks or months and it is advisable to seek professional help if the disruption is extreme.

Stress related physical illness can also occur during this time and the importance of emotional and psychological support as well as the need to take care of yourself physically and medically cannot be overemphasized..

It can also be expected that after the divorce has taken place there will be significant changes in social patterns. Getting involved in the singles' world is often difficult and can engender feelings of anxiety as well as pleasure and excitement. Often, relationships with friends, family and colleagues change, and you may find that you are treated differently because of your new marital status. Old sources of support may no longer be available, and new ones need to be developed.

EFFECTS ON CHILDREN

Divorce always has an effect on children. Sometimes children appear to be unaffected but, in almost all cases, the reality is that the feelings are either suppressed or there is a process of denial in place. Children usually feel confused and unsure as to how they should feel about each parent and how they should act toward the other parent. This is especially true around visitations and you should expect a period of testing the limits. In this way, children determine what the new boundaries are in the new situation. Some children become depressed. Others become angry and many blame themselves for the fact that the divorce took place. It is extremely important during this time that parents be as supportive and nurturing as possible for their children. They should be aware that there is often an attempt on the part of the children to manipulate by playing "the two ends against the middle."

It is especially important to be sensitive to the fact that children may have trouble recognizing and expressing their feelings to newly divorced parents. Professional help should be sought if there is an indication that a child is experiencing a great deal of difficulty.

Sometimes a child's feelings are displayed through changes in behavior such as sleep or eating behavior. There may be changes in social patterns, and often there is a change in the way they relate to peers and authority figures in school. Deterioration in school grades may be seen and this too should be a sign to the observant parent that a problem is developing and professional intervention should be sought.

Various physical or psychosomatic illnesses may appear as a result of the stress or tension of the divorce. This is prevalent among children and also happens to the adults involved. Again, the observant parent will seek professional counseling for the child when stress related illness occurs such as headaches, stomach aches, allergies, or frequent accidents.

In summary, divorce is a stressful and traumatic life change, the effects of which can surface in many ways. Be prepared to help yourself and your children through this difficult time.

CHAPTER THREE

DECIDING HOW TO PROCEED

Most people believe that when anybody gets divorced or separated it has to be a battle. The traditional way of getting a divorce in the United States is to hire the "toughest attorneys in town" and fight it out to the finish. This process itself is extremely destructive. In fact, many psychologists and mental health workers believe that the adversarial process, rather than the fact of a divorce or separation, is the more destructive force, both for the couple and the children. If a divorce or separation can be accomplished with a minimum of rage and adversarial posturing, then people may have an opportunity to get through the process and get on with their lives while still able to have civil communication with each other. This is important, especially, if there are children.

I've been told by many people who have recently gone through either mediated or self directed divorce that the divorce process accomplished in a non-adversarial setting had actually taught them more about communicating with each other than they had learned during all the years of their marriage. People have come through a divorce and been able to say that the very fact that they had been able to accomplish all the things they did during the negotiation gave them added confidence and a sense of security. After the separation or divorce they were able to get on with their lives and conduct themselves in a satisfying way.

While working with children who have been the subject of custody battles lasting many years, it become very clear that these children are irreparably harmed. On the other hand, I've worked with children who have gone through divorces where their parents were less adversarialy inclined and in those cases the children managed to get through the process relatively intact and within a short time afterward had continued with their lives in a constructive way. They were subsequently able to make good adjustments to the post divorce situation.

The bottom line is that no matter what you've been taught, you really don't have to fight during a divorce or separation process. However, you do have to discuss things with your spouse and the early discussions often set the tone for future negotiations during the divorce process.

CONSTRUCTIVE DISCUSSION

Before proceeding to discuss the issues that are important in determining how your divorce or separation is going to take place, I'd like to give you some tips on constructive discussion. Some of the techniques I've learned over the years are as follows:

1. AVOID BLAMING

Blaming the other person does no good and always escalates the level of hostility. Talk about how you feel and what you want to have happen.

2. FOCUS ON THE DESIRED OUTCOME

Keep clearly in mind what you want to accomplish and find the best way to achieve it.

3. TIMEOUTS.

One of the most helpful techniques for non-argumentative and non-destructive discussion is to agree before hand that no matter what, either party may ask for and receive a "timeout". This means that before discussing important issues it should be agreed that if either person needs or desires a rest from the discussion, then he or she can request it and take a ten or fifteen minute timeout while considering options and possibly "cooling down".

4. MAKING APPOINTMENTS.

Another technique which can often help discussion move along constructively is to make appointments with your spouse as to the time and place when discussion will take place and to set aside a particular amount of time during which the discussion will go on. By setting up an appointment and presetting a time limit, arguments and destructive interaction can be avoided.

5. SETTING AN AGENDA.

Another valuable technique is to set - in writing and in advance - an agenda for each meeting during which discussion will take place. By setting forth an agenda and accomplishing whatever is on the agenda, and no more, each party has an opportunity to prepare.

With preparation you can usually achieve far more than if you come into a discussion cold. Using these simple techniques you can move the discussions along rapidly and avoid much pain. More details on constructive discussion are given in Chapter 11.

THE ECONOMICS OF DIVORCE

As most people contemplating a divorce find out, the economics of divorce can sometimes be very difficult to overcome. In general the fact that there will be two family units where one existed before, means that the money available may not be able to provide the same lifestyles to which you have been accustomed. It also becomes apparent that the less money spent in obtaining the divorce, the more there is to divide between spouses. The use of lawyers, mediators, or some combination of professionals in obtaining a divorce means that the more time spent with these professionals, the more fees will be charged. For all practical purposes time equals money. Therefore, it makes economic sense to try to accomplish as much as you can on your own, or with relatively inexpensive mediators before heading for the enormous expenses of an all out adversarial legal battle. The premise of this book is that the more you can prepare yourself, the more you can decide on your own, and the more able you are to avoid long drawn out arguments while paying professionals, the less costly will be the divorce or separation process and the more spendable money that will be left at the end of this process.

TELLING THE CHILDREN AND FAMILY

Once the decisions have been made to get a divorce or separation and it's been decided how you're going to proceed, it becomes important to consider communicating with other family members and friends.

Obviously the most important people to deal with are your children. It would be foolish to think that children are unaware that there is a problem. I've often had couples come to my office and tell me they have been talking about divorce for some time but they don't think their children understand that anything whatsoever is wrong. I've asked them whether they've fought over the last year or so and they say, "Of course, everybody fights". I've also questioned whether they've spent less time together and the reply usually is, "Of course we spend less time together." In many cases people say they are not even sharing the same bedroom anymore. I then say, "Well, how is it that your children don't know that you're planning a divorce or separation? The answer is, "We always try not to fight in front of the children and they've never told us that they suspected anything".

In these cases about ninety five percent of the children over seven or eight years old have been living with the expectation that their parents were going to get a divorce. In fact, most have discussed it with their friends, especially those friends who they know have been through a similar process. With younger children I often find that while the kids have not been conscious or specifically aware of the process which is about to take place, they have been living in a state of tension and may be terrified or confused about what is going on in their home. The fact is that most kids already know that something is going on and the older children know, pretty much, what is going on. However, it becomes very important once the decision is firm to let the kids know *from you* what is about to happen and to give them an opportunity to get used to the idea and give both parents feedback.

In my experience children are best told about an up coming divorce or separation as soon as parents are *sure* that it is going to take place. It's usually best if kids are told by both parents together and it should be understood that older children must be told in a somewhat different way from younger children. A trip to the library can sometimes be very helpful as there are a number of children's books, usually including pictures, simple statements, and graphic illustrations to help parents tell their children what is about to happen. With older kids it is important to sit down and make it clear that the decision is made by the parents and not the children, and to reassure the children that the decision had nothing to do with anything that they might have done wrong. Children should always be reassured that they will still have two parents to love and that they still have two parents who love them. Ideally this could be accomplished in a family setting. However, if great difficulty exists in communication within your family, a divorce counselor or a child therapist (psychologist or social worker) might be very helpful. Some churches and synagogues provide these services and it is often a source of comfort to children to know that they have someone else with whom they can discuss these confusing events. Schools should also be informed and many schools have school psychologists, social workers, and guidance counselors experienced in helping kids and families through these difficult times.

Generally one of the first things that happens in a divorce or separation process is that one parent decides to leave the home. This is, again, a very important issue to deal with children on. I often suggest that kids can be allowed to have an active part in looking for, or selecting the new residence for the parent who is moving out. This allows children to understand that they will still have a place in the life of the parent who is leaving. It reassures them that their interests are being considered and that their opinions are being sought. This is not to say that children should be given the impression that they can make or change the decisions regarding the divorce or separation. It is quite important that kids understand that while their love and affection is important and their security is to be protected, the decision to divorce or separate is one that is made by parents not children.

TALKING TO OTHERS

Sometime people have the greatest difficulty discussing their plans to separate or divorce with their parents or other family members. In this case it is usually best if both spouses can make it clear that the divorce or separation is a mutual decision. I understand that this may be very idealistic but I have learned in many years of practice and experience that this is the best way to avoid the difficulties that arise when inlaws and parents become polarized. This is most important when there are children involved.

Remember, though the marriage may end, the family continues. This is the most important reason to prepare the way for a successful divorce or separation by informing family, extended family, and friends before the reality takes place. When people are confided in they usually have better feelings afterwards. While it may mean there will be some unsolicited advice, it usually means that there will be more support available to both parties as well as the kids than if friends and families were left out of the process altogether.

CHAPTER 4

THE OPTIONS AVAILABLE

SEPARATION VERSUS DIVORCE

The first important issue that usually comes up is whether to pursue a separation or a divorce. In most jurisdictions the main difference between separation and divorce is that when two parties are **separated** they may not marry another party. When they are **divorced**, they are free to marry someone else. In addition, there are tax and insurance ramifications which might be important. In general, the difference between a legal separation and a divorce is minimal from the legal point of view.

The big difference between a separation and a divorce is an emotional one, the feeling of finality. A divorce is a final break-up of the marriage whereas a separation generally leaves people feeling like they have some time to think things over and, possibly, reconcile. Very often one party desires a separation and the other a divorce. In cases like these it is very important to discuss the reasons, the ramifications, and the feelings involved in great detail. If a clear decision can't be reached then some professional help might be in order.

ANNULMENT

The termination of a marriage may also be accomplished in special circumstances through the process of **annulment**.

Generally, a marriage may be declared null and void when at the time of the marriage one party was not capable of entering into the union due to any one of the following: a) a former spouse of either party was still living and the former marriage was never terminated; b) one or both of the parties were under the age of consent; c) one of the parties was either mentally retarded or mentally ill; d) one of the parties was physically incapable of entering the marriage; e) one of the parties consented to the marriage by use of force, duress or fraud.

The process of annulment is not as accessible to the lay person as is an action for divorce, and it is recommended that the reader seek counsel before attempting to initiate such a proceeding.

DIVORCE COUNSELING

Psychologists, social workers, and religious counselors have begun to develop a specialty known as "divorce counseling". The object of divorce counseling is usually not to save a marriage but rather to help people to recognize the reasons for, and the need for ending the marriage. When one party is convinced of the need for a divorce and the other party isn't, divorce counseling can be helpful in learning to accept the new reality and prepare for the inevitable divorce. In addition, divorce counseling can help people who know they want a divorce, to work through some of the anger and rage before they actually start negotiations. In this way, it enables them to proceed with the divorce in a less adversarial manner. Professional divorce counseling can also help people to talk to their children, families, and friends. It can enable them to take what might have been an angry, rageful, and destructive adversarial situation and turn it into a relatively constructive, less adversarial divorce.

HOW TO GET THERE

Once you as a couple have decided that a divorce or separation is the course of action that you want to take, the next step is to decide the best way to get there. As already stated it is best to proceed in the least adversarial, least destructive way possible, so it is wise to consider the options and the advantages of each approach for your particular situation. Remember that you will be dealing with the after-effects of your approach for a long time. So while you may want to "kill" your spouse now with legal maneuvers, years later you will be living with the effects wrought by increased hostility, delay and expense.

USING LAWYERS:
THE ADVERSARIAL APPROACH

Traditionally, divorce has been accomplished with both parties hiring their own lawyers to represent them. This adversarial approach emphasizes that each party has conflicting interests in a divorce situation. Lawyers are trained to protect their client's rights and to strive to "win" a decision in their client's favor. When people are unable to discuss issues with each other or rage and anger are so extreme so as to not allow communication even with the help of a trained third party, then the use of separate attorneys may be the only way to proceed. In especially difficult situations such as domestic violence or severe alcohol or substance abuse it may be especially important to make sure that parties are represented individually and not left subject to physical or emotional damage which could result in an out of control battle.

MEDIATION

Mediation has been a rapidly growing factor in the matrimonial field. In a mediated divorce the two parties either hire or are assigned by a state or county agency to a neutral party known as a mediator who can help and guide the individuals with all of the issues. The mediator will also help to decide all of those issues in a fair and equitable way so that a legal separation or divorce agreement can be drawn. Mediation is a far less rageful process then is the adversarial divorce. It can often be accomplished in such a way that parties can talk to each other in a more civil way afterwards than if they have gone through a "battle royale" in the courts. It is also generally believed that mediation is a more constructive route than adversarial battling for children who might be victimized by a divorce process. Mediation can be used to resolve individual issues or it can be used as a means of resolving the entire divorce situation. Mediation is often conducted by mental health professionals, attorneys, or teams of mental health professionals and attorneys together.

DOING IT YOURSELF

The premise of this book is that it is possible for people to accomplish all or most of the important aspects of a divorce or separation by themselves. Using the guidelines set forth here it should be possible for most people to decide all or most of the issues themselves. There are also guidelines for drawing an agreement and for processing that agreement through the legal system so as to obtain a final divorce decree without the need of using any professional counsel.

Doing your own divorce can lead to a sense of accomplishment. It certainly allows you to keep absolute and complete control of the outcome but it can also lead to inadvertently creating an agreement which might not be as constructive for the future as if you received some professional advice.

COMBINED METHODS

Consider using a combination of the different methodologies described above. Most couples, especially those utilizing this book, should be able to decide many of the issues on their own. Sometimes issues that can't be decided on your own can be worked out with the help of a mediator. With the help of the mediator, agreement can usually be reached on all issues. It might also make sense to get some help from a legal advisor, not only to assure both parties that their agreement conforms to the legal necessities of their state, but also to help them draw that agreement in language that is clear and concise. The process of filing your agreement might also be made smoother by using the help of an attorney.

In these issues you must weigh the expense against the difficulty of doing it yourself and the convenience of the help.

NOW WHAT?

If you've gotten this far reading this book then you've probably made a decision to divorce or separate. You've learned something about how to prepare yourself for it. You've learned the possible routes to obtaining a divorce or separation. You've learned how to discuss the situation with the important others in your life. The next task is to learn something about the law governing separation or divorce in your jurisdiction.

In most jurisdictions divorcing couples may agree to almost any terms, as long as they are fair and equitable. Their agreement, again assuming that it is fair and equitable, will be accepted by the courts. However, it is still important to understand that in most jurisdictions there are certain requirements of the law which must be upheld in order to obtain a legal separation or divorce and these technical aspects of the law must be understood. The next section of this book will deal with some of the concepts and issues involved in the divorce law of various jurisdictions of the United States.

STEP II
UNDERSTANDING THE LAW

CHAPTER FIVE

GROUNDS FOR DIVORCE

A divorce can only be granted by a Judge in the county or area where you live. A divorce may be based on certain grounds; i.e. there must be a reason for the divorce.

The grounds or reason for the divorce is usually categorized as **fault grounds** or **no fault grounds.**

NO FAULT DIVORCE

A no fault basis for divorce is one wherein the parties allege that the marriage is irretrievably broken down; or that the parties have irreconcilable differences; or that the parties have lived separate from each other for a period of time, i.e.; one year, eighteen months, etc. No fault grounds for divorce vary from state to state and you must check the appropriate laws in your state (refer to Table 2 in the Appendix).

Most states recognize no fault as the basis for divorce. It is a method of obtaining a divorce without blaming one party or finding fault in one party, but rather reflects of recognition that the marriage is over without the finding of fault.

No fault states permit either spouse to initiate action for divorce. The effect of the new no fault legislation has been to abbreviate the time it takes to complete an action for divorce and to diminish the acrimonious tone of the proceedings. It permits the parties to move on to the financial and custody issues which must be addressed.

FAULT GROUNDS

The other basis for securing a divorce is predicated on "fault ground" which in essence requires that one party accuse the other of certain improper conduct which would justify the first party in securing a divorce.

New York State for example is one of the few states in the country that requires a fault basis for the granting of a divorce. The grounds for divorce in New York State are found in the Domestic Relations Law, Section 170 and are as follows:

1) The cruel and inhuman treatment of one spouse by the other such that the conduct of the one spouse endangers the physical or mental well being of the other spouse and renders it unsafe and improper for that spouse to further cohabit with the other spouse;

2) The physical abandonment of one spouse by the other for a period of at least one consecutive year or more;
   In addition to the **physical abandonment** of one spouse by the other, there is **sexual abandonment** which is the unjustified refusal of one spouse to engage in sexual relations with the other spouse for a period of one consecutive year.

3) The confinement of one spouse in prison for period of three or more consecutive years after the marriage;

4) Adultery.

NO FAULT BASIS

1) Where the parties having lived separate and apart pursuant to a judgement of separation issued by the court for a period of one year or more following the granting of the judgement;

2) The husband and wife having lived separate and apart pursuant to a written agreement of separation subscribed by the parties and notarized.

The parties "having lived separate and apart pursuant to a separation agreement" is the closest that New York State comes to a no fault divorce. Implicit in this section of course, is the fact that the parties must agree to all the terms of their marital settlement and voluntarily sign an agreement. If the parties cannot agree, they will not sign the agreement, and they would be relegated to proving grounds for divorce.

Where grounds must be proven in fault states, there is a general principle of law that the longer the marriage, the stronger the grounds that are required.

Several fault states require that the party seeking a divorce demonstrate **misconduct** on the part of the spouse. Misconduct regularly includes adultery, failure to consummate the marriage, drug or alcohol abuse, confinement for insanity or severe mental illness, desertion or abandonment, conviction or confinement for a felony, incest, sexually deviant behavior, neglect or failure to support, fraud, a wife's pregnancy by another man at the time of the marriage, a concealed pregnancy, physical or mental abuse and cruel and inhuman treatment.

In the majority of states where marital fault may be grounds for divorce, such misconduct will have little effect on the distribution of marital property or the granting of maintenance unless the misconduct is egregious.

Please refer to Table 2 in the Appendix to this book in order to ascertain whether your state is a fault or no fault state.

CHAPTER SIX

CHILD CUSTODY AND VISITATION

One of the most important, if not the most important, issues in a matrimonial dissolution is the resolution of matters concerning the welfare of the children. Primary, of course, is the issue of where the children will live and with which parent the children will live.

The word "custody" is the legal word that continues to be used to describe which parent the children will live with.

There several kinds of custody arrangements: joint custody or shared parental custody; sole custody, and joint custody with primary residency with one parent.

I will now discuss the different forms of custody that are commonly used in matrimonial matters, and then describe what occurs in a contested custody matter.

JOINT CUSTODY

Joint custody in its truest sense is an arrangement whereby the parents equally share the physical presence of the children, and equally share in all important decision making as well. Whether the parents share the children for one week at a time, two weeks, one month, or six months, there is a true sharing of the physical presence. This may require that parents reside in the same school district, or if not, that one parent may have to transport the children to and from school.

JOINT CUSTODY WITH A CHILD'S PRIMARY PHYSICAL RESIDENCE WITH ONE PARENT

This is an arrangement whereby the children reside *primarily with one parent*, with the other parent enjoying visitation rights. However, this arrangement contemplates that both parents will share in all major decision making regarding the children, with the primary custodial parent having the right to make day to day decisions. The parent who is not the primary residential parent enjoys visitation rights which are spelled out in an agreement.

In both forms of joint custody, both parents retain their full legal rights to the children.

SOLE CUSTODY

Sole custody is when the children live with one parent, with the other parent entitled to visitation rights. The parent who has sole custody also has the right to make all major decisions affecting the health, education and welfare of the children, with the other parent not having those rights, unless an agreement provides that the noncustodial parent share in certain major decision making issues concerning the children. A visitation schedule will be set out in the agreement or by the court.

VISITATION RIGHTS

Visitation rights for the noncustodial parent have become broader in recent years. The notion of a visiting parent being entitled to have the children one day a week, or that a father is not capable of having visitation with infants or very young children, is no longer recognized in most instances. Visitation schedules have become expansive, and it is not uncommon for a non-custodial parent to have visitation rights even with infants, and certainly with children one, two and three years of age.

This does not mean that if an individual is not capable of supervising an infant or young children that they will nevertheless have that right. If there is a reason why visitation should be denied or curtailed, then that should be discussed and appropriate arrangements should be made.

A typical visitation schedule might reflect the following:
- Alternate weekends Friday 5 p.m. through Sunday 7 p.m.
- One afternoon during the week 5 p.m. to 8 p.m. Alternating holidays - civil, religious, school
- Two to four weeks during the summer
- Father's Day - Father
- Mother's Day - Mother
- Children's Birthday - Share
- Father's Birthday - Father
- Mother's Birthday - Mother

Visitation is optional with the visiting parent, and can not be ordered or forced upon such parent.

Parents should be aware that children look forward to the visiting parent picking them up and being with them during visitation times, and are disappointed when the visiting parent fails to honor the schedule.

Children are also disappointed when they are picked up to be with their father or mother, and then are left with a girlfriend, aunt, uncle, or grandmother, while the father or mother engages in an activity independent of the children.

As children get older, and into their teenage years, they are not always amenable to following a visitation schedule that has been agreed upon by lawyers and others. Whether a teenager visits with a parent or not often depends on the relationship between the teenager and the parent. A good relationship between the noncustodial parent and the children during the child's earlier years, will enable the noncustodial parent to continue to enjoy a close relationship as the years go on following the divorce.

Courts are reluctant to order an older teenager to go with a parent where there is an unequivocal desire by the child not to visit with the parent, particularly where there has been, for example, an erratic visitation pattern by the noncustodial parent, or the failure to pay child support. Whether a court will order a child to visit is a matter which must be decided on a case by case basis.

Where parties agree on the custodial arrangement, whether it be sole, joint or joint with residential custody in one parent, the issue of custody can be resolved without court intervention. The agreed upon custody arrangement will become part of an agreement to be signed by the parents.

WHEN CUSTODY IS IN DISPUTE

When the issue of custody cannot be agreed upon, it becomes the most difficult issue in the divorce. Where there is animosity between the parents and an inability to agree, the courts will rarely award joint custody. In those instances, the court will decide the issue of custody in favor of one parent or the other..

When the issue of custody must be decided by the court, there are various procedures that are usually followed prior to the time that the court will hear the issue of custody and make a determination. Perhaps the most common procedure is that of **forensics:** the psychological evaluation of the children and the parents, and the preparation of a report which is submitted to the court.

In a custody dispute, children aged about seven and older, will be interviewed by a psychologist or social worker in order to obtain information which is necessary for them to make an evaluation. The children will of course be drawn into the marital fray and cannot be shielded from this aspect of the dispute between the parents.

If the report submitted to the court is noncommittal, or, notwithstanding the recommendation in favor of one parent, the other parent does not want to settle the matter, the court must then conduct a hearing at which time most Judges will interview the children in chambers.

Thus, the children will be brought into the matter for a second time, and actually have to appear in the court house and speak with the Judge privately during a procedure usually referred to as an "in camera" interview. During this interview parents are not present, and sometimes attorneys are excluded as well.

The court may appoint a special lawyer to represent the childrens' interest, called a **law guardian**, who may also make a recommendation to the court with reference to the issue of custody. Most jurisdictions also permit litigants to engage their own private psychologist in addition to those recommended by the court. Where there is a contested custody case, legal fees as well as psychological and counseling fees can run into the tens of thousands of dollars and have a tremendous emotional impact on both parties as well as the children.

Where children are older, usually thirteen, fourteen, or above, the expressed preference of children usually carries great weight, and in some cases, depending upon the maturity of the child, the court is almost bound to honor the wishes of the older child.

If a mature young teenager of thirteen, fourteen, or fifteen expresses an unequivocal preference to be with one parent rather than the other, it is difficult to envision a court directing the child to live with the other parent, overriding the child's expressed preference.

Older children can usually help resolve the custody issue if they are able and willing to express a preference. An unequivocal preference by such a child would usually result in the attorney for the other parent advising the client that the chance of a Judge overruling the wishes of a child of that age would be minimal, and that continued litigation would not be in the best interests of the child or of the parties, nor would it curry favor with the court.

The law is gender neutral in all jurisdictions, and there is no preference that custody should be awarded to one parent or the other. However in most instances custody is still awarded to the mother and the father receives visitation rights.

In view of the enactment in many states of child support guidelines, noncustodial parents have been ordered, or have been agreeing because of the new law, to pay more child support than ever before. This has resulted in many more applications for custody being filed by fathers who ordinarily would not be doing so. The intent of filing such applications is to try to use the threat of a custody battle to negotiate a better child support settlement, one that perhaps is lower than what the guidelines would dictate that the noncustodial parent should pay.

CHANGE OF CUSTODY

As with the issue of support, the issue of the change in custody status is one that is always subject to be heard by the court as it is in the best interest of children that their needs be addressed.

Change of custody is not granted merely because one parent requests change, but it must be predicated on a meaningful and substantial reason.

For example if one parent who receives custody at the time of the divorce, subsequently becomes a drug addict or an alcoholic or engages in other antisocial behavior which has an impact upon the children, a change in custody may be warranted.

The important criterion with regard to this issue is that the behavior which is being attacked by the noncustodial parent must impact on the children negatively. If the custodial parent engages in behavior which the noncustodial parent disagrees with, but there is no detrimental impact on the children, then such an application will not be successful.

As with the determination of custody in the first instance, change of custody applications can also involve psychological and home study evaluations as discussed earlier in this chapter.

SEPARATION OF SIBLINGS

As a general rule, the separation of siblings is frowned upon. However, where circumstances warrant, and if it is in the best interest of the children, separation of the siblings can be mediated or negotiated between the parties, and indeed could be ordered by a court.

CHAPTER SEVEN

CHILD SUPPORT

Child support is a concept that deals exclusively with the parents' obligation to support the children. It is independent of and totally separate from the issue of maintenance or spousal support.

The child support law has created two descriptive categories of parents; the noncustodial parent, and the custodial parent. The **custodial parent** is the parent **WITH WHOM THE CHILDREN WILL LIVE** and who will be **RECEIVING** child support on behalf of the children. The **noncustodial parent** is the parent **WITH WHOM THE CHILDREN DO NOT LIVE** and who will be **PAYING** the child support.

Although most statutes refer to both parents having an obligation to support the children, in actual practice, one parent will be paying child support, and the other parent will be receiving child support. Of course, the parent receiving child support will be utilizing his or her own income as well as the child support monies received from the noncustodial parent to support the children.

As a result of federal law, the Family Support Act of 1988, each state has been directed to enact a set of guidelines or formula for the purpose of establishing child support. The purpose of the federal legislation was to remedy deficiencies and inequities in establishing child support from state to state and within different jurisdictions in the same state, and to adopt guidelines that establish minimum and meaningful standards of obligations on behalf of both parents.

Some states have general guidelines, and some states have enacted specific formulas with mathematical computations for the purpose of computing child support. Child support by agreement can be set outside state guidelines, providing the amount agreed to is fair and reasonable. The court also has the power to set support outside the guidelines provided special circumstances are demonstrated.

Notwithstanding guidelines or formulas, general factors that must be considered with regard to the issue of child support, and which are always present in the minds of Judges are the following:

1) The financial resources of the custodial or noncustodial parent, and those of the child;

2) The physical and emotional health of the child, and his or her educational/ vocational needs and aptitude;

3) Where practical and relevant, the standard of living a child would have enjoyed had the marriage not been dissolved;

4) Where practical and relevant, the tax consequences to the parties;

5) The non-monetary contribution that the parents will make towards the care and well being of the child.

Child support is a concept that contemplates change, in view of the changing needs of the children, and the changing income of the parents. Clearly the cost to raise a child of three years of age is not the same as the cost to raise a teenager. Accordingly, applications for child support modifications are common, and the criteria one must demonstrate in order to qualify for a modification change from state to state.

It is the intent of the law to assure that children receive adequate support and that both parents make a fair and reasonable contribution to the support of the children.

Accordingly, it would seem that the intent of the federal mandate is to provide for increases in support by way of modification where parental income increases, and where the children's needs increase. Downward modification applications are also permitted where warranted, but are usually looked upon with skepticism, unless clear and convincing proof of the necessity of the application is demonstrated.

Agreements by parents which provide for less child support than contemplated in the the laws of their state may be subject to attack by the custodial parent seeking more support predicated on public policy considerations. Agreements that seek to prevent modification of child support awards, and which attempt to fix child support at one level for the duration of the child's minority, may also be subject to attack predicated on public policy considerations.

Public policy considerations regarding child support simply means the following: that children are wards

18

of the court and will not be bound by agreements made by their parents if the agreement is to the detriment of the children; that children should be supported by parents, and not by third parties or the taxpayers.

The concept of **child support** consists of not only the direct payment of monies for the basic needs of the children, such as food, clothing, shelter, and education, but in addition, includes the obligation of both parents to provide medical insurance, pay for uncovered medical expenses, special needs, and other reasonable expenses.

Some states also include in their statutes the obligation of the noncustodial parent to contribute to child care expense if the custodial parent incurs that expense as a result of working.

Although most statutes provide a mathematical formula or guideline for computing child support, there is usually a provision which permits the court to deviate from the mathematical formula and apply a more traditional "needs basis" standard in setting child support if a special reason or extraordinary circumstance is shown to warrant it.

Child support is a parental obligation until the child is emancipated. Emancipation could be eighteen or twenty-one depending upon which state you live in. See Table 2 for your state.

The issue of emancipation is one that could be very clear, (for example, that at the age of twenty one a parent is no longer obligated to support a child), or, on the other hand, the age of emancipation could be a difficult issue, where for example, the age of support is twenty one, and a child is eighteen, not in school full time, and not able to support him/herself. An issue may arise as to whether or not a child between eighteen and twenty one is emancipated and should continue to receive support from the noncustodial parent, or whether that child should be working full time and be self supporting.

This issue is not easily resolvable, and we must look to the facts and circumstances of each case. For example, is the child who is not in college full time capable of being self supporting? Can a child in this category secure a job and earn enough to support him or herself? Will supplemental support from the noncustodial parent be needed? Is the child not seeking a job and not working because the child does not want to or because the child cannot reasonably secure a position?

These and other questions may arise concerning the issue of whether or not a child is emancipated prior to the age beyond which a parent is no longer obligated to support the child.

If a parent believes that a child is emancipated and that the parent should not be contributing money towards the support of that child, a proceeding may be commenced wherein a hearing will be held in order to ascertain whether the child is actually emancipated.

MEDICAL INSURANCE

In addition to direct child support, health insurance has become a primary concern due to its high cost and the fact that most if not all children are in need of health care during their minority.

Accordingly, most jurisdictions consider health care in the same category as child support. Parents are responsible for the health care of their children, and can be ordered to maintain a health policy and share uncovered health care, including deductible costs.

In order to decrease the amount of out of pocket expense that parents may incur for health care, it may be in the parents' best interests if they are both employed to maintain two separate health insurance policies. In that way, claims can be submitted to both health care carriers with a view towards minimizing the out of pocket cost to the parents.

Since the issue of health care is so important, it is recommended that your agreement have a detailed health care article, which addresses major areas of dispute that frequently arise in connection with this issue. Please refer to Chapters 14 and 17 for a discussion of the health insurance clause.

One of the problems which is commonly encountered with regard to this issue, is that of reimbursement to the custodial parent for fees advanced to a doctor, dentist, or other health care provider.

In many cases the father provides for medical insurance through his place of employment, and the reimbursement checks are forwarded to the father's residence. In order to attempt to avoid the problem of the father not remitting the money to the mother and the mother having to call, write or perhaps even sue to recover monies that she is entitled to, you should attempt to mediate or negotiate a clause in your agreement which directs the health care provider to remit payments directly to the party who advanced the money. Some health care providers will acknowledge this provision and remit the monies to the party who advanced the monies, thereby eliminating the problem. Other health care providers will not honor the agreement, and the parties will be left to work this out between themselves.

Another issue that should be clarified is what is to be paid by the parties with reference to health care. Health care can be defined broadly as described in the agreement, (see appendix), or health care can be limited. Finally, there must be a statement as to how the parties will share uncovered health care: equally, pro rata to the income of the parties, etc.

LIFE INSURANCE

The noncustodial parent who is paying support may be required to maintain a life insurance policy in order to provide the amount of support anticipated to be paid during the minority of the children in the event of the death of the noncustodial parent.

TAXES

The payment of child support is a **nontaxable event,** that is to say, that the payor parent cannot deduct the amount paid for support and the parent receiving the money need not include that money as income.

The Internal Revenue laws now provide that the custodial parent automatically has the right to claim the children as dependents. In order for the noncustodial parent to claim one or more of the children as dependents, the agreement must give the noncustodial parent that right, and the custodial parent must sign an Internal Revenue form that is filed together with noncustodial parent's tax return wherein the custodial parent consents to the other party's claiming the children as dependents.

COLLEGE EDUCATION

Most parents want their children to go to college and such a goal is laudable. However, in the throws of a matrimonial dissolution, with the division of one family into two families, and the maintenance of two homes with its attendant costs, a college education may become difficult to afford.

Where the parents do wish to provide for college education, it is usually recommended that the agreement provide that the parties agree to share equally or pro-rata to income, or in some other ratio, the cost of college, but in an amount that does not exceed your state college costs for room, board, and tuition in the state where you live, after grants and other aid are received.

Care should be given to define what is meant by **college education**, as disputes easily arise if the intent of the parties is not clear. For example, does college education mean tuition, room, and board only, or does it mean activities, travel expenses, and

SAT costs as well? What about graduate school? This issue should be clarified so that there will be no misunderstanding or dispute between the parties.

People who divorce, and who have children who want to go to college, can "benefit" from the divorce with reference to college aid and grants. In most cases, the custodial parent is the mother who, in most instances, earns less money than the father. The mother can apply for college aid predicated upon her income, excluding the father's income, and the child would be entitled to receive aid and grants which sometimes can be enough to pay for college tuition room and board.

College aid advisors and planners are professionals who specialize in counseling students to secure maximum aid and grants. You should seek the advice of a college aid planner in your area as benefits may be available to people far beyond their expectations.

If the custodial parent should remarry, the remarriage does not alleviate the obligation of the noncustodial parent to pay child support. The noncustodial parent will be required to maintain his/her obligation notwithstanding the remarriage of the custodial parent.

COLLECTION OF CHILD SUPPORT

Nonpayment of child support is commonplace throughout this country. Various measures have been enacted by statute in order to collect child support.

BY GARNISHEE

One of the most common methods of collecting child support is to garnishee the salary of the nonpaying parent, which can include current payments and an additional payment representing arrears. This technique is very effective where the paying parent is an employee who is "on the books" and whose employer will honor the garnishee and not attempt to frustrate the collection of money.

However, where the nonpaying parent is being paid in cash, or partially in cash or the nonpaying parent owns the business, the effectiveness of a garnishee is greatly reduced.

BY JUDGEMENT

Another means of attempting to collect child support is by securing a judgement (representing accrued unpaid child support) against a nonpaying spouse. This judgement would constitute a lien against that person's interest in real property, be it marital or separate, and once entered in the County Clerk's records, would collect interest. In addition the entry of a money judgement for child support would adversely affect that person's credit.

BY A TAX REFUND INTERCEPT

In addition, once a child support award has been reduced to a judgement, there is the referral of the nonpayment of child support to the federal government, and if the nonpaying spouse is entitled to a tax refund, there may very well be an intercept of the tax refund in order to satisfy in whole or in part the outstanding child support arrears. An intercept is effective even if the nonpaying spouse has remarried and filed a joint return with the new spouse.

BY CONTEMPT

The remedy of contempt, that is, the jailing of the nonpaying spouse, may be the only remedy that would effectively compel the payment of money. However to secure contempt, the party seeking to enforce the child support award needs to petition the court and the court must hold a hearing. Such a procedure is costly and time consuming, and in general the courts are loath to incarcerate an individual for nonpayment of child support.

CHAPTER EIGHT

MAINTENANCE OR SPOUSAL SUPPORT

Most states now recognize marriage as an economic partnership, and have enacted legislation that provides for sharing - based on either community property, or equitable distribution principles - of the assets acquired during the marriage. This is covered in detail in the next chapter.

With the sharing of all assets acquired during the marriage, a new concept has been adopted regarding what was formally referred to as alimony, and now commonly referred to in most states as **maintenance** or **spousal support**.

While under the old laws, alimony was awarded for the lifetime of the spouse, to be terminated only upon death or remarriage, the thrust of legislation in most states today is for maintenance or spousal support to be awarded for a limited period of time (See Table 2). This period is designed to enable the needy spouse at the time of the divorce to become self-supporting, or to become rehabilitated in an economic sense, and enter the labor force.

Accordingly, lifetime alimony, to be awarded until death or remarriage, is now the exception. The general rule in most states today is to award maintenance on a **needs basis**. Needs basis is not easily definable and must be considered in the context of the facts of the marriage.

CONSIDERATIONS IN ARRIVING AT MAINTENANCE

General considerations in determining the amount and duration of maintenance are as follows:

1) The income and property of the respective parties including marital property distributed pursuant to the marital dissolution;

2) The duration of the marriage and the age and health of both parties;

3) The present and future earning capacity of both parties;

4) The ability of the party seeking maintenance to become self-supporting and if applicable the amount of time and training necessary;

5) Reduced or lost lifetime earning capacity of the party seeking maintenance as a result of having forgone or delayed education, training, employment or career opportunities during the marriage;

6) The presence of children of the marriage in the respective homes of the parties;

7) The tax consequences to each party;

8) Contributions and services of the party seeking maintenance as a spouse, parent, wage earner and homemaker, to the career or career potential of the other party;

9) Wasteful dissipation of marital assets by either spouse;

10) Any transfer or incumbrance made in contemplation of a matrimonial action without fair consideration; ie. - any other factor which the court shall expressly find to be just and proper.

In short we must consider the length of the marriage, the ability of each spouse at the time of the divorce to be self supporting, the potential earning ability of each spouse, and of course, any other considerations that would be pertinent to this issue.

Thus, maintenance could be awarded for what is referred to as a durational period, as opposed to a permanent period. That is to say, maintenance could be awarded for a period of three years, five years, or seven years, and then terminate, regardless of remarriage. Maintenance could be awarded for a number of years in one amount, with a reduction over a period of years, and eventually phased out.

Of course, maintenance can also be awarded permanently, until death or remarriage where warranted.

For example, a person in the mid-fifties or older who has never worked, or only worked part-time may be a candidate for lifetime maintenance. An infirm person, a disabled person, or someone who is not able to generate enough income to become self-supporting would also be a candidate for lifetime maintenance.

Where the disparity in the income is great between the two spouses (for example, where one spouse has an earning history of one hundred thousand dollars and another spouse has an earning history of fifteen thousand dollars), in most jurisdictions a long term award, and possibly a permanent award, might be warranted in view of the probability that the lesser income earning person would not be able to generate an amount of money which would enable that person to enjoy a standard of living that was enjoyed during the marriage.

Following are several examples to illustrate the concept of an award of maintenance based on needs.

MR. AND MRS. JONES

At the time of divorce, Mr. & Mrs. Jones were married thirty years. Mr. Jones had been an executive with the XYZ Corporation and had always earned a handsome living. At the time of the divorce Mr. Jones was earning approximately one hundred thousand dollars. Mrs. Jones is fifty three years of age, has not worked since the birth of her children over twenty years ago, has raised a family and was involved in several volunteer community organization programs.

In this example, Mr. Jones will be obligated to support Mrs. Jones for the rest of her life, and his obligation will terminate only upon Mrs. Jones' remarriage or death. There may have to be an adjustment upon Mr. Jones' retirement.

We have not considered the issue of distribution of assets with reference to the issue of maintenance in this example. However, if Mr. & Mrs. Jones had acquired substantial assets over the course of their marriage such that upon distribution of the assets Mrs. Jones would have monies that would generate significant income, this would be taken into account and might reduce Mr. Jones' obligation.

MR. AND MRS. UNHAPPY

Mr. & Mrs. Unhappy have been married for five years. Mrs. Unhappy is a teacher with a Master's degree, and Mr. Unhappy is also a teacher with a Master's degree, both degrees acquired prior to the marriage. Mr. Unhappy earns fifty thousand dollars in his field of endeavor, and there is a position open for Mrs. Unhappy at a nearby school with a comparable salary.

Mr. Unhappy & Mrs. Unhappy have three children, ages three, two, and one, none of whom are ready for full-time kindergarten.

In this example, Mr. Unhappy might have to support Mrs. Unhappy, providing his income is sufficient, until the youngest child is in school full-time, after which it is expected that Mrs. Unhappy will secure full-time employment in order to support herself.

(Mrs. Unhappy will still be entitled to receive child support as discussed in chapter 7).

Thus, Mrs. Unhappy would be entitled to receive durational support notwithstanding the fact that with the Master's degree she would be able to support herself. It is not to be expected that she should place three children of such tender years in day care or secure a full-time babysitter if that is not her preference, and if the father's income is adequate. The courts would hold that very young children should be able to enjoy the care of their mother at least until the time the youngest child is in school full-time.

MR. AND MRS. DIDNMAKEIT

Mr. & Mrs. Didnmakeit have been married for eighteen years. Mr. Didnmakeit is a policeman who earns fifty thousand dollars a year and Mrs. Didnmakeit has worked at a part-time job in a department store earning fifty dollars per week for the past three years. This couple has three children ages sixteen, fourteen, and twelve.

Mrs. Didnmakeit has the ability to take classes in order to receive a promotion where she would be entitled to a full-time job at a department store which would pay twenty thousand dollars per year.

In this example, Mrs. Didnmakeit has the ability to become rehabilitated and to become self-supporting. Thus, durational maintenance would be appropriate, for a period of time, after which Mr. Didnmakeit will not be obligated to support Mrs. Didnmakeit, but will be obligated to continue to support the children.

Other factors that may have a bearing on maintenance are marital fault, and economic fault. See Table 2 for your state's guidelines.

The concept of **marital fault** means behavior that would constitute grounds for divorce in states that require grounds, such as adultery and cruel and unusual treatment. Even in fault states, such as New York, however, marital fault has generally been held not to have a bearing on an award of maintenance, unless the marital fault rises to the level of egregious or outrageous fault. **Egregious fault** is conduct that shocks the conscience of the court. Many cases decided today indicate that even sexual activity between a spouse and a third party would not have a bearing on the award of maintenance.

The degree to which fault may or may not be considered in an award of maintenance is not easily definable, and the specific case law of each state should be reviewed in connection with this issue.

Economic fault or **misconduct** is generally conduct by one spouse which results in a wasting or a loss of marital assets. If a spouse is guilty of such conduct, this may also have a bearing on the award of maintenance.

The discussion thus far pertains to an award of maintenance that becomes effective as of the date of trial, (the conclusion of the case), and the date of execution of the agreement of settlement.

TEMPORARY MAINTENANCE WHILE A CASE IS PENDING

While the case is pending and before final judgement, or execution of an agreement, there may be a need for one spouse to request temporary or **pendente lite** maintenance from the court. This type of maintenance is awarded while the case is pending, to enable one spouse to sustain him or herself during the course of the action.

The amount of the pendente lite award is not necessarily the same amount as the permanent award. Most pendente lite orders are awarded based on affidavits submitted to the courts, and not after a trial or a hearing where the parties have an opportunity to testify and are subject to cross examination. Accordingly the pendente lite award may be adjusted either upwards or downward at the time of the entry of the final judgement of divorce.

In cases where one party may attempt to deceive the court or actually lie in an affidavit attesting that income is far less than the income actually provable at trial, the court has the authority to award the full amount of maintenance ascertained after the trial retroactive to the date of the application for maintenance.

MAINTENANCE DISTINGUISHED FROM CHILD SUPPORT

Maintenance or alimony is money paid by one spouse to the other spouse for the support of that spouse. It is distinguished from child support which is money paid by one spouse to another spouse for support for the children.

When the person receiving maintenance remarries, or the support terminates by the terms of the

agreement or court order, maintenance will terminate, but child support will continue until the children are emancipated.

HEALTH AND LIFE INSURANCE

It may be proper in some cases to provide that the spouse who has an obligation to pay maintenance should maintain a life insurance and/or disability policy for a period to correspond to the time during which maintenance is being paid and/or a distributive award is being paid. The underlying principle of course is that in the event of the death or disabiliy the payor spouse, a fund would be available to compensate the other spouse for loss of income and/or benefits from the payor spouse.

In many situations the receiving spouse may not have a job or might not have a job that entitles such spouse to medical benefits. The payor spouse, who presumably is employed, would have the opportunity through Federal law, commonly referred to as COBRA, to secure medical insurance for up to thirty six months through the employer-sponsored health insurance policy for the benefit of his/her spouse.

The obligation to maintain medical insurance and/or life insurance would terminate upon the payor spouse's fulfillment of the maintenance and/or distributive award obligation.

Where a spouse is unable to secure life insurance because of physical condition or age, other means should be found, if possible, to secure the obligation, i.e. - mortgage on property owned by the payor spouse.

TAX CONSIDERATIONS

Payments of maintenance - either pendente lite or permanent - are deductible by the person paying. Payments that are deductible by the payor spouse, are included in the income of the spouse receiving the money.

Monies expended by a spouse for the payment of medical insurance and/or life insurance pursuant to court order, are also treated as maintenance since these payments are deductible by the payor spouse and included as income by the receiving spouse.

Remember, child support payments are **not deductible** by the payor and are **not** included as income to the receiving spouse.

CHAPTER NINE

PROPERTY DISTRIBUTION

MARITAL PROPERTY

Underlying the concept of property division is the premise that a marriage is an economic partnership, and that assets acquired during the marriage will be divided between the parties regardless of whose name the asset is in, and regardless of whether one party worked in the labor force, and the other party was a homemaker.

This concept is to be distinguished from the "title concept" which resulted in property being awarded to the person whose name the asset was in, with the other party not having a claim to such property. See Table 2.

The laws in most states now view marriage as a business partnership with each party contributing in his or her way to the continuation of the "business," i.e.: the well being of the family, and/or the acquisition of money and/or property. Accordingly if it is decided that the business entity should cease, a dissolution of the business entity must be achieved, either by judicial decree, or by agreement of the parties.

Thus, the assets acquired during the marriage must be "marshalled" or identified, valued, and distributed.

Assets means anything of value, and includes the marital home, savings, pension - retirement benefits, jewelry, stocks, bonds; coin collection, collectable trains, antiques, or licenses (i.e.: Law, Medical, RN) earned during the course of the marriage. All assets (except separate property as defined below) acquired during the marriage are marital property regardless of whose name the asset is in.

All states but one (Mississippi) are either **community property** states or **equitable distribution** states. Community property states are generally those states that recognize all property acquired during the marriage to belong to both of the parties equally and divided on a fifty-fifty basis. (See Table 2 in the Appendix regarding your state.)

Equitable distribution states are those states that treat all property as marital, yet permit discretion to the parties or the court to divide the property other than on a fifty-fifty basis. Most equitable distribution states do not have a defined mathematical formula for the division of marital property. Rather, certain factors have been enacted by the legislature of each state which are considered by judges and lawyers in determining how property is to be shared. Examples of typical factors to be considered are as follows:

1) the income and property of each party at the time of marriage, and at the time of the commencement of the action;
2) the duration of the marriage and the age and health of both parties;
3) the need of a custodial parent to occupy or own the marital residence and to use or own its household effects;
4) the loss of inheritance and pension right upon dissolution of the marriage as of the date of dissolution;
5) any award of maintenance;
6) any equitable claim to, interest in, or direct or indirect contribution made to the acquisition of marital property by the party not having title, including joint efforts or expenditures and contributions and services as a spouse, parent, wage earner and homemaker, and to the career or career potential of the other party;
7) the liquid or non-liquid character of all marital property;
8) the probable future financial circumstances of each party;
9) the impossibility or difficulty of evaluating any component asset or any interest in a business, corporation or profession, and the economic desirability of retaining such asset or interest intact and free from any claim or interference by the other party;
10) the tax consequences to each party;
11) the wasteful dissipation of assets by either spouse;
12) any transfer or encumbrance made in contemplation of a matrimonial action without fair consideration;
13) any other factor which the court shall expressly find to be just and proper.

It is critical to insure that all assets acquired during the marriage are listed and accounted for prior to the time that the agreement is signed by the parties or adjudicated by a court. If an asset is not accounted for in the divorce proceeding or settlement, then it is presumed subsequent to the execution of the agreement or adjudication by the court, that the asset will be owned by the party in whose name the asset is in.

SEPARATE PROPERTY

Contrasted with marital property, defined above as all property acquired during the marriage regardless of whose name the asset is in, is the concept of separate property.

Separate property in most states is defined as property owned by each spouse before the marriage; property received by one spouse from a third party (not the other spouse) as a gift or inheritance; or compensation received by a spouse for disability awards or negligence awards.

The distinguishing feature of separate property is that it is a limited kind of property, usually limited specifically by the statute dealing with the issue of property in your state. All property not specifically defined as separate, is presumed to be marital property.

Further, when one party to a marriage receives separate property it must be received in that person's name alone. The property must remain in the name of the person receiving the property. In other words, if Bob receives a gift from his mother of fifty thousand dollars, and places the fifty thousand dollars in a bank account in his name alone, and the money remains there for a period of ten years, after which Bob and his wife become involved in a matrimonial dispute, the money in Bob's separate bank account, that was received by him from his mother, remained in Bob's name and will be Bob's at the time of the divorce and not subject to marital distribution.

CONVERSION OF SEPARATE TO MARITAL PROPERTY

Separate property can be converted to marital property, thus becoming subject to property distribution in the matrimonial proceeding.

Money which is separate property, used to purchase an asset to which both names are then placed in title, may very well be transmuted or converted to marital money. For example, if Mary withdraws her separate money to purchase a home, and title to the home is in the names of Mary and her husband, the money that was separate will in all probability be considered marital property.

There is a possibility that Mary may receive a credit for the separate money that was used to purchase the house, but the issue of credit for the separate property must be decided on a case by case basis.

APPRECIATION OF SEPARATE PROPERTY

Another concept in property distribution is that of appreciation of a separate asset. This concept can best be explained by the following illustration:

Jack works with his father in a one man auto repair shop. Jack's father eventually passes away and bequeaths the auto repair shop to Jack. Two years after Jack receives the auto repair shop by way of inheritance, Jack marries Sally and they live together as man and wife for the next twenty years. During this twenty year period, Jack devotes all of his marital work effort to his auto repair business, and eventually increases the operation of the business from a one man operation, to a shop that grosses over one million dollars a year and employs fifteen mechanics.

Obviously, the value of the business has increased substantially from the time Jack acquired it prior to the marriage. The business increased as a result of Jack's direct efforts in working the business. Jack's wife Sally was a homemaker during the twenty years of marriage, raised four children, and provided for their care and needs as well as the care and needs of the home.

As a result of Jack's active efforts in the appreciation of what was separate property, and Mary's contribution to the marriage by raising the children and maintaining the home, Mary will have an interest in the appreciation of the value of Jack's business.

MARITAL LIABILITIES

All liabilities incurred during the marriage, with certain exceptions, are marital liabilities and must be taken into consideration along with the distribution of marital property.

Generally, as in the dissolution of a business, we must provide for the sharing of the marital liabilities as well as the marital assets.

Some situations make it impossible to truely share liabilities, and adjustments must be made.

For example, Mary and Joe decide to divorce at a time when Mary is home with three minor children and does not work. Joe has been the sole wage earner in the home and is the only person who has an income with which to continue to satisfy marital liabilities. In this case, Mary may be awarded a share of marital assets, while Joe assumes most of the marital liabilities.

Another situation which may affect the sharing of marital liabilities, would be where one party incurs liabilities which are the result of **wasteful dissipation of a marital asset**: the wanton loss of money or property; an unjustified disregard for prudent judgement. For example, Bob has borrowed from credit cards or from a bank for purposes of gambling, and has caused an indebtedness which can be verified from his gambling activities. He, and not his wife, may be solely responsible for the liquidation of these obligations.

The above general guidelines provide you with a working knowledge of property law. We must now apply our knowledge of the law to the specific facts of your case in order to proceed with the dissolution of your marriage.

We will now detail two areas of property distribution common to most people.

THE MARITAL HOME

Perhaps the most common marital asset is the marital home. Certain propositions have generally been accepted by the courts in most of our states regarding the disposition of the home.

Where there are minor children in the home, the courts will generally not order the marital home sold. The custodial parent will usually be permitted to remain in the home with the minor children until the emancipation of the youngest child. The rationale underlying this principal is that the children's lives will be disrupted by the divorce, and that to relocate the children from their community, friends, and home would be an additional trauma which should be avoided. In addition, it may be cheaper for the custodial parent and the children to remain in the home than to sell the home and purchase another, or rent an apartment.

In many cases, the noncustodial parent may seek to have the home sold in order to receive his or her share of the equity in the home. The general rule is that where there are minor children, the home will not be sold and the custodial parent will be permitted to reside there with the children.

Where the continued residence in the home of the custodial parent and the children would be impracticable, notwithstanding the presence of children, the home may be sold.

For example, where parties live in a home that is worth a substantial amount of money, the mortgage payment may be substantial, requiring an inordinate amount of maintenance and/or child support to be used to pay the mortgage. There may be a direction that the home be sold in order to relieve the parties of the continued burden of an excessive mortgage payment. At the same time, the "freeing up" of what might be substantial cash equity would allow both parties to acquire separate accommodations.

If the home was acquired during the marriage, with marital monies, then as a general proposition, the parties should share the equity (the amount left after payment of mortgage and closing costs) in the home at the time of sale.

PENSION AND/OR RETIREMENT BENEFITS

Another common asset in matrimonial proceedings is a pension, or other retirement benefit.

A pension or a retirement benefit acquired during the marriage as a result of one person's employment is a marital asset. The employed spouse who earns this benefit will have only his or her name on the retirement plan. As discussed earlier, title is immaterial (except in Mississippi) in matrimonial law, and the retirement benefit will be subject to distribution.

With regard to the disposition of a pension, we must look at two factors: first, the value of the pension, sometimes called present day value; and second, what the pension benefit will pay or yield at the time the employed spouse will become eligible to receive the pension benefits (valued as of the commencement of the matrimonial proceeding).

Valuation of a pension during a marriage generally means the value of the pension from the time the parties were married and the employed spouse participated in the pension, up to the time of commencement of the matrimonial proceedings. In other words, the value of the pension prior to the marriage and after the commencement of the matrimonial action is excluded in the pension valuation.

Most matrimonial practitioners use the services of an actuary or a CPA to compute the present day value of a pension. The present day value of a pension tells us the value of the pension in dollars at the time of the commencement of the matrimonial proceeding, although the pension may not be in pay status; may not be vested; and may never pay a cash value, but only a monthly benefit at the time it goes into pay status.

The largest company doing this pension valuation work is Legal Economic Evaluations, Inc. of Palto Alto, California.

In Table 6 we have included pension valuation forms for your convenience.

The actuary will also project what the pension will pay at the time the pension goes into pay status, i.e. on a monthly basis. For example, the actuary may tell us that after a twenty year marriage Mr. Jones, who is a fireman, may have a pension with a present day value of one hundred and fifty thousand dollars, and that the pension in pay status will pay two thousand dollars a month.

There are basically two ways to deal with the distribution of the pension: Pay Status Sharing or Exchange.

In Pay Status Sharing arrangements the parties agree or the court may order, that upon retirement and at such time as the pension is in pay status, the monthly pension payment will be shared by the parties equally, or in some other ratio, i.e. sixty-forty or seventy-thirty. This means that subsequent to the divorce and until the employed spouse retires or is eligible for retirement, the nonemployed spouse will not receive any benefit from the pension whatsoever, but will await actual retirement, or the earliest retirement age of the employed spouse, to receive his/her monthly pension benefit.

In many jurisdictions, a special court order is secured, commonly referred to as a **Qualified Domestic Relations Order (QDRO)**, which is served upon the pension administrator, and directs the administrator to pay to the nonemployed spouse, sometimes called the "alternate payee", a certain percent, or an amount of money each month when the pension goes into pay status, or at such time as the employed spouse is eligible to receive pension benefits.

For example, if the actuary advises that the pension will pay two thousand dollars a month upon retirement, the court order may provide that Mrs. Jones will receive fifty percent of the pension benefit at the time Mr. Jones retires, or at such time as Mr. Jones is eligible to retire but does not actually retire if Mrs. Jones exercises her option to receive her share of the pension at that time.

Most pensions permit the nonemployed person, the alternate payee, to receive his or her benefit at the time the employed spouse reaches retirement age although he or she does not actually retire. In this case the benefit may be less than if the nonemployed spouse waited until the actual retirement of the employed spouse.

Thus Mrs. Jones will receive her share of the pension at one of the occasions mentioned above, and will receive monthly pension checks directly from the pension administrator.

Several safeguards must be followed in connection with pension matters. One primary concern is that the Qualified Domestic Relations Order provide that the employed spouse elect a survivor benefit option to the pension. This ensures that if the employed spouse dies before the pension reaches pay status, or during the time the pension is in pay status, that the nonemployed spouse will receive his or her share. If the survivor option is not elected, and the employed spouse passes away prior to or during retirement, the nonemployed (alternate payee) spouse's interest in the pension may also "die" and he/she may no longer receive any interest in the pension.

If the nonsurvivorship election is made prior to the time the parties become involved in their matrimonial matter, the election is in all probability irreversible. In such cases, it is recommended that life insurance on the life of the employed spouse be secured to guarantee the alternate payee's interest in the plan.

The survivorship option results in a lower monthly payment when the pension goes into pay status. In cases where the parties want to receive the maximum amount of monthly benefit payable by the pension, the non survivor option may be the preferred choice, providing life insurance can be secured and paid for at a reasonable cost to guarantee payment to the alternate payee in the event of death of the other spouse.

Another area of concern occurs when the employed spouse is a participant in a governmental pension which is not subject to the federal pension law, known as Erisa. State and local governments are not obligated to honor a Qualified Domestic Relations Order. Governmental agencies can however elect to recognize a Qualified Domestic Relations Order, or a comparable order. Care must be given to inquire specifically as to the rules and regulations governing your pension plan.

Qualified Domestic Relations Orders are complicated instruments and should be drafted by the actuary or the attorney, and preapproved by the pension administrator of the pension plan.

Other retirement benefits such as IRA's, 401 K

28

plans, and KEOUGH plans are much easier to value (look at the balance on deposit and divide). These benefits require the transferring or rolling over from one spouse's individual name of a portion of the monies to the other spouse's IRA, or retirement vehicle, or the rolling out of a joint IRA into two individual IRA accounts.

The second method to provide for the distribution of a pension is to trade or exchange the value of the pension for another asset.

For example, assume that the marital home is worth two hundred thousand dollars and has a mortgage of one hundred thousand dollars. The difference between the mortgage and the fair market value of the home is one hundred thousand dollars. We call this the equity in the home.

Assume that the employed spouse is the husband and that the actuarial report provides that the present day value of the pension is one hundred thousand dollars.

The parties may agree, or the court may direct, that the pension be retained by the husband for his benefit, while the home becomes the sole and separate property of the wife for her benefit. Thus, the sharing of marital assets of almost equal values will have been accomplished.

There are other ramifications to exchanging the pension for the home which are not the subject of this work, but which should be considered when discussing distribution of such an asset. Tax considerations and liquidity are two major issues which might best be discussed with your accountant before committing to an exchange involving tax sheltered or illiquid assets.

THE LICENSE OR ENHANCED EARNINGS AS A MARITAL ASSET

Many states now recognize a license that one earns during the marriage, (or the enhanced earning capacity that the license generates), to be a marital asset.

The license can be in medicine, law, accounting, or virtually any other area.

The principle behind this concept is as follows:
If one party to the marriage earns a license during the marriage, and the other party has aided in some manner towards the acquisition of the license (efforts as a homemaker are considered to be contributions towards the acquisition of a license), then the license is considered an asset, and will be valued and "distributed" with other marital assets.

If the person who holds the license will earn more money by virtue of that, license then the difference between what the holder of the license will earn over his or her work life, and what a person without the license would earn, represents **enhanced earnings**.

To illustrate: during the course of the marriage, Mary attends college and earns her college degree, and a teaching license in special education. Bob is gainfully employed and also helps take care of the home and the children during the time Mary is studying, writing papers or otherwise engaged in school. Mary, having earned her license during the marriage, will earn a salary which will be more than a female of Mary's age in her geographical area without a license. The difference between what Mary will earn, for example, forty thousand dollars a year, and what a comparable person without a license will earn, for example, twenty five thousand dollars a year, is fifteen thousand, and the enhanced earnings of fifteen thousand dollars per year will be projected over Mary's work life expectancy of perhaps twenty years. The total amount of money, i.e.: three hundred thousand dollars, reduced and adjusted for taxes and present day value, will represent an asset to be considered in the context of the overall distribution of marital assets.

THE BUSINESS AS AN ASSET

It has been well established in law that a business that was started during the marriage is a marital asset. In addition even a business that was acquired prior to the marriage but which has appreciated in value during the marriage due to the active efforts of either spouse, is be deemed marital with regard to the appreciation. A business should be valued by an accountant or economist for purposes of marital distribution as this is a complex task and the value may be nominal or substantial.

A Business, in regards to marital law, may be any form: a one person operation, a partnership, or a corporation - small or large. Almost any business can be valued.

THE DISTRIBUTIVE AWARD

In most cases the non-licensed or non-titled party is not going to become a partner in the license or business, and the business will not be sold as a result of the divorce. How then, does a spouse receive his or her interest in the business or the license? The answer is that the spouse who does not hold the license or is not active in the business will receive other assets, i.e.: house, savings, etc. in exchange for his or her interest. When these other assets are not sufficient to effect an equitable exchange, a distributive award may be provided for. This means that the person who holds the license, or owns the business, will pay to the other party a certain amount of money over a period of time. The payment of this money is independent of the payment of any maintenance or alimony and could be paid with or without interest.

Table 3 in the Appendix to this book contains a listing of marital assets which should be considered. This list is not exhaustive of all possible and conceivable marital assets, but is illustrative of such assets, and will help you begin to gather your materials.

STEP III
REACHING AGREEMENT AND MAKING DECISIONS

INTRODUCTION

Now that you've decided to divorce or separate, learned about preparing your family and yourself for the process, and learned about the law, it's time to start working out agreement on all of the issues so that you and your spouse can successfully separate or divorce. The purpose of this section of the book is to take you step by step through decisions on all of the issues. There will be a number of suggestions along the way regarding how you might decide, and there will also be some indications of the various alternatives available to you. Remember that the basic task is to reach an agreement that is fair and equitable for both of you and that meets the special needs of your situation. As you saw in the previous chapters the law in different states sets rules and guidelines regarding divorce and separation. However, in general, all jurisdictions will accept any agreement that the two of you have reached as long as that agreement is fair and equitable, and as long as both parties to the agreement understand what is written and have agreed to the various parts without undue pressure from some outside source. In most jurisdictions, issues which affect children may be open to far more scrutiny from legal authorities than would other areas of your agreement. The issues may also be open to modification, at any time, after the agreement is finalized. This is because circumstances change and children's needs change over time.

It is also important for both of you to be aware that there may be significant disparity between you in terms of the power that you exert in negotiations. Frequently marriages evolve in such a way that one spouse has significantly more ability to sway the other than vice versa. In cases like this, it is very easy for an agreement to become one sided and lose its sense of fairness and equitability. This can happen even without conscious awareness on the part of either party and must be guarded against with great care.

If there is any doubt as to the fairness or equitability of any agreement it should be understood that a neutral third party, such as a professional mediator or attorney, or a close friend of both of you, will be consulted for an outside opinion as to the fairness or equitability of the agreement you have reached.

Once more, remember your task is to reach a fair and equitable agreement on all issues. In this way you and your spouse can have a successful divorce and will be best able to go on with your lives afterwards. The agreement that you are about to reach will most likely end your marriage but, if you have children, the family will continue, and it is extremely important that you be able to communicate with each other in the future.

CHAPTER TEN

GROUND RULES

YOU DON'T HAVE TO FIGHT

The traditional adversarial view of divorce postulates conflicting interests between parties. The entire adversarial process is designed to create a winner and, as a by-product of this victory, a loser. Great care is taken to protect each party's separate interests.

In reality, it is clear that parties involved in a separation or divorce action retain more mutual interests then conflicting ones. Children, the conservation of the marital estate, future emotional and financial well being, extended family and mutual friends, as well as whatever warm feelings are left between you - all demonstrate that both parties share many mutual interests which probably outweigh the conflicting ones.

The premise of this book is that by emphasizing the mutuality of your interests you can promote agreement and end up in a "win- win" position. In this "win-win" situation there are no losers and each of you can go on with your life while maintaining a sense of self-respect in the knowledge that your interests have been protected without the need to hurt and maim your spouse.

It is still obvious that there are very strong negative emotions involved in any divorce or separation proceeding. The feeling which usually comes to the fore-front is a sense of hurt. Hurt feelings usually lead to anger, and anger often leads to fighting.

The main object of setting ground rules is to avoid fighting, or if it can't be avoided completely, to at least limit the fighting and the destructiveness that it causes.

The following are some rules for you to consider before starting your negotiation.

THE GROUND RULES FOR SUCCESSFUL AGREEMENT

1. AVOID BLAMING THE OTHER PARTY

At this point it serves no useful purpose, and will actually work against your interests by escalating discussion into fighting. So hold your tongue and focus on the present and the future, not the past! If your spouse starts name-calling or blaming, calmly label it as such and repeat that you would like the discussion to focus on reaching satisfactory solutions to the current issues.

2. FOCUS ON THE DESIRED OUTCOMES

Keep your goal in mind: the resolution of your situation and the reaching of equitable agreement on all the issues so you can all go on with your lives. Do what you need to do to reach this goal.

3. MEETING TIMES

It is always important to agree, beforehand ,on the time of a negotiation session and the length of time it will take. It is suggested that one to one and a half hours is an ideal time for negotiation and the time chosen should be set so that outside distractions can be minimized and the pressure to finish quickly and get to somewhere else can be minimized.

4. THE SETTING

Pick a place to do your negotiating that is comfortable but not "too comfortable". It's usually desirable to have a table and chairs so that you can take notes; the room should be well lit and distracting influences should be minimized. The place should be a "neutral corner". It is best to negotiate in a place which does not give either side an unfair advantage. This means that both parties should be equally comfortable within the setting.

5. TIMEOUTS

Both parties should agree before any negotiations start that at any time during the negotiation either party may call for and receive a timeout. This means that each of you will have the opportunity to take a few minutes to collect your thoughts, get yourself together, and if necessary, end the negotiation meeting. Obviously it would be best if the timeout rule is not abused, but it is important to know that if either of you gets upset you have the right and the opportunity to stop and come back at another time to complete your task.

6. THREATS

The great enemy of agreement is "the threat". Always avoid making threats during negotiation. Threats only serve to increase hostility and to increase defensiveness. This is antithetical to the openness and feeling of trust which is needed to arrive at a successful agreement. Try to avoid making threats, and if your spouse uses them against you, calmly identify them and ask that threats not be used in negotiation.

7. STRUCTURED DISCUSSION

There will probably be times during the negotiation process when the normal give and take of conversation and discussion will become overly heated. At these times it is often helpful to use a structured discussion process. This means that each party will be given a set period of time, usually five minutes or less, during which time he or she may speak uninterrupted while the other party listens. This structured discussion can be alternated and continued for as long as necessary until the particular issue being dealt with is completed. Remember, listening is as important as talking. Structured discussion also means structured listening.

8. NOTE TAKING

Each party should keep careful notes during the entire negotiating process. As agreement is reached on each issue the result should be written down and both of you must read what has been written and agree as to the validity of the content. If, as the negotiation proceeds, either one of you finds that there is wide divergence with regard to your notes or understandings, it may be helpful to agree to record the sessions so you can check back periodically. Recording should only be used in extreme cases and is not usually necessary.

9. RECAPPING

As has already been stated it is important to make sure that both parties concur on what is written and agreed upon for each issue. It is also important to recap at the end of each negotiating session what has been agreed upon and a note should be made as to what will be discussed at the following session.

10. ONE ISSUE AT A TIME

It is usually helpful to stick to the issue at hand. When you are negotiating a particular matter, stay with that topic and don't bring in others if you can help it. Dealing with one issue at a time means that you will progress step by step to a successful conclusion.

11. INVOLVING THIRD PARTIES

It is usually best **not** to involve related third parties, especially the children, in any of your negotiating sessions. The exception to this rule, which will be discussed later, is the involvement of professional help or neutral third parties as evaluators of fairness.

12. OPENNESS

It is important to be open and honest during the negotiating process. However, do not confuse honesty with hurtfulness. You can be honest about your needs, your feelings, and your opinions while still trying not to be hurtful to the other party. By limiting the hurtfulness of your statements, it is likely that you will be more successful in reaching agreement.

13. SETTING AGENDAS

Setting agendas is recommended throughout the negotiating process. Agendas can be set for each negotiating session as well as for each topic to be negotiated. It is suggested that you negotiate topics in the order in which they are presented in this book. Many years of experience have shown that by utilizing the order suggested, topics can be completed with the least amount of dissention and with the greatest likelihood of success. A certain amount of homework will be necessary in order to prepare yourself for each negotiating session. By referring to the topic outlines at the beginning of each chapter you will know what homework has to be done, and by setting agendas for each session you will know what is called for each time you meet.

14. PROFESSIONAL HELP

(a) Mediation

When negotiations bog down or when there is doubt as to the fairness of an agreement, professional help may and probably should be sought. Divorce or family mediators, as well as matrimonial attorneys are available to help you reach agreement on specific issues. You can use professional help not only to ascertain the fairness of an overall agreement but also to help break impasse on a particular issue which represents only a part of your total agreement.

(b) Arbitration

When an impasse cannot be broken, even with the help of a professional mediator, then it may be necessary to use arbitration. **Arbitration** is a method whereby two parties agree to hire an expert in the area being discussed and abide by the finding that the expert makes when presented with both sides of the disagreement. Binding arbitration may be used in extreme cases but it should be emphasized that most people would rather decide an issue themselves then allow a third party to decide it for them. Therefore, this method of breaking impasse seldom is needed or utilized.

(c) Professional Counseling

Very often while negotiating, strong emotions can come to the fore. If you feel yourself becoming uncontrollably angry, depressed, anxious, or simply upset, then you should consider using a professional counselor to help you deal with these feelings. Very often uncontrolled feelings lead to threats, and, as we have said before, threats can prevent successful negotiation. In addition, a counselor can often help you to organize and prioritize your thoughts and needs with regard to the negotiating process.

15. VIOLENCE

While it may seem almost unnecessary, it should be mentioned that violence or physical abuse as well as verbal or emotional abuse constitute good cause to immediately end all negotiations and obtain appropriate professional help. No one should be expected to negotiate under the threat of physical or emotional harm.

Now that we've set the ground rules and understand some of the issues involved in negotiating, it's time to start gathering information so that we can proceed with the decision making process step by step.

CHAPTER ELEVEN

ORGANIZING YOUR DATA

Before starting your negotiation you will have to collect and organize a lot of information. The task ahead of you, getting all the financial and household records together, may be unpleasant, but it is essential. Therefore the sooner and more thoroughly you do it, the better off you will be.

It is often helpful to organize the various papers and information that you will be collecting either by using an accordion file available at stationary or business supply stores or by setting up a filing system using large envelopes or folders for each category.

Some of information you will be collecting and documents you will be needing are valuable and it is worth making a photocopy of the important ones so that originals can be maintained in a safe place.

WHAT TO COLLECT

The following information should be on hand:

1. TAX RETURNS

The prior three years' federal income tax returns should be available so that you can refer back for the purposes of making financial decisions.

2. INCOME RECORDS

The three most recent pay stubs for you and your spouse should be available as well as records of other income received over the prior twelve months.

3. BUSINESSES, PROFESSIONAL CORPORATIONS, PARTNERSHIPS, AND SOLE PROPRIETORSHIPS

Records of ownership as well as income from all partnerships, private practices, professional corporations, family owned businesses, or hobby businesses should be available for the previous year.

4. TITLES AND DEEDS

Copies of deeds or titles to all real estate, automobiles, boats, recreational vehicles, time shares, or other possessions of significant value which have titles or deeds should be collected and copies made.

5. INVESTMENTS

The latest monthly, quarterly, or annual statement for all investment accounts, brokerage accounts, limited partnerships or other investment vehicles should be collected.

Check the list for most common investments in the Financial Statement Form included in Table 5 of the Appendix.

6. BANKING RECORDS

The latest statements for all savings, money market, or checking accounts should be available.

7. PENSIONS AND RETIREMENT ACCOUNTS

The most recent statement for all defined benefit, defined contribution, 401 K, 401 W, KEOUGH, IRA, tax deferred savings or annuity accounts, and profit sharing plans should be collected. In addition, a social security benefits projection should be obtained. This can be requested from your local social security office.

8. HOUSEHOLD INVENTORY

An inventory of all household items should be taken and appraisals obtained depending on circumstances. A form to help you with this is given in Table 4 in the Appendix.

9. SAFE DEPOSIT INVENTORY AND CASH ON HAND

An inventory of all items kept in safe deposit boxes or cash on hand should be available.

10. JEWELRY

An inventory of all precious jewelry should be made and appraisals obtained.

11. COLLECTIBLES

All collectibles such as antiques, fine art, stamp collections, coin collections, baseball cards, etc. should be inventoried and valued separate from regular household items.

12. ACCOUNTS RECEIVABLE

Any loans made to others or debts owed to either spouse should be known and recorded.

13. EMPLOYEE BENEFITS

Any statement of employee benefits or policies relating to either party should be on hand.

14. LIFE INSURANCE

All life insurance policies especially those with cash value should be on hand and the cash value for each policy should be ascertained by contacting your insurance agent or issuing company.

15. MEDICAL INSURANCE

A copy of any medical insurance policies for either of you or the children should be on hand.

16. EDUCATIONAL RECORDS

Any school transcripts, degrees, licenses, or special vocational certificates should be on hand or copies made.

17. EMPLOYMENT HISTORIES

Dates of employment for both parties for the entire duration of the marriage should be available with special reference to any employment which might have involved retirement or pension benefits. Also include a salary history for both spouses as well as adolescent children, and have available any military discharge papers and records relating to military pensions or disabilities.

18. PERSONAL PROPERTY AND AUTOMOBILE INSURANCE

Copies of these policies as well as the schedule of payments should be on hand.

19. PRIOR FINANCIAL STATEMENTS

If any financial statements have been filled out and filed within the past few years it would be helpful to have them on hand.

20. ACCOUNTS PAYABLE

Records of all mortgages, home equity loans, promissory notes, personal loans, business loans, educational loans, auto loans, boat loans, and other loans should be on hand. In addition, all balances due on bank cards, credit cards, department store accounts, and personal charge accounts should be available. Membership cards, travel cards, airline accounts, rental car accounts, and gasoline credit cards should be listed and the most recent statements available. Lastly, any loans received from family members or friends which might require repayment should be listed and any notes or agreements relating to these loans should be available.

21. PERSONAL PAPERS

Marriage certificates, birth certificates for yourself and children, adoption papers, baptismal certificates, citizenship papers, passports, visas, green cards, social security numbers, social security benefit records, drivers license, name change papers, wills and codicils, medical records or any other personal records which might effect the decision making process should be available.

22. INFORMATION RELATING TO THE CHILDREN

All records regarding child care, educational expenses, or special medical expenses, etc. for the children should be kept on file.

23. PAYMENT RECORDS

All canceled checks, bills, bank statements, and other records which will be helpful in calculating budgets and future needs should be on record and available.

24. COLLEGE EXPENSES

One of the most important future investments for many families is the college expense for children and sometimes educational and college expenses for one or both spouses either during or after the separation or divorce. Any records of college expenses or estimates of future expenses which have been obtained should be made and it might also be valuable to consult a specialist in calculating future college expenses with special emphasis on financial aid in order to determine what those expenses might be.

Now that you have collected all of this data it is important to start organizing some of the numbers.

THE DETAILED FINANCIAL STATEMENT

One of the most important tools for organizing your data is the detailed financial statement. The financial statement lists and organizes all of your assets and liabilities in such a way that a net worth can be calculated. In addition, the financial statement will show in whose name various assets and liabilities are. It also provides an income record and will enable us to calculate the means to meet future needs for both of you.

The following pages are a sample "Financial Information and Income Statement."

There is a blank set of forms for your use in Table 5 in the Appendix.

FINANCIAL INFORMATION AND INCOME STATEMENT

ASSETS

Estimate the value of each of the following items of property, and place value in appropriate column on right. If any item is located in a jurisdiction other than in which you live, indicate where such item is located, and, if necessary, give details on a separate sheet.

	Husband	Wife	Joint
A. Bank Accounts, Savings, and Cash on Hand:			
FIRST NAT. BANK #123400 SAVINGS	3000		
" " " #04999 "			5500
BANK OF COMMERCE #7777 MM		2600	
FIRST NATIONAL #1223 CKING			756
CASH ON HAND			500
B. Notes, Accounts Receivable (i.e. money owed to you. Indicate by whom payable, amount, and date or dates payable):			
NOTE FROM SALLY		500	

C. Stocks, Bonds, Mutual Funds:	Husband	Wife	Joint
MERRILL LYNCH (see attached schedule)			35,823
SAVINGS BONDS " " "	3027	6550	
MUTUAL FUNDS " " "	10,425	9850	

D. Real Estate (Home and other):			
MARITAL HOME - 200 APPLE CT			209,000

E. Life Insurance - Name of Company, policy number, face value, type (i.e., "term", "ordinary life," etc.) Place cash value on right:

	Husband	Wife	Joint
ACME LIFE TERM 50,000 FACE			
ACME LIFE WHOLE LIFE 50,000	15,821		
" " " " 50,000		15,821	

F. Business or Professional Interests. (Please furnish last balancesheet and P&L statement, tax return, buy-sell agreements,etc.):

	Husband	Wife	Joint

	Husband	Wife	Joint

G. Licenses & Degrees: List any licenses, college degrees, or professional degrees awarded during the marriage. Include the date of award:

	Husband	Wife	Joint
_____	_____	_____	_____
_____	_____	_____	_____
_____	_____	_____	_____
_____	_____	_____	_____

H. Pensions and Tax Deferred annuities: Include all pensions, IRA's, Keoughs, 401Ks, tax deferred annuities, or any other retirement accounts. If value is unknown, leave right hand column blank:

	Husband	Wife	Joint
IRA	_____	12,800	_____
DEFINED BENEFIT	62,000	_____	_____
_____	_____	_____	_____
_____	_____	_____	_____

I. Miscellaneous Property: Patents, trademarks, copyrights, royalties, employee benefits (furnish last statement and descriptive booklet), stock options, etc:

	Husband	Wife	Joint
FIGURINES	_____	_____	10,000
_____	_____	_____	_____
_____	_____	_____	_____
_____	_____	_____	_____

37-3

J. Automobiles:	Husband	Wife	Joint
1990 FORD TAURUS	11,000		
1988 CHEV.		7000	

K. Personal Effects, and Tangible
Personal Property:

	Husband	Wife	Joint
PERSONAL PROPERTY			5000
JEWELRY		3000	
HOUSEHOLD ITEMS			10,000
BOAT			7000

L. Other:

	Husband	Wife	Joint

	Husband	Wife	Joint
TOTAL ASSETS	105,273	58,121	283,579
TOTAL			446,973

LIABILITIES

A. Mortgages on Real Estate:

	Husband	Wife	Joint
200 APPLE CT 1st MORTGAGE			26,000
200 APPLE CT 2nd "			9,000

	Husband	Wife	Joint	
B. Notes Payable to Banks and Others:				
AUTO LOAN ON FORD	4000			
CHASE - EDUCATION LOAN		700		
MOM + DAD SMITH			3000	
C. Loans on Insurance Policies:				
D. Credit Card Debt:				
AMEX	2000			
MASTERCARD		800		
VISA			1000	
SEARS		650		
E. Other Debts:				
HARVARD UNIV - PLEDGE	1000			
MISC. BILLS			3000	
				TOTAL
Total Liabilities:	7000	2150	42,000	51,150
Net Worth (Assets minus Liabilities):	98273	55,971	241,579	395,82

Annual Income

	Husband	Wife
Gross Salary	85,000	35,000
Less:		
Withholding	(20,000)	(7,000)
FICA	(5600)	(3250)
Other Deductions (Itemize):		
_____	(_____)	(_____)
_____	(_____)	(_____)
_____	(_____)	(_____)
_____	(_____)	(_____)
Net Salary	59,400	24,750
Dividend Income*	_____	_____
Interest Income*	_____	_____
Income from Trusts*	_____	_____
Rental Income*	_____	_____
Other Income (specify)*	_____	_____
Total Annual Income	_____	_____

Less Deductions for:	Husband	Wife
Estimated Taxes	(_____)	(_____)
Other Deductions for Tax Payments on Income Not Subject to Withholding	(_____)	(_____)
Total Deductions	(_____)	(_____)
Net Annual (take home) Income	59400	24750
Average Monthly Net (take home) Income (1/12th of Annual Figure)	4950	2062.50

* If this income is received jointly, so indicate ( ) and divide between husband and wife.

FILLING OUT THE FINANCIAL STATEMENT

As you can see the financial statement is organized into three major parts: assets, liabilities, and income. Within each of these are numerous sub-headings. The sub-headings (real estate, bank accounts, pensions, etc.) enable you to list each item and then, on the right hand side of the form, insert a value for each item. When inserting the value, the dollar value should be put in the "husband", "wife", or "joint" title column depending on whose name the holding is in. Thus, if an automobile is titled to the wife, the valuation should be put in the wife column; if a home is held jointly (i.e., the title is in both names) then the value of the home should be placed in the joint column.

This process will enable us to total the three columns "wife", "husband", and "joint", so that we will have a listing and totals for all assets, liabilities and income.

While most of the items in the financial and income statement are self-explanatory it might be helpful to discuss a few of them which sometimes give people difficulty.

In order to exemplify how the financial information and income statement may be filled out let's examine a typical situation together.

Mr. & Mrs. Ordinaire are seeking to complete a successful divorce agreement. They have collected all of the information which we have listed previously and are now ready to fill out their financial and income statement. Let's go through it step by step and see how it is done, referring to the sample form shown on the previous pages.

BANK ACCOUNTS, SAVINGS, AND CASH ON HAND

Mr. & Mrs. Ordinaire have looked through their accounts and have discovered that Mr. Ordinaire has a savings account in his name at the First National Bank. The account number is 1234. The amount in the account is three thousand dollars as per the savings book. Mrs. Ordinaire does not have a savings account in her name but the couple does have a joint account also at the First National Bank which they also list. Mrs. Ordinaire has a money market account at the Bank of Commerce and, in addition, the couple has a joint checking account at First National Bank. Mr. & Mrs. Ordinaire also keep a five hundred dollar cash emergency fund in the tin cup over the sink and this is duly listed under cash on hand.

ACCOUNTS RECEIVABLE

Mr. & Mrs. Ordinaire usually do not loan money to anyone but, about a year ago, Mrs. Ordinaire loaned seven hundred and fifty dollars to her sister and has since received two hundred and fifty dollars back. This leaves a balance of five hundred dollars which is still owed to her and she has a note which her sister signed indicating that this money is owed.

STOCKS, BONDS, AND MUTUAL FUNDS

The Ordinaire's have been investing in stocks and bonds for some time and have most of their holdings in a brokerage account with Merrill Lynch. In addition they have stock certificates for several hundred shares of IBM which they keep in their safe deposit box. They also have some series E savings bonds in the safe deposit box and they have some mutual funds which were purchased over the years. With holdings this significant the Ordinaire's decide that it would be best to list these stocks, bonds, and mutual funds on a separate sheet of paper which they attach to the back of the financial information and income statement. They total these numbers and include the totals on the financial information and income statement.

It should be noted that the monthly statement from their stock broker gave the accounts' net worth and the monthly statement from their mutual fund company also gave them a current net worth. In order to value the savings bonds and stock certificates held in the safe deposit box they had to look up the values in the daily listings of their local newspaper for stocks and consulted with their banker in order to calculate the value of the bonds. The Ordinaire's main stock fund at Merrill Lynch was held jointly. The mutual funds had been purchased at different times in different names, and the savings bonds had likewise been purchased in different names at different times. The totals again are listed on the financial statement.

REAL ESTATE

For most people the most important real estate holding and often the only one which they have is their marital home. Some people also have second homes, investment properties, or land held for possible retirement. Real estate can include land, homes, commercial property, condominiums, or co-operative apartments. The listing process is the same for all of these types of real estate holdings. The property is listed at its fair market value. Any liens or mortgages held against the property are listed later in the liability section.

In order to obtain fair market value for real estate two methods are generally used. The first option is to hire a licensed real estate appraiser who, for a fee, will give you a valuation of your property. The second option, the one most often chosen, is to contact a local real estate broker or perhaps two local real estate brokers and ask for a fair market evaluation of the property explaining that a sale is being contemplated. The brokers should go over all local records, finding comparable sales in recent months and base an estimate of market value on these comparable sales. This system of using "comps" is facilitated by public records and multiple listing records by associations of real estate brokers. If you obtain two evaluations and they are widely separated it might be in order to get a third evaluation so that true market value can be approximated. If the two valuations are close, then the two should be averaged to find Fair Market Value.

The Ordinaire's marital home was valued by two brokers who came in with estimates of two hundred and ten, and two hundred and twenty thousand dollars, respectively. The two were averaged giving them a value of two hundred and fifteen thousand dollars. The Ordinaire's recognized that if they chose to sell their house there would be a real estate commission of approximately six thousand dollars and so they deducted that amount from the fair market value in order to get a truer valuation of what they might receive if they sold the house through a broker. The resulting value of two hundred and nine thousand dollars was placed on the asset list.

LIFE INSURANCE

Life insurance comes in many forms. Many people have life insurance coverage through their employer; they may have some form of insurance on their mortgage or they may have purchased life insurance in some other way. Many life insurance policies are "term" policies and do not accumulate any cash value. Others such as whole life, or universal life may accumulate substantial cash value over the life of the policy. For the purposes of asset evaluation only the cash value or, what some people call the loan value of the policy, is relevant. However, for purposes of planning in a divorce or separation situation policies without cash value may also be important. We therefore suggest that all policies be listed but that only those with cash value will be shown on the asset evaluation side (right side) of the financial statement.

Mr. & Mrs. Ordinaire looked over their life insurance situation and found that Mr. Ordinaire had a term life insurance policy through his employer with a face value of one year's salary. Each had a fifty thousand dollar "whole life" policy which they purchased on the day of their marriage having equal

cash value of fifteen thousand eight hundred and twenty one dollars.

BUSINESS OR PROFESSIONAL INTERESTS

Neither Mr. or Mrs. Ordinaire were in business, nor did either one of them own part of any professional practice. Therefore this section for them would be left blank. However, many people who are in business for themselves, own a part of a professional practice, or small closed corporation, have an interest in a partnership, or sole proprietorship would have to value these assets for the purposes of their agreement. In these cases it is best to consult with your accountant and seek professional help in arriving at a valuation.

LICENSES AND DEGREES

Neither Mr. or Mrs. Ordinaire had obtained a college degree or a professional license during their marriage. Therefore this section is left blank. However, if either of them had obtained a license or degree during the marriage, they would have had to arrive at a value. This is a complex procedure and would require consultation with their accountant.

PENSIONS AND TAX DEFERRED ANNUITIES

Under this heading we will be listing all pension monies or tax deferred annuity monies which have been put aside for a later date. This includes IRA'S, KEOUGHS'S, 401 K'S, 401 W'S, tax deferred annuities, defined contribution pension plans, defined benefit pension plans and many profit sharing plans. It should be noted that most of these pensions can be valued by simply looking at the latest statement which is usually provided on an annual basis by the pension administrator, usually a bank or insurance company. However certain kinds of pensions, most notably, defined benefit pensions, are not so easily valued. These types of pension plans usually require the services of a actuary in order to make an exact evaluation. Actuaries are not always easy to find, but in the Appendix, Table 6, we have supplied the informational form required by "Legal Economic Evaluations Inc.", the largest company of its kind. They can value your defined benefit plan for a relatively low fee in a few days.

The Ordinaire's used an actuary and listed their pension holdings accordingly.

In addition it should be noted that most pension monies are "pre-tax" dollars. While we do not necessary take this into account when simply listing the assets this does become an important issue when the distribution of marital assets takes place. This will be discussed later in the book.

MISCELLANEOUS PROPERTY

COLLECTIBLES

Mr. & Mrs. Ordinaire have spent a number of years collecting china figurines. They had their collection valued and found that it was worth a considerable sum, which is listed under assets.

AUTOMOBILES

As with so many other families in this country, Mr. & Mrs. Ordinaire have two cars. In order to ascertain the value they called their insurance broker and got the "blue book" retail values of the cars and used these values. They could have also gone to a local library or contacted their bank to find out the values.

PERSONAL EFFECTS AND TANGIBLE PERSONAL PROPERTY

Mr. & Mrs. Ordinaire each have a considerable amount of clothing, jewelry, and other items of personal property. As is often the case they decided that their personal property was held in approximately equal shares with the exception of some jewelry held by Mrs. Ordinaire. For that reason they simply estimate the value of personal property less the jewelry based on a guess. The jewelry had been appraised by a jeweler for insurance purposes in the past but they recognize that the resale value of the jewelry is only about half of what it had been appraised for and used this estimated resale in their asset list. In addition the Ordinaire's have their list of household effects including furniture and other household items and they estimated a value based on what they thought it would be worth if they sold at auction. They understood that if they wanted a true evaluation they could bring in an auctioneer, or tag sale expert who would give them a professional estimate of value. However, they chose not to do this.

The Ordinaire's also own a small boat which they estimated could be sold for about seven thousand dollars. The boat was also listed.

OTHER

While the Ordinaire's felt they had listed all of their assets some people find that they have property of value which may not be completely tangible. Patent trademarks, copyrights, royalty agreements, employee benefits, employment contracts, stock options, and many other nontangible assets may accrue to one party or the other over the years of a marriage. These assets should be listed at this time.

ASSET TOTALS

As you can see three columns have been created and the columns can now be totaled quite easily.

COMPUTING LIABILITIES

Now that you've had the fun of adding up everything you own, we have to go on to the sad part, what you owe.

MORTGAGES ON REAL ESTATE

Most people in this country who own real estate have a loan or mortgage against that real estate. There may be more than one loan outstanding against real estate. This generally constitutes a second mortgage.

On the liability statement the important number is "how much is owed currently" on each mortgage, not the amount that was originally borrowed. The current liability or "pay off" can be obtained by contacting the lender. This amount should be recorded on the liability statement.

The Ordinaire's originally had a mortgage of fifty thousand dollars on their house. When they contacted their bank, they found out they still owed twenty six thousand dollars. In addition, three years ago the Ordinaire's had taken out a home improvement loan which was registered by their bank as a second mortgage. They owe nine thousand dollars on this loan. This should also be recorded on the statement.

NOTES PAYABLE TO BANKS AND OTHERS

In this section all bank loans, automobile loans, credit union loans, or loans made from other parties should be listed. The Ordinaire's found that they owed the bank four thousand dollars on the auto loan they had taken out when they purchased their ford. Mrs. Ordinaire still owed seven hundred dollars on her education loan that she had taken a number of years before when she went to college. In addition, Mr. & Mrs. Ordinaire had borrowed three thousand dollars from Mrs. Ordinaire's parents. They had yet to repay this loan. All of these loans are recorded.

INSURANCE POLICY LOANS

The Ordinaire's as we have mentioned before, had two life insurance policies with cash value. In their case they had never made a loan against these policies but many people do. The amount of the loan against your insurance policy can be checked with your insurance company. Usually, there is a yearly, monthly, or quarterly statement which the insurance company sends showing the amount of the loan.

CREDIT CARDS

Credit card balances are sometimes significant for people going through a separation or divorce. It is important to carefully look at credit card debts and ascertain what is owed. Fortunately it is a relatively easy process because the monthly statement lists the total owed and the Ordinaire's were able to calculate these debts and duly record them.

OTHER DEBTS

Over the years people accumulate debts or make pledges which obligate them for payments over a period of time. Installment payments, pledges to educational institutions or charities, payments of membership fees over a period of time, and normal monthly bills to doctors, lawyers, shopkeepers, etc. are included in this category.

The Ordinaire's had pledged money to Mr. Ordinaire's alma mater. They also calculated that they owed approximately three thousand dollars in bills which they did not bother to list separately. These debts were recorded.

TOTAL LIABILITIES

The total liabilities for the couple can now be calculated by totaling the columns.

NET WORTH

Net worth is calculated by subtracting total liabilities from total assets.
Total liabilities plus net worth should equal the total assets.

TOTAL ASSETS, LIABILITIES, AND NET WORTH

The total assets for the couple may be calculated by adding the assets for each party and the assets held jointly. The total of those three numbers equals the total assets for the couple.

The total liabilities can be obtained similarly. Net worth for the couple equals the total assets minus the total liabilities. Total net worth represents the true value of all holdings owned by Mr. & Mrs. Ordinaire. It should be noted that this does not indicate which property is marital and which is not. Nor does it take account of the tax liabilities which might be owed on tax deferred or pension monies.

ANNUAL INCOME

The income part of the financial statement can be relatively simple or it could be quite complicated. In the case of the Ordinaire's it is simple because both parties are employed by large companies, they can calculate their income simply by looking at their most recent pay stub.

In some cases people have income from different sources and the calculation can be more complex. If your income statement is complicated it may be beneficial to consult with your accountant especially when estimating taxes or other deductions.

It is now evident that the monthly income can be calculated by simply dividing the annual take home pay by twelve.

The Ordinaire's have now finished their financial information and income statement.

BUDGETING

The next step in preparing for the negotiation is to put together the living expenses for you and your family. One way to do this is to compute a monthly budget. The monthly budget should include not only the expenses and bills which you pay out each month but also seasonal expenses, emergency expenses, and plans for future needs. Calculating expenses is sometimes difficult but it's worth the effort.

Your canceled checks for the past year should enable you to analyze fairly accurately how much money is spent for different things. In addition, you might want to keep records for a month or two of how much money is spent at the supermarket or on sundries. If you tend to use cash for auto or other expenses you might want to keep records for a couple of months of how much you spend on gasoline and routine maintenance for your cars, as well as lunches, tolls, and other daily expenses. In the following section we will go through a typical budget situation. It is important to note that many expenses may be divided between each spouse and the children. Keep in mind that once the separation occurs, the housing requirements will change dramatically. For this reason each of you should calculate your own monthly budget using estimates of what it will cost you after the separation has taken place. If one party stays in the marital home, the payments which have been made in the past will probably be comparable to those which will be needed in the future. If one spouse leaves the home he or she may have to investigate the rental market in order to calculate what housing might cost.

Remember, we use monthly budgets primarily to give each of you a basis on which to estimate your future needs. Estimates should be realistic and should not be inflated or grossly underestimated. Doing either will effect future negotiations negatively.

To help you calculate your monthly budget we have included some forms which have been used by many people. It is usually advisable to start by filling out Schedules A, B, and C, Emergencies and future goals, Seasonal expenses, and Installment Debt payments, first. Then proceed to fill out the Monthly Expense Budget. Blank forms are included for your use in the Appendix, Table 7.

SCHEDULE A

EMERGENCIES AND FUTURE GOALS

The purpose of schedule A is to help you to estimate what you may need in the future. It is very important when filling out Schedule A to be realistic. You know what your assets are and you also know your income. You must keep both of these in mind when planning for the future. For example, if you already have a substantial amount of money in retirement funds and savings you may not have to plan for future savings or investments. On the other hand, if you have very little money set aside then it may become more important to budget for future savings and investment. If educational funds have been set aside for the children, you may not need to consider budgeting additional monies. If your car is brand new you may not need to plan on a replacement vehicle for a number of years. If, on the other hand, you have a "real clunker" then auto replacement may become a priority. Fill out Schedule A as carefully as you can remembering that you "can't get blood from a stone". This means that if your income is insufficient even to meet certain priority everyday needs then it doesn't make sense to consider setting aside large amounts of money that are not there. One last hint is that since you can't always foresee the future, allow for a small emergency fund to give you a cushion for the inevitable unforseen need.

SCHEDULE B

SEASONAL EXPENSES

Schedule B is designed to remind you about those seasonal expenses that come up almost every year but are not necessarily present each month. Each family has its own seasonal expenses. These may not be the same for everyone. Such things as summer landscaping cost, or pool maintenance should be considered and can be listed in the "other" category. Remember as with Schedule A, you can't anticipate everything and you must be reasonable. With this in mind fill out Schedule B as best you can.

SCHEDULE C

INSTALLMENT DEBT PAYMENTS

Schedule C is self-explanatory for the most part. The purpose is to put together and analyze your installment debt. You should list all of the regular monthly payments which you are required to make except mortgage and rent which are not considered installment debts. Installments debts consist of monies that you owe to someone else, which are being paid off over a period of time. You may include leases here, such as car or other major equipment. Keep in mind the payoff date. If the last payment is only a couple of months away it's not necessary to calculate that debt in the long term planning. If, on the other hand, an installment debt isn't going to be paid off for a long period of time, it is important to consider it when working out your monthly budget. With this in mind fill out Schedule C.

MONTHLY EXPENSE BUDGET FORM

As we've mentioned before, the best way to estimate for the future is to look at the past. Therefore, its important to go over your last year's checks so that you know what it costs for the various items in the budget. As we've already suggested, keeping track of your grocery bills for a couple of months, as well as clothing, sundry, and other cash outlays will help in making these estimates.

As you can see, the monthly expense budget is constructed so you can list anticipated expenses for yourself and your children separately. It is anticipated that after your separation or divorce you will become two separate households.

Therefore each spouse should complete a monthly expense budget. For this reason we have included two copies of the monthly expense budget in the Appendix. If you do not anticipate that your children will be living with you, complete only column A, an expense budget for yourself only. If you do anticipate that the children will be living with you, then attempt to distribute your estimated monthly needs between columns A & B. This may be difficult with some of the expenses such as rent but you can usually estimate by assuming that the difference between what you would spend on yourself alone versus what it would cost for you and the children together would be the cost for the children. In other words, if you were living alone and needed a one bedroom apartment which cost five hundred dollars a month but if you were living with your children and needed a two bedroom apartment which would cost seven hundred dollars a month then you can allocate two hundred dollars per month in rent to the children while keeping five hundred dollars for yourself.

Again remember that when you estimate budgetary needs it is important to be realistic. The object of filling out this budget form is to give you a basis for estimating what you will really need to live, on a month to month basis. Certain things may be necessary and others may be luxuries. You may have to make changes after the divorce. It may be impossible to provide exactly the same level of living style for two families that you had with one family. This is something which will have to be dealt with based on your particular situation. With these guidelines in mind, fill out the Monthly Expense Budget form. When you finish make sure that you and your spouse have not duplicated or left out any expenses such as installment debt payments or seasonal expenses.

Once you've finished this process you should have two monthly expense budgets which, when totaled together, will give you the total expenses for you, your spouse, and your children. This total represents the estimated monthly needs for your entire family.

By accurately assessing and scheduling those needs, you will be able to negotiate more effectively and work out the support and maintenance aspects of your agreement with some surety. We've now pulled together all of the data and we're ready to start the process of making the important decisions.

CHAPTER TWELVE

MAKING THE DECISIONS

THE MEMORANDUM OF AGREEMENT

Before we start dealing with specific issues it's important to understand that the decision agreement process will be broken down into several steps. The first is the development of your **Memorandum of Agreement**.

The Memorandum of Agreement is a form, contained in Table 8 of the Appendix. It lists all of the decisions made on all of the pertinent issues. Using it you can draw up your final agreement of separation or divorce. The Memorandum is divided into sections each containing the important issues which must be dealt with. I suggest that you prepare for each negotiation meeting by deciding in advance which part of the Memorandum you are going to deal with. Limit your discussion to that part of the Memorandum. Once you've reached agreement on a particular issue write it down in the clearest terms possible on the Memorandum form. Then, make sure that you're both in agreement as to the content. Only then should you move on to the next section. Once the Memorandum is completed you will be able to review it and make sure that you are still in agreement on all parts of the Memorandum. You may signify your agreement in the Memorandum by signing off and proceeding to the next phase of your action, the drawing of the final agreement.

GETTING STARTED

Lets get started with the memorandum of agreement.

First, look at the Memorandum. You see that the first part contains spaces for some general information: name, address, the date you start this negotiation, date of marriage, etc.

The next section of the Memorandum is the listing of marital assets. You see there are spaces for all of your assets and, eventually, you'll be filling in all of ones that apply.

Next we have a listing of all of the marital liabilities and these too will be filled out.

The next section of the Memorandum is a summary table which organizes the marital assets and liabilities according to title.

Now we get to the various issues that must be dealt with starting with child custody and support, and including each of the areas that must be covered. Space is left in each section for you and your spouse to write in what you've agreed to.

At the end of the Memorandum is a place for you and your spouse to sign and date the Memorandum when you have completed it, gone over it to make sure that it states exactly what you want, and agreed to end your decision making process.

If at any time you need extra space you can insert pages or change the spacing of various sections to suit your needs. Now let's get started.

BASIC DATA

The basic data on the Memorandum of Agreement is self-explanatory. Fill in names, address, date, employment, social security numbers, the date of your marriage, etc. The only significant thing to remember here is that people usually agree that the date they start negotiating is the date used for evaluation of assets. This is not a hard and fast rule and you can pick any convenient date such as the date of signing the agreement, the last day of the year, or any other convenient date which is in close proximity to this process. This is up to you but remember the date of the start of negotiation is one of your options.

The next significant issue to be decided is the type of action you wish to take. Most people starting negotiation have an idea about whether or not they want to go for a legal separation or a divorce. As you've seen in the law section there are some legal differences between a legal separation and divorce but probably the most important difference is the emotional one. In a divorce the decision is final and is viewed by most people as relatively irrevocable. While a legal separation carries most of the same legal ramifications as a divorce it is viewed by most people as less final.

I generally recommend that if either party to this negotiation is unsure or less than positive about getting a divorce, then using a legal separation is a good interim step to take.

If you decided that divorce is the course of action you wish to pursue then you must be aware that in some jurisdictions there is a requirement for grounds. Check Table 2 in the appendix to see if your jurisdiction requires grounds. If required, you must decide what grounds you would like to use for your divorce. You may also decide which of you will be the plaintiff and which of you will be the defendant. In most agreed-upon divorces the significance of who is the plaintiff and who is the defendant is purely technical. However, when a no fault divorce is not available to you, it may be necessary to make this decision. Chapter 5 will help you decide on the grounds you wish to use. Keep in mind that it generally makes for a better atmosphere for negotiation if the grounds are as free of blame as possible. Further, consider that the children may be affected if you choose grounds which are overly onerous.

LISTING OF MARITAL ASSETS

We are now ready to list all of the marital assets. Remember that a listing of assets does not constitute a decision on how those assets are going to be distributed. It is simply a list to be used later when the distribution of marital assets is discussed. The important principal right now is to make the decision of which assets are marital and which are not. You already know from your reading that the definition of marital assets varies from state to state. However, there is a general principle which holds that marital assets are assets which were acquired during a marriage. Furthermore, it is the marital assets that are subject to distribution at the time of a legal separation or divorce. It is also generally accepted that if you as two adult, informed parties decide that a particular item of property is marital and thus subject to distribution or if you, together, decide that a particular article of property is separate or non-marital and, therefore, not subject to distribution, this decision will be accepted when your divorce or separation is finalized. Therefore, in listing the marital assets it will be necessary to make joint decisions whether or not particular assets are marital. Remember that the longer you've been married, the greater the likelihood that assets will be marital. There are some exceptions to this, and you may refer to the law section for guidance. You may also adhere to the general principle that the two of you together have the right to decide which articles of property will be subject to distribution and which will not.

In preparation for the listing refer to your financial statements and start listing each of the assets on the Memorandum of Agreement. As you consider each item, come to agreement on whether or not the item will be a marital or separate property. Only list the marital items here. This decision does not involve the title of the particular piece of property, nor does it mean that we are deciding at this time who gets what. It merely means that the property listed is marital and therefore subject to distribution when we discuss distribution of assets. For example: if the two of you each work at a job and through your employers you each have a pension, then you should list the pensions at this time even though the title is in only one name.

You may eventually decide that you're each going to keep your own pension without sharing it, but it is important to write it down as an item to be included in the pool of marital property which will be later distributed.

Notice that the listing here is somewhat more detailed than the listing in the financial statement. This is done to enable you to segregate various items of property so that final distribution can be more easily accomplished.

LISTING OF MARITAL LIABILITIES

Make your decisions and list all liabilities in the same way that the assets were listed. Once again, liabilities are generally seen as marital when they were acquired during the marriage. This usually means that they will be shared as part of the marital distribution in the same way as assets.

Once you've listed the assets and liabilities you are ready to reorganize them in the asset and liability tables located in the next section.

THE ASSET AND LIABILITY TABLES

The asset and liability tables may be completed by going through the listing of marital assets and liabilities and placing the values in the appropriate columns. Within subsections that contain more than one item, such as real estate or CD's, total the amounts of each, that are in either individual or joint name. According to title, list the assets and liabilities in the proper column. For example; if you as a couple own three pieces of property, a marital home which is jointly held, a piece of vacant land which is in the husband's name alone, and a vacation home which is in the wife's name alone, on the asset and debit tables the full value of the vacant land would be listed in the husband column, the full value of the marital home would be listed in the joint column, and full value of the vacation home would be listed in the wife column.

Note that the pension and the tax deferred annuities are listed on the bottom and are segregated from the rest of the property. This is done because pensions and annuities generally contain monies which were not taxed. This means that when the final distribution of assets takes place, untaxed assets may be worth less in today's dollars than already taxed assets. In addition, on the liability side of the tabulation, mortgages are segregated out because they may be treated somewhat differently from other liabilities at a later point in the negotiation.

Once you've tabulated all the marital assets and liabilities in the table add up the columns and go onto the next chapter.

CHAPTER THIRTEEN

PARENTING FOR THE FUTURE

In the traditional adversarial approach to divorce or separation the issue of "who should get the children" or "child custody" is often the most difficult, complex, and traumatic part of the process. Given that people who are utilizing Step III of this book have a commitment to working together towards a fair and equitable agreement for their separation or divorce, it would not be appropriate to treat the issue of parenting in the same way as do adversaries in court. Therefore rather than discussing the issue as one of "who should get the children" we shall strive here to reach agreement on how the future responsibilities for parenting will be shared between you.

This approach is consonant with a growing tendency across the nation toward parental sharing in the form of joint legal custody and sharing of physical custody when it meets the best interest of the child. Our task here is to reach agreement on how best to share future parenting responsibilities. We should do it in such a way as to best meet the needs of your children and of yourselves, and take into consideration all the special circumstances which effect your family.

Before proceeding it would be helpful for both of you to do the following homework:

1) Read this chapter before proceeding.
2) Work out a weekly schedule for yourself noting the times when you have to be in work, when you can be home, and when you have other activities. Use the form in Table 9, Schedule 1. Make special note of times you have to spend with your children on Schedule 2.
3) Make a list of all the special days and holidays on which it would be important for you to spend time with your children. Use table 9, Schedule 3 to help you.
4) Develop a schedule of vacation times that you might have, and list all of the extended school vacations on Schedule 4.
5) List the significant others such as grandparents, aunts, uncles, and cousins with whom the children have contact on Schedule 5, and consider when this contact can take place.
6) Think about and define what moving would mean for you.

7) Re-read Chapter 6 on Custody.

After you've completed this work make an appointment to have your next negotiation session and start working on parenting for the future.

SOME GENERAL PRINCIPLES TO GO BY

The first important principle is the principle of "best interest of the child". The "best interest of the child" underlies all good parenting agreements. It must be agreed and in, fact, it is usually taken for granted that both parents are concerned for the children's welfare. Therefore any decision that is made will consider what is best for the child before considering what is best for the parents.

The next important principle is that children have rights, including the right to two parents. This means that in no way should an agreement limit the children's rights to love and be loved by two parents. Only in very exceptional circumstances, where there might be danger, should the right to two parents be abrogated.

The next principle to consider is the rights of the parents. While we are saying that parental rights come second to the "best interest of the child", parental rights are still very important and no agreement should unfairly or unnecessarily limit contact or the rights of a parent to take part in the parenting process.

Lastly when considering the parenting agreement you should remember that grandparents also have rights, and often it's very important to children to be in contact with grandparents and other members of the extended family.

In preparation for making important decisions, remember that you will have to deal with each other and the children after the separation or divorce takes place. While the marriage may be breaking up the family will still exist. Therefore it is especially important that in this negotiation process and afterwards neither parent should do anything to undermine or downgrade the other in the eyes of the children. It is important to understand that once the separation takes place many children go through a "two home syndrome" which includes a period of adjustment. During this time, limits will be tested as children learn how to behave in the two different environments. Don't hesitate to be specific about the different rules in the two homes. This doesn't mean that one way is right and the other is wrong. Very often when two separate households form, children will be tempted to be manipulative. Often parents get into a pattern in which they communicate with each other through the children. This should be avoided whenever possible. Confer with each other and listen to the children and understand their needs whenever possible.

Most people entering into negotiation on parenting will be concerned with what's best for their children. This is a very difficult question to address. It is important that the children understand that they have access to both parents, can talk to both parents, and can depend on both parents, no matter what. Younger children need more frequent contact with both parents in order to maintain a relationship. Older children are able to go for longer periods of time without contact and still not have a sense of abandonment. As children get older, friends become more important. They have more connections to school and they develop a greater need to follow their own schedule of events. It's important that in whatever agreement is reached with regard to parenting, there should be some flexibility so that children's needs as well as parents needs, both of which change over time, can be accommodated.

PHYSICAL CUSTODY OR ESTABLISHING THE HOME BASE

Most people who have reached this point have already formed a clear idea of where and with whom they want their children to be living. Usually, the considerations of stability within the home, continuity of friendships, continuity of schooling, and the wishes of the children, as well as availability of parental time dictate which parent will have primary physical custody. If this is the case, then let us start by deciding that primary physical custody will be with one parent or the other.

It is important to understand that primary physical custody does not mean "total ownership" or even total physical custody. It simply defines for both of you and for the children where their "official" home base will be.

In cases where this is not a foregone conclusion you may consider sharing the physical custody.

SHARED OR JOINT PHYSICAL CUSTODY

When it is not clearly defined for both parents that one or the other will be the primary physical custodian of the children, then the issue of how the physical custody will be shared becomes important. At this point it is important to look back at the time availability schedules 1 through 5 in Appendix 9 which you completed at the beginning of this chapter. Compare your availability for child contact and also compare your work schedules with regard to travel and late night or emergency needs. Based on this, start to discuss the sharing of the children.

Following are some examples of how other couples have handled shared custody:

FRAN AND BOB

Fran and Bob were living separately for almost a year before they started their divorce proceeding. During that year the children lived with Fran, attended school, and saw Bob mostly on weekends. Fran worked in a part-time job which did not occupy her other than during school hours, while Bob often had to travel and work late, seeing clients. By the time they started working on their divorce agreement Fran and Bob had already reached a "defacto" understanding that the children would be best off continuing with Fran but Bob was uncomfortable with the idea of giving Fran sole physical custody. After discussing it for some time it was agreed that they would draw up a "shared custody" agreement in which Bob would have the children from Friday evening to Sunday evening every week and Fran would have the children from Monday through Friday. It was also mentioned in the agreement that on weekends when Bob had to be out of town Fran would be given three days notification and that she would then take the children on those weekends. The agreement stated that Bob could visit with the children on any evening during the week when he had available time but he was required to give Fran at least six hours prior notification so as to protect her privacy.

LAURA AND TED

Laura and Ted both work full-time as professionals. Each one can be required by his or her work to go out of town on weekends and both are subject to evening hours with clients or customers. Neither parent wanted to give up care of their two children aged eight and eleven and the children had made it quite clear that they wanted as much contact as possible with both their mom and dad. After much soul searching Laura and Ted decided that the only solution for them would be to share the physical custody of their children approximately equally. In order to accomplish this it was decided that while Laura would remain in the marital home, Ted would rent a home only a half mile from the marital home. It was decided that the children would spend alternate weeks with each parent and still be able to attend the same school and keep contact with their friends.

Flexibility would be necessary so that on weekends or evenings when one parent was required to be away, the other would be available to care for the children.

Laura and Ted entered into this agreement with some trepidation and for that reason made it clear that it was a trial which would last only as long as the children seemed happy. Approximately one year later they both felt that the kids had adjusted well and the situation was working for them. Laura and Ted also included an agreement stating that if either parent felt the children were suffering by this arrangement, then a child psychologist or family counselor would be sought out who could help them decide how best to deal with the situation.

MATT AND SARAH

Matt and Sarah had been separated for several months before starting work on their divorce agreement. Matt was living at his mother's house while Sarah was at home with the kids. The children, two boys aged eleven and fourteen, said very often that they really missed being with their father. At the same time, it was very clear that the children needed a great deal of contact with their mother. Matt worked a full-time job while Sarah was not employed outside of the home.

The solution for this family was that the children remained in the marital home with Sarah during the week. Remember Matt lived with his parents. On weekends Matt moved back into the house to stay with the children and Sarah left. Both parents realized that this solution would be short term. It was agreed that if it became unworkable because of difficulties with the living accommodations or one of them became involved with a new significant other, then the physical sharing would have to be renegotiated.

TAMMY AND SETH

Tammy and Seth had a son aged sixteen and a daughter of twelve. Tammy worked in a daytime job from which she was off at approximately four thirty, while Seth had a job which occupied him for many hours but he could be flexible with his schedule. The couple realized that they could not manage to keep up their marital home after the divorce and it was placed on the market. Neither parent wanted to limit their contact with the children and the children were old enough and verbal enough about their wishes to make it clear that they wanted to be able to have contact with both parents. They also wanted to remain in contact with their friends.

Tammy and Seth decided that after the marital home was sold Tammy would rent an apartment near the marital home and Seth would reside about forty-five minutes away. They agreed that the children would establish a home base with Tammy but that anytime they wished they could spend weekends with their father. During long school holidays including the summer, the children would spend the majority of the time with their father. Seth agreed to curtail his work schedule during those periods.

As you can see a number of different solutions can be found to deal with the sharing of physical custody. Sharing the children does not necessarily mean that the children will be shifted back and forth irrationally. Nor does it mean that they lose a sense of having a home base. When the needs of the children as well as the availability and needs of the parents are taken into consideration, there are many unique and workable solutions that can be created to enable parents to share the physical custody of their children.

VISITATION SCHEDULES

Visitation is a concept which is closely tied to traditional custody solutions wherein one parent has the primary physical custody of the children and the other parent becomes the visiting parent. If you've chosen this type of parenting situation then it becomes important to work out a comprehensive schedule of visitation entitlement for the "noncustodial" parent. However, even if you have worked out a sharing of the physical custody this does not mean that certain aspects of visitation do not have to be attended to. Different family traditions or special occasions such as birthdays, confirmations, bar mitzvahs, weddings etc. may require that the children visit with a particular parent on a particular day or occasion. This may be true no matter what kind of parental sharing you have agreed to.

We should differentiate between the concepts of access and visitation entitlement. Access implies having the ability to be in touch with or be in contact with one another. Most agreements accept that children should have access to either parent at anytime, unless it is unreasonable to have access at that time. For example, you might agree that your children should be allowed to phone either parent at anytime and this telephone access should be unlimited and should not be denied unreasonably.

BOB AND MARY

Bob and Mary had been separated for sometime and had agreed at the time of their separation that the children should have unlimited phone access to their parents. In addition, they agreed that each parent should have unlimited phone access to the children. This access was not to be unreasonably denied.

One evening when their son decided that he didn't want to do his homework, Mary told him that he had to continue doing his homework until it was finished. Not only was it important to do homework generally, but he also had a social studies test the next day. The child said that he did not want to continue his homework because he wanted to call his father. Mary said "you cannot call your father right now and you must finish your homework before you call your father". Bob and Mary agreed at a later time that this was a reasonable denial of access.

The concept of access may also apply to actual physical visitation. Many couples agree that both parents should have unlimited access to the children and that the children should have unlimited access to the parents and this physical access is not to be unreasonably denied. The most important condition in this case is that prior notice may be required. This is done in order to protect the privacy of the parent who has custody at the time of access.

SETH AND MIRIAM

Seth and Miriam were both very close to their children before they were divorced and wanted to remain close to their children afterwards. The children were living with Miriam who had primary physical custody. They had agreed that either parent had unlimited access to the children providing that six hours notification was given. This access could not be unreasonably denied.

Seth's job was such that he occasionally had days off, but he often did not know until the same day. He developed a pattern of calling Miriam first thing in the morning when he knew he would be having a day off. He told her that he would like to see the children that evening and take them out for dinner. On occasion Miriam would have to tell him it was impossible because the children had prior plans either with friends or some other special commitment. Seth agreed that this was reasonable. On most occasions when Seth called it was agreed that he would pick the children up two hours after school so that they would have a chance to do their homework. He took them out and returned by nine o'clock.

On a few occasions Seth did not realize that he would be free to see the children until only an hour or so before he wanted to see them. On these occasions he called Miriam anyway, knowing that the six hour prior notification rule was not being followed. However, even though Miriam knew that

she could deny the access without reasonable cause she had no reason to do so and on most occasions Seth was given access to the children and had his visitation.

As you can see from the example above access between parents and children is an important aspect of the relationship and usually involves contact on an irregular and non-preordained schedule.

In contrast to this we have another kind of contact called **scheduled visitation or visitation entitlement.** A scheduled visitation is a time when the children are scheduled to be with a particular parent. This schedule is agreed to well in advance and becomes an entitlement for both the children and the visiting parent. Some visitations involving special occasions, emergencies, or certain holidays may not be scheduled but remain entitlements nevertheless.

WEEKENDS

Scheduled weekend visitation applies primarily in cases where the shared parenting agreement has not already allocated weekends. In cases where primary physical custody is with one parent and the other parent wants to have substantial time with the children and the children are not deemed harmed by this practice, then scheduled weekend visitation becomes the primary vehicle through which the noncustodial parent maintains contact. Keep in mind that many tasks performed by parents for their children can only be performed when they are residing together. For example, having breakfast together, tucking children into bed, reading a story at bedtime, sitting around watching TV, or helping children with their studies are behaviors which usually don't occur unless there is an overnight visitation. Weekend visitation becomes the primary vehicle for maintenance of these kinds of parent-child contacts. It should also be noted that weekends are often thought of as "fun time" which implies that a parent who gives up all weekends may be giving up all of the enjoyable time with his or her children. This should be considered when making arrangements for weekend visitation.

SETH AND MIRIAM

As discussed before Seth and Miriam both wanted contact with their children although Miriam was the primary physical custodian. Both children were school aged and weekend time was important not only for Seth but also for Miriam. Miriam had the children Monday through Friday and Seth reasoned that it was important for him to have the children on weekends. Miriam acknowledged that she had the children the majority of the time and that Seth loved

50

the children and was a "good father". However, she said she was not willing to allow the children to be with their father every weekend because that would mean that she would never have a chance to spend a Saturday or Sunday afternoon with the kids doing a fun, family activity. Miriam also acknowledged that the children's being with Seth on weekends gave her an opportunity to go on some trips and visit with friends.

Seth and Miriam agreed that while the children would be with Miriam every week from Monday through Friday Seth would have the children two out of three weekends from Friday evening at five o'clock through Sunday evening at eight p.m.. Every third weekend Miriam would have the kids. On the weekends when Seth had the children he agreed to both pick them up and drop them off at Miriam's house. Seth and Miriam also agreed that the schedule could be changed depending on Seth's business obligations and Miriam's ski trips, with two weeks' notification.

Seth and Miriam developed a plan that was unique to them, and it has worked out quite well. Note Seth and Miriam's attention to detail. They designated who would be picking up the children and who would be dropping them off. If the distance between parental homes was considerable it might be important to share the transportation responsibilities. When distances are especially great it might also be important to work out a sharing of travel expenses during visitations.

MID WEEK VISITATION

While mid week visitation is usually covered under access there are times when it should be scheduled.

SETH AND MIRIAM

As we described before Seth and Miriam had agreed that the children would be spending two out of three weekends with their father. Seth was uncomfortable about the two week hiatus during which time he might not see the children. He, therefore, requested that there be a scheduled mid week visitation during the week when he would not have the children for the weekend. This was agreed to and became part of their agreement.

HOLIDAYS

Holidays are important. They often involve family traditions as well as days off from school. Look over the list of holidays that are important to you. It may be that holidays which are important to one parent are not so important to the other. If that is the case it may influence who will be scheduled to be with the children on a particular holiday. Think not only of the usual major holidays such as Thanksgiving, Christmas, Easter, New Year's, and Labor Day but also of other holidays which may have special significance such as religious holidays or Memorial Day, if that's when you traditionally get together with your parents for a weekend picnic. Look over your list and try to establish a pattern which would enable each of you to be with the children on the holidays with special significance to you but not to your spouse. In cases where a holiday holds special significance to both of you, you can consider alternating the holiday so that each of you will have the children on alternate years, or splitting the holiday so that part of the day is spent with each of you. In general one day school holidays which fall on a Monday are considered part of the weekend. If a parent has a scheduled weekend visitation it might be best resolved that the holiday weekend be stretched for an extra day. This will depend on your special circumstances.

Long school vacations such as Christmas, Easter and February break, not only represent an opportunity to have a lengthy visit with the children, but they also represent a responsibility to provide child care, especially when children are young. Often people use a long school holiday to take a trip or family visit. In these cases you might consider your usual pattern and agree that the children will spend the extended vacation with one or the other of you. Here too alternating by year might work.

JOE AND MARY

Joe and Mary have two children aged seven and eleven. They were concerned not only about who should spend the various holidays with the kids, but also about taking care of the children during the holidays. After much discussion they agreed that all the holidays which fell on Monday would be taken by whichever parent had the children for that weekend. In cases where they both had to work on the Monday, it was agreed that a baby sitter would be hired to watch the children and that the responsibility of getting the baby sitter would be with the parent who had the children on that particular weekend.

Joe and Mary also ascertained that the holidays which were important to them during the year were Thanksgiving, Christmas, Easter, and Memorial Day. They agreed that Thanksgiving, Easter and Memorial Day would be alternated on a year by year basis. With Christmas they wanted to make a special arrangement.

Joe's family always celebrated Christmas eve with a big dinner. Mary's family celebrated on Christmas day. It was, therefore, agreed that Joe would have the children every Chrismas on Christmas Eve and that the children would spend the night with him. He would bring the kids to Mary's house at nine thirty Christmas morning. The children then spent the balance of Christmas day with their mother and her family. It was also understood that if anytime in the future the situation changed, then this part of the agreement would be renegotiable.

While both Joe and Mary would have liked to have taken extended vacations every winter with the children they realized that for financial reasons it might be impossible. Therefore, it was agreed that the two lengthy vacations would be alternated. The parent taking the children for the holiday would be responsible for providing day care during that school vacation.

SPECIAL OCCASIONS AND EMERGENCIES

The next issue to be dealt with is special occasions and emergencies. Special occasions usually include such things as parents birthdays, mother's day, father's day, children's birthdays, confirmations, family celebrations, and times of illness.

Look over your list of special occasions and important times and try to work out a schedule for guaranteed access on those special occasions.

JOE AND MARY

Joe and Mary worked out schedules for the major holidays quite well. They also had concerns about a number of special occasions which were going to take place. Joe was concerned because his sister was getting married in a few months and he wanted to make sure that the children were available. This was especially important because they were going to be part of the wedding party. It was agreed that both parents would be entitled to have the children for special family occasions such as weddings, bar mitzvahs, confirmations, funerals, and family birthday celebrations, providing reasonable notice was given.

Joe and Mary also decided that on special occasions for their own children such as confirmation or birthdays they, Joe and Mary, were on good enough terms so that they could share the occasions with their children. It was, therefore, agreed that on the children' birthdays both parents would have access to the children and this would also be true for other special occasions for the children. Joe and Mary took into account the possibility that their relationship might deteriorate. They agreed that if either one felt uncomfortable sharing an occasion, that person would have the right to opt out of the celebration or party but would still have some access to the children on that day. There were also some concerns about Mother's Day, Father's Day, and parental birthdays so it was agreed that Mary wouldhave the right to have the children on Mother's Day and her birthday and Joe would have the children on his birthday and Father's Day.

It was also agreed that if the children should become ill for more than twenty-four hours, then the noncustodial parent would have the right to visit with the children in the custodial parent's home given three hours prior notification.

EXTENDED VACATIONS

Most people want the right to take their children with them on an extended vacation at least once per year. We've already talked about extended vacations during the school year, but most often extended vacations take place during the summer months. For that reason its important to consider providing an entitlement to each parent to have the children for an extended vacation each year. The important issues here are whether the children want to go on the vacation and that the non-vacationing parent is informed well in advance of the vacation and also of the location so that the children can be reached in case of emergency.

JOE AND MARY

In addition to the other aspects of visitation Joe and Mary agreed that each of them would have the right to take the children during the children's summer vacation for a period of two weeks. Both Joe and Mary understood that they might not use this entitlement every year but they wanted it in case they decided to use it. Each would inform the other, as well as the children, at least six weeks in advance so that adequate planning could take place. They agreed that the address and phone number where the children would be staying would be supplied and that the children would call home at least once during the vacation at a prearranged time.

VISITATION WITH RELATIVES

So far we've dealt with issues involving access and visitation between parents and children. For some people it might be important to include some thoughts regarding visitation with grandparents or other special people. Keep in mind that children often have meaningful and sometimes very important relationships with family members other than their parents. Therefore, no matter how you might feel about in-laws, it is often important to provide the children with access to important others.

SALLY AND SHELDON

Sally and Sheldon had completed all aspects of their visitation agreement when they suddenly became aware that Sheldon was uncomfortable with allowing visitation to Sally's mother and father. Sheldon claimed that Sally's mother and father were probably the biggest reason they were getting divorced in the first place. He felt that they were forever influencing the children against him. Sally claimed that her parents were merely supporting their daughter and that Sheldon probably "deserved" anything he got in the way of criticism. After some discussion Sally and Sheldon realized that the issue of visitation to Sally's parents could result in a major impasse and create difficulty with the overall divorce agreement.

Following the ground rules that they had established, Sally and Sheldon called a "timeout" and put off any further negotiation on the issue until the following week. One week later, they were still both upset about the matter, but Sheldon had had a chance to talk to his children. He mentioned to them that their mother would be taking them to their grandmother's house the following weekend. Sheldon observed that the children were pleased and were looking forward to the visit. This made him realize that it would be unfair to the children to deprive them of visitation to their grandparents.

Sally and Sheldon agreed that Sally could take the children to visit their grandparents any time she had the children but Sheldon did request that the children not be left overnight in the sole care of their grandparents unless Sheldon had given his approval. Sally was able to agree to this and the couple were able to move on to the next issue.

CHANGE OF RESIDENCE OR MOVING

Once a divorce or separation agreement is finalized and a pattern of sharing the parenting has become established, one of the most difficult circumstances to deal with is if one or both parents have to change their place of residence. Change of residence is often necessitated by job requirements, the ending of a lease, or remarriage. The move could be a relatively minor one or it could be over a great distance. Obviously, if one parent has to move a long way it creates problems which are more difficult to deal with than if the move is a relatively short one.

At this time it would be very important for you to establish guidelines as to what would constitute a move or change of residence. Some people use distance and others travel time as a measure. It would be important for you to establish that if a move greater than a certain magnitude takes place, then certain changes in the visitation or physical custody arrangements might have to be made.

You could agree as to what those changes would be or it could be left open for future negotiation.

STEVE AND CLAUDIA

Steve and Claudia had completed their agreement except for the issue of what would happen if one of them had to move. Steve's job was with a large corporation and he knew that he might be called upon to move to another state. Claudia was employed in an office and did not anticipate a move under any circumstances.

They started with an understanding that all aspects of their agreement would stay in force unless one of them moved more than twenty five miles from their present location. They felt that everything they agreed to could continue to take place within that distance. They also agreed that if Steve was called upon to move to another state then Claudia, who had primary physical custody of the children, would also move to that state if possible. Steve was willing to pay all of Claudia's moving expenses and would also support her during the time it took her to find new employment up to a period of six months. Claudia accepted this situation as it would allow them both to continue their parenting. However, she also insisted that she not be "obligated". It was understood that if Steve moved and Claudia didn't, it would necessitate some major changes in the visitation schedule but they were not prepared at this time to work those out. Therefore, they decided that if Steve had to move out of state and Claudia didn't go along that the parenting would be open to renegotiation.

At Steve's insistence the agreement was made gender neutral. Therefore if by some chance Claudia had to move, the same conditions would apply.

MARY AND SAL

Mary and Sal reached a difficult point in their negotiation when they started to talk about the idea of moving. Mary had met and was dating a man who lived three hundred miles away and had his own business at that location. Mary was a professional and knew that if she established a permanent relationship with her new boyfriend, she would be able to start a practice where he lived. Sal realized that he could not move and understood that if Mary left with their two children aged ten and fifteen, he would be cut off from them for long periods of time.

The couple discussed this at length and decided to talk to the children about how they would feel if Mary chose to get married and move. Their fifteen year old made it very clear that he would want to be with his father while their ten year old daughter stated that she would want to be with her mother.

Sal and Mary decided that in the event that Mary moved more than fifty miles away, the custody of the children would be split with their son staying with Sal and their daughter going with her mother. Suitable visitation and access schedules were also set up and, in this way, the parents resolved the issue.

Splitting siblings is something that is done infrequently and sometimes can have negative results for one or more of the children. However, when a situation develops where one parent is forced by necessity to move a great distance then unusual and not totally desirable solutions may have to be sought.

RENEGOTIATION AND IMPASSE

In all situations involving children it must be understood that circumstances change over time. This applies not only to the sharing of parenting and visitation but also to issues involving decision making and support. It is, therefore, suggested that all agreements made between separating or divorcing parents include an agreement to renegotiate if an impasse is reached with regard to the children. Renegotiation in times of impasse or disagreement can be very difficult. It is recommended that at the time you formulate your separation or divorce agreement, you agree that if at anytime in the future a disagreement regarding the children reaches the level of impasse, then a mediator will be chosen to help the two of you reach agreement on the particular issue of impasse. If mediation should fail then you could provide for the use of either binding arbitration or litigation.

THE SHARING OF INFORMATION

Almost everytime a divorce takes place it results in some diminution of contact between parent and child. Whatever time is spent with one parent leaves the other somewhat in the dark as to what has gone on with the children. For this reason it is important to agree to share certain kinds of information. It is fairly obvious that information about medical matters, educational matters, and special events should be shared. What might not be so obvious is that information about disciplinary situations and emotional health should also be shared. It is important that parents confer not only to have the opportunity to participate in special situations and know about their children, but also so children know that both parents are informed and united on important issues.

SAL AND EMILY

Sal and Emily decided that Emily would have sole custody of their three children. However, Sal did not want the children to think that he had "abandoned" them. In discussion with Emily it was decided that Sal should continue to participate in a number of events most importantly school conferences, spring concerts, and after school sporting events. Therefore, it was agreed that Emily would share with Sal all of the information needed as to time, schedules, and import of all such events.

DECISION MAKING OR LEGAL CUSTODY

As has been discussed before, custody is separated into two different concepts, physical custody, and legal custody. For our purposes legal custody is separate from the physical sharing of the children and is related to the making of important decisions. Thus legal custody involves the rights and responsibilities of both parents to take part in major decisions involving religion, education, medical treatment, standards of behavior and social activity. When we talk of **sole legal custody**, we are referring to a situation in which the sole responsibility and right to make decisions belongs to one parent or the other. When we discuss **joint legal custody**, this means that both parents retain the right to make decisions and both parents have responsibility for such decisions.

Let's understand that we are talking about major decisions and non-emergency decisions which effect the children. We are not referring to normal, day to day decisions or emergency medical decisions which must be made by whichever parent has physical custody of the children at a particular time.

In our experience the most important consideration regarding joint legal custody is whether or not the two parties can communicate well enough to discuss matters. This implies that there must be some semblance of agreement beforehand, not diametrically opposed stances on major issues. In cases where joint legal custody is decided upon, the advantage is that both parents and children have a sense that there is a continued cooperation between parents and a continued involvement with children. This certainly enhances the feeling for children that they have not been "abandoned" or "left" by either parent. On the other hand, if every time a major decision has to be made the result is fighting and bickering, then joint legal custody would not be an enhancement for either parents or children.

SYLVIA AND JOEL

Sylvia and Joel have two children aged five and seven. They have always disagreed on almost everything regarding the children. Sylvia was brought up Catholic and Joel was brought up in the Jewish tradition. In the past they had agreed that the children would be raised as Unitarians but neither had been particularly happy about this decision. Now that they were getting divorced they were concerned that whomever had the children the majority of the time would probably enforce his or her views.

Joel reasoned that since they had been able to compromise in the past and since neither one of them wanted to face the eventuality that the other would enforce his or her views on the children, they should develop a joint custody or joint decision making agreement thus insuring that both parents would have input into all major decisions. Sylvia reasoned that since they tended to argue about almost everything, and this fact had led to their divorce, the arguments would not end. She felt that an agreement to share decision making jointly would mean endless arguing and bickering. After a half hour argument regarding this point both parties took a timeout and resumed negotiation a week later.

At the resumption of negotiation the argument continued. Neither party was able to agree to the other's point of view and each felt that the children would be damaged irreparably by giving in. It finally dawned on both that the very fact that they could not agree here meant that they probably would not be able to agree later. They realized that sole custody in regard to decision making would be the only workable choice and agreed that Sylvia, who had the majority of the physical custody, would make all of the major decisions on her own. Although he agreed to it, this did not sit particularly well with Joel and he did insist that during his weekend visitations he would be allowed to bring the children to religious services of his choice. This was included as part of the agreement.

LUKE AND JOAN

Luke and Joan were involved in a divorce which had been sparked by unfaithfulness on one of their parts, and there was a considerable degree of enmity. They had one child aged seven. While neither Luke nor Joan had much regard for each other, they both loved their daughter deeply and wanted to be involved in every part of her upbringing. Despite the fact that they disliked each other intensely, they recognized that they both had the best interest of their child at heart. They also understood that before she was born and until until she was two years old, they had discussed at great length their plans and expectations for her. During those discussions they had generally agreed. For this

reason, they felt that, where their daughter was concerned, they could still agree. Luke and Joan decided on a joint legal custody agreement wherein they would make all major decisions regarding religious training, educational training, non-emergency medical decisions, behavioral standards, and social behavior as well as all other major decisions by consensus.

They also realized that they might disagree in the future and included in their agreement a clause which stated that in case of disagreement or impasse they would utilize the services of a child psychologist or family mediator to resolve the dispute. They went even one step further by saying that where the welfare of their daughter was concerned they would abide by a recommendation of a child psychologist or family mediator if they could not reach agreement on their own.

FINALIZING YOUR PARENTING AGREEMENT

We've now agreed on all of the issues involved in parenting, visitation, and legal custody and are ready to move onto issues of child support. However, before moving on I think it's important to state that children do grow up. Throughout the ages there has been considerable disagreement as to when they are grown up. Usually the children claim grown up status far earlier than the parents want to allow it. However, the truth is that as children reach adolescence they become far more able to make decisions for themselves and also far less willing to have decision forced upon them. For this reason it is very important to remember that when parents agree, it may be binding on the parents but it is not necessarily binding on the children. These realities are the same whether the parents remain married or not. They must learn to cope with the difficulties of adolescence and with the need to let go and allow children to start to forge their own way in life. When a divorce has taken place this can be extremely painful and difficult to deal with but it can help if all of us remember it.

Remember that there are trained professionals in every community. I strongly recommend that anyone who is having difficulty dealing with children's growing sense of maturity or anyone who feels that the divorce or separation has wrought considerable harm on their children seek the services of a good child psychologist or family counselor and not hesitate to do so. I would also like to point out that the material in this chapter regarding decisions on custody, parenting, and visitation is very difficult. Therefore if having used all of the hints in the book with regard to reaching agreement you still cannot make all of the necessary decisions then I strongly recommend that you seek the services of a mediator to help you reach agreement.

CHAPTER FOURTEEN

CHILD SUPPORT

Now that you've worked out how you will be sharing the responsibilities of parenting and how much of the time each child will be spending with each parent, you are ready to look at how the children are going to be supported and by whom.

Almost everyone will agree that parents are responsible to support their children until they reach a certain age. The legal age, called emancipation, to which children have to be supported varies from state to state, but is generally either eighteen or twenty-one. See Table 2. It is also usually agreed that the support of children is a shared responsibility. The degree to which each parent shares that responsibility is the main issue to be dealt with in this chapter.

Remember that child support is a right of the child. It is never related to fault. Nor is it related to punitive action or feelings between spouses. Child support should be based on the needs of the child and the financial means of the two parents - not other circumstances of the divorce.

HOMEWORK

Before discussing child support with your spouse, do the following homework:
1) Go over the budgets you've already prepared.
2) Taking into consideration the parenting arrangements, you may want to recalculate some of the expenses attributable to the children. For example, if you've agreed to physical sharing both parents must calculate the cost of room and board as well as certain other expenses.
3) Total the expenses for the child or children and make sure that you and your spouse have not duplicated any child related expenses.
4) Check Table 2 and know what the age of emancipation is in your state as well as whether there are any statutory guidelines for child support (see Chapter 7).

WHO SHOULD PAY?

Traditionally child support was money paid by the divorced father to his ex-wife in order to support the children of the marriage. The amount paid was set at the time of the divorce and was paid until the children reached majority or were otherwise emancipated. This arrangement is based on the traditional sole custody model. The wife in this case had "sole custody of the children" and the payment was made to the custodian and she was given complete responsibility for seeing to it that the money paid in support was, in fact, used for the children.

In recent years the traditional sole custody model has changed for many divorcing couples and the traditional child support model may no longer be completely valid in these cases.

STAN AND MADELINE

Stan and Madeline as part of their divorce agreement decided to share physical custody of their children on approximately a fifty-fifty basis. This required that both parents maintain residences in which their two children had their own rooms and clothing. It also meant that during the time the children were with each parent, that parent would be responsible for supplying their food, allowance, social needs etc.

As a result, Stan and Madeline decided to disregard the traditional child support model and agreed that each would total the monies spent on the children and that these monies would be shared equitably.

Based on the sharing of the physical custody Stan and Madeline decided that it would be inequitable for them not to share the costs of supporting the children no matter who the children were residing with at any given time.

This is a good example of how changes in the model of custody can effect the way child support is viewed. For Stan and Madeline it was clear: they wanted to share the cost of supporting their children. Both of them were employed and made reasonable salaries and both felt that a sharing of the expenses of the children was fair and equitable. The question however, of how those expenses should be shared is another matter entirely.

PRO-RATA SHARING

One way of sharing child expenses is based on the computation of a pro-rata share. **Pro-rata** sharing means sharing according to the income of each party. For example; if Stan earns one hundred thousand dollars per year and Madeline earns fifty thousand dollars per year, then Stan would contribute two thirds of any expenses and Madeline one third of any expenses attributed to the children. This would be a pro-rata sharing according to income. Thus, if Stan and Madeline agreed to share all child expenses on a pro-rata basis, and the expenses attributable to the children amounted to fifteen thousand dollars per year, then Stan would pay ten thousand toward the expenses of the children and Madeline five thousand.

OTHER WAYS OF SHARING

While pro-rata sharing is generally considered to be very fair it may also be complicated to figure out. It involves calculations of income and sometimes projections of income (this is covered in the chapter on spousal support and maintenance).

Some people feel that simply splitting the cost of certain items fifty-fifty is a lot easier. At other times, it is agreed that one parent or the other will bear the full burden of some aspects of child support. In general the greater the disparity of income between the two spouses, the more likely it is that one spouse will bear greater responsibility for payment. However, each situation has its own special circumstances which must be examined.

STATUTORY GUIDELINES

As already discussed in Chapter 7, many states have adopted statutory child support guidelines. These guidelines generally calculate child support as a percentage of income with the percentage growing as the number of children increases. If your state has such a statute it may be helpful to look at it. This will help you understand the customary child support guidelines for your jurisdiction.

NEED BASED GUIDELINES

In many cases child support can be calculated according to the needs of the children. This was obviously done by Stan and Madeline and may work very well for you. Keep in mind that even if your state has percentage based guidelines for child support, this does not mean that your agreement must reflect those guidelines. In most statutes there is an option for people to waive the guidelines in favor of their own decision as long as their decision is fair and equitable for the children. As in most other issues regarding children, "the best interest of the child" must be protected when calculating support.

WHAT HAS TO BE PAID FOR?

While most people understand that child support covers the cost of raising a child it is important to understand that the things that have to be paid for vary from situation to situation.

Basic child support usually includes such things as room and board, clothing, allowance, and recreational expenses - in other words all of the day to day expenses attributable to the children's upbringing.

Medical insurance and medical cost are another aspect of child support which must be considered separately.

Child care or day care when required by the work schedule of the custodial parent is another item of child support which is usually considered above and beyond basic child support.

Education, whether it be private schooling or college, is also is generally calculated separately from basic child support.

Other items including sports, music lessons, tutoring, or summer camp are additional items attributable to the raising of children and are generally considered separately from child basic support.

All of these must be dealt with and should be included in your agreement. In addition, it's important to take account of the fact that as children get older or circumstances change, the children's needs change.

MODIFICATION OF SUPPORT

As circumstances change, child support may also need to change. Circumstances change as a child grows older. A twelve year old or a sixteen year old needs a great many more items of clothing and food then does a two or three year old. In addition, parental incomes can change significantly, either up or down. This too might necessitate a modification of child support. In most jurisdictions, child support is statutorily open to modification based on changed circumstances. Certainly it would be good for you to take this into account in your agreement and allow for changes in child support as circumstances change for better or worse or simply due to the passage of time.

CHARLES AND DORIS

Charles and Doris divorced at a time when their children were aged three and seven. Doris had primary physical custody. Although Charles had alternate weekend visitations as well as vacation time in the summer, it was felt that he should pay child support to Doris based on his income and the children's needs. They lived in a state which had a statute outlining child support as a percentage of the income of the non-custodial parent. For the two children it was agreed that Charles would pay Doris approximately twenty-five percent of his gross income from all sources. Since he earned approximately eighty thousand dollars a year this amounted to about four hundred dollars per week basic child support. In addition they agreed that until the children reached age twelve, they should not be left alone while Doris was working. Therefore, they agreed that child care expenses necessitated by Doris' work schedule would be shared by the two of them on a pro-rata basis according to income. They further agreed that shares would be modified yearly according to the incomes shown on their federal tax returns to calculate the pro-rata sharing for the previous year.

Charles was self-employed and did not have any medical insurance. Doris, on the other hand, was a civil service employee and had a medical insurance plan which allowed her to cover the children at the expense of her employer. They agreed that all medical expenses not covered by Doris's health insurance would be born by Charles. They reasoned that since Doris was supplying medical coverage, he should pay for the balance of all of the medical expenses.

They also agreed that it was extremely important for them to send their children to college if their children wanted to go. They, therefore, agreed that they would set aside one hundred dollars per month shared pro-rata according to their income and place that money in a college fund to be used for the children's education. They also agreed that at the time the children started college, if there was not enough money in the fund to pay their expenses they would share any additional college expenses pro-rata according to income up to a total of five thousand dollars per year. This did not mean that they could not spend more than the five thousand per year but it put a limit on their liability.

The last aspect of the support agreement was that of modification. This couple agreed that if at anytime either one of them felt that circumstances had changed significantly, then the agreement regarding child support could be opened to modification. They agreed that if they could not concur on a modification, then they would use the services of a mediator. If the mediator was unable to help them reach agreement they could utilize binding arbitration with a appointee of the American Arbitration Association or if that was not feasible they could open the matter to litigation.

STAN AND MADELINE

Stan and Madeline had already agreed to share all expenses for their children pro-rata according to their income. Their agreement stated that basic child support, child care expenses necessitated by the work schedule of the custodial parent, or any other agreed-to costs of child care would be shared pro-rata.

Stan and Madeline also agreed that they would set aside money each month for college, and in this instance decided to contribute fifty dollars each. They further agreed that any additional expenses for the undergraduate college of their children would be paid by both of them on a pro-rata basis according to income but they limited the amount paid to whatever they could reasonably afford at the time. Stan and Madeline also agreed that their support agreement was open to modification at anytime in the future if circumstances changed substantially. they said mediation would be utilized prior to arbitration or litigation in the settling of any impasse that they might reach in regard to child support.

In general, child support and the issues surrounding it are a difficult matter to decide upon. We strongly recommend that if you and your spouse can't reach agreement any aspect of child support, that you should seek out a mediator to assist you.

CHAPTER FIFTEEN

DECIDING ON DISTRIBUTION OF MARITAL PROPERTY AND LIABILITIES

In Chapter 9 the concepts of marital property and liability have been explained. You've also seen that the definition of what property is marital varies from state to state and the guidelines for distributing marital property and liabilities also vary from state to state. In the Appendix (Table 2) you may check what laws and guidelines apply in your state, but in general, the courts in all jurisdictions will accept any property distribution agreement that is presented to them by two divorcing spouses as long as that agreement meets the broad definition of fair and equitable.

While the definition of "fairness" or "equitability" may seem quite different for different people, certain general precepts must be considered.
1) In order to be considered fair and equitable an agreement reached between two parties must contain no element of duress or force.
2) The agreement must be understood by both parties involved and both parties must be aware of their rights, obligations, and the options available to them to resolve the issues.
3) The special circumstances affecting their decision should be understood by both parties to the agreement.

If the above conditions are met and if the two people concur, then most jurisdictions will accept whatever distribution of marital assets and liabilities you have agreed to. Chapters 5 through 9 of this book, attempt to help you understand the legal options and guidelines, as well as your rights and responsibilities, so that you can reach agreement in a fair and equitable way. However, since the distribution of marital assets is such an important part of your agreement and because it involves the financial stability and wellbeing of the entire family, it is suggested that if any misunderstanding, disagreement, or impasse should arise, then you should seek the assistance of a professional mediator to aid you in this task.

COMMON ASSETS AND LIABILITIES

The most common marital assets are:
1) Marital home
2) Individually held pensions and retirement accounts
3) Home furnishings
4) Personal Property
5) Savings
6) Businesses and Practices

The most common liabilities dealt with in marital distribution are:
1) Home mortgages
2) Bank loans
3) Auto loans
4) Credit card balances
5) Household bills

These assets and liabilities as well as others which are less common are the subject of our distribution of assets and liabilities agreement.

THE SUCCESSFUL AGREEMENT PROCESS

Over many years of helping people to reach agreement on property distribution as well as with many other issues, we have found that using a structured process in reaching your agreement will be helpful in achieving a successful ending. Our steps for success are:

Step 1: Each of you should think about and write down what kind of a distribution of assets and liabilities you think would be fair. In consideration of fairness you should think about, a) the value of the total marital estate, b) the length of time you've been married, c) your personal needs and income, and d) the nonmarital estates that each of you possess.

Step 2: With your concept of fairness in mind, make a list of all the assets and liabilities which you would like to have at the end of the distribution, using the worksheets in Table 10 of the Appendix.

Step 3: Total the values (taken from your listings of marital assets and liabilities) of all of the assets and liabilities that you have listed on your "want" list above.

Step 4: Compare your lists to see if you have each laid claim to the same thing and also to see the relative values of the assets minus the liabilities which you have requested.

Step 5: Work out trades and sharing agreements for those assets in which you have both voiced an interest.

Step 6: Equalize your holdings or bring them to the percentage levels that you have agreed would represent a fair and equitable sharing.

During the equalization process keep in mind that you may share assets at a later date, create payments (distributive awards) over a period of time, or make up for apparent inequities elsewhere. For example: You may use increases or decreases of maintenance in return for greater or lesser shares of marital assets. You've already seen some of the options available for dealing with distribution of assets and liabilities. However, a few additional examples may be helpful.

THE FURNITURE QUANDARY OF BOB AND JOAN

Bob and Joan have been married nine years and in the past two years had completely furnished their home. They have decided that they are going to sell their house and split the net equity equally. They have each waived rights to the other's pension even though Bob's pension is worth some five thousand dollars more than Joan's in present day value. Each of them needed whatever savings they had accumulated in order to pay for moving expenses, and for setting up separate apartments. The couple has no additional assets. It has been agreed that each would take their own personal property and they calculated that the personal property which each owned was of approximately equal value. The last item to be dealt with was home furnishings.

Bob and Joan recognized that they had spent more that twenty thousand dollars furnishing their home over the last couple of years. They also realized that the sale of the contents of the home would have netted them a very small part of what it would cost to replace the furniture. They also recognized that over the years they had accumulated a great many other household items which would also cost a great deal to replace. The problem was that each of them wanted the same items and neither one of them wanted certain other items.

Bob and Joan decided to resolve the situation as follows: In order to equalize the inequity that had been created when each waived rights to each others pension, Joan claimed the living room furniture. It was decided that the balance of the furniture and household items would be distributed on an item by item basis with the two parties taking turns selecting items. The household inventory that had been created earlier (see Table 9) was used as a check list and Bob and Joan flipped a coin to see who would go first. Bob won and chose the large screen T.V. Joan then made her choice and they continued to alternate until all items desired were chosen. Bob and Joan decided that whatever neither one of them wanted would be sold and the proceeds divided equally.

THE BIG DEBT PROBLEM: SAL AND ANGELA

Sal and Angela had resolved all of the issues separating them with the exception of some twenty-five thousand dollars in accumulated debt. They had almost no savings to cover those debts. It had already been decided that Angela would be getting sole occupancy of the couple's home until their youngest child reached age eighteen or graduated from high school. It had also been decided that Sal's pension would be divided via a QDRO (Qualified Domestic Relations Order: See Chapter 8) at the time it went into pay status.

Sal earned about sixty thousand dollars a year and Angela, who had to stay home to take care of the children, earned only twelve thousand dollars a year at her part-time job. Both realized that for Angela to stay in the house she would have to use most of her child support, spousal maintenance, and income, and would have little left over for debt reduction. Both also agreed that the debts should be marital and that they both had responsibility to pay them off.

Sal and Angela agreed as follows: An equity loan was taken against the house and a second mortgage created in the amount of twenty-five thousand dollars. The twenty-five thousand dollar proceeds of the mortgage were used to pay off the marital debts. It was agreed that this mortgage which was amortized over fifteen years would be paid by Sal, and at the time the house was sold, Sal would be reimbursed for what he spent paying off this second mortgage. The reimbursement would come directly from the proceeds of the sale of the house before the net equity was split fifty-fifty. In this way Sal and Angela managed to arrive at an equitable solution.

PENSION DECISIONS: MARY AND BILL

Mary and Bill had agreed on everything with regard to their distribution of assets, except how to deal with their pensions.

Bill was a New York City fireman and had acquired over the fourteen years of the marriage a substantial pension benefit which was payable when he attained age fifty-five (he is now forty-five). Mary worked for a bank and had acquired approximately thirty-five thousand dollars in assets in a 401K plan. In addition, Mary and Bill each had about seven thousand dollars in IRA plans. Bill's pension was valued by an actuary who placed its present day value at eighty-five thousand dollars. In addition, the actuary projected that at age fifty-five Bill would get approximately two thousand dollars a month for the rest of his life from the pension. The couple did not want to disturb any other aspects of their distribution of assets plan.

Bill and Mary decided to do the following: Each kept their own IRA plans. They decided to split Mary's 401K plan by rolling over half of it to an IRA rollover plan in Bob's name. This was allowed both by the IRS and by her pension plan administrator without any tax penalty. The couple then contacted an attorney who drew up a QDRO directing the administrator of Bill's pension (a New York City plan) to segregate the contents of the plan in such a way that upon Bill attaining age fifty-five each of the couple would receive checks for one half of the marital share (about one half of the amount that Bill would have received on his own). In doing this the couple had to select the appropriate pay out option and recognized that there would be some reduction in total pension payout. This was traded off for the security of knowing that they would each have pension income for the rest of their lives.

Another option to consider in pension situations is the use of single payment annuity policies to achieve equity, as in the following example:

SALLY AND RAY

Ray was a New York City fireman whose pension was valued similarly to Bill's at eighty five thousand dollars. The actuary who valued it also projected that there would be a two thousand dollar a month payout at age fifty five. Sally had no pension plan of her own but the couple had accumulated substantial savings which was held in CD's at their local bank. Ray and Sally analyzed the situation and realized that Ray was planning to retire in North Carolina at age fifty five and was counting heavily on the two thousand dollars a month that he would receive from his pension. Sally did not want to deprive Ray of any of that money because she recognized how hard he had worked for it. Consultation with the actuary revealed that if they decided to split Ray's pension then Sally would be entitled to eight hundred and fifty dollars a month for the rest of her life once Ray achieved the age of fifty five. Sally, at that time, would be fifty four. The actuary discussed the fact that they might use a single premium annuity plan to resolve their problem. Ray invested his share of

their savings purchasing a single premium annuity plan which would pay Sally eight hundred and fifty dollars a month for the rest of her life starting on the date that Ray retired. This resolved the problem, and Ray still has his pension plus a small amount of savings. Sally waved her rights to Ray's pension and kept and kept 50% of the accumulated CD's.

Another issue which sometimes arises when dealing with pensions is the tax impact. The following illustrates this.

JOAN AND DAVID

Joan and David had resolved all of the issues regarding their divorce with the exception of distribution of assets. The couple had a house which was valued at about two hundred thousand dollars and David had a pension which was valued at about two hundred and fifty thousand dollars. They had decided that they wanted to trade the house for the pension. Joan was pleased at the prospect of owning the house outright and David very much wanted to have clear title to his pension. The problem was that the house encumbered by a fifty thousand dollar mortgage, had a net equity of only one hundred and fifty thousand dollars, while the pension had a present day value of two hundred and fifty thousand dollars. Joan and David could figure out no way of coming up with the one hundred thousand dollar difference. Consultation with their accountant revealed the fact that the present day value of David's pension, two hundred and fifty thousand dollars, was calculated in pre-tax dollars. The accountant suggested that in order to create an equitable trade off the two hundred and fifty thousand dollar value should be tax impacted. What this means is that the accountant calculated how much would be left of the two hundred and fifty thousand dollar present day value if taxes were paid on that money thereby making it more comparable to the hundred and fifty thousand dollar after tax value of the house. The accountant had previously explained that Joan would not have to pay any taxes or capital gains on the equity in the house because she would get a one hundred and twenty five thousand dollar tax deduction when the house was sold. The accountant explained that because of their tax brackets, the two hundred and fifty thousand dollars in the pension was actually worth about two thirds of that amount or one hundred and sixty five thousand after tax dollars. Joan and David agreed that David would keep his interest in the pension which was calculated at one hundred and sixty five thousand tax impacted dollars and Joan got the equity in the house which was valued at one hundred and fifty thousand after tax dollars. The fifteen thousand dollar difference was equalized through a redistribution of some of the couples savings.

THE FAMILY BUSINESS

Very often businesses are owned and run by one or both members of the family. Both husband and wife may have an emotional as well as a financial stake in the success of a family business. We've already discussed in Chapter 9, some of the concepts involved in distributing family businesses but an additional example might be helpful.

PAM AND MIKE

Pam and Mike opened a stationary store shortly after they got married. Throughout their fifteen year marriage Mike worked six days a week in the store and Pam worked evenings and weekends as well as other hours, as permitted by the children's schedules. The couple had, over the years, invested most of their capital and profits back into the business and the business had a substantial inventory as well as considerable good will value. In addition the business, a corporation, had an option to extend the lease on the store for another ten years. Pam and Mike asked their accountant to value the business and as they both had intimate knowledge of the workings of the business including its cash flow and potential, they did not feel the need to get additional evaluations. The accountant valued the business at four hundred thousand dollars. Pam and Mike also had a marital home which was valued at about one hundred thousand dollars net equity as well as furnishings and other household items valued at thirty thousand dollars. The couple also had savings of approximately fifty thousand dollars.

It was decided that Pam would keep the house as well as all of the furnishings giving her an equity of one hundred and thirty thousand dollars. In addition the couple split their savings equally.

Mike and Pam felt that it would be best if Mike continued to operate the business on his own as Pam was still very much involved in child care. Therefore it was agreed that Mike would get full title to the business. This created an inequity in the distribution of assets whereby Mike was getting approximately two hundred and seventy thousand dollars more value than Pam.

The couple realized that they did not have sufficient assets to equalize this inequity, nor did they have sufficient credit for Mike to borrow the hundred and thirty five thousand dollars he would need to pay off Pam for her fifty percent interest in the business.

What they decided was for Mike to pay Pam over the next ten years for her interest in the business. This "distributive award" was paid out as a self-amortizing loan over a period of ten years with the interest being set at what was then the going rate for ten year treasury bills, eight and one half percent. It was further agreed that if at anytime prior to the loan being paid off the business was sold then the balance of the loan would be paid from the proceeds of the sale.

Pam and Mike understood that Pam's share of the business was a property right and that Mike might be personally liable for the balance of the loan even if the business went bankrupt. Pam and Mike discussed this at great length and agreed that if the business should go bankrupt, then Mike would not be personally liable for more than twenty five thousand dollars of the balance of the loan. This was the approximate amount of cash that he was getting from savings in the distribution of assets.

MAKING IT ALL LEGAL

As you've seen the distribution of assets and liabilities can be accomplished in many different ways. The main requirement is that the two of you agree to the fairness of the distribution with full knowledge and understanding of your rights, responsibilities, and the ramifications of your decisions. Once all of those decisions have been made it's important that the proper steps be taken to "make it all legal".

When properties are transferred it is important that deeds and titles be changed and registered in the appropriate way. Beneficiaries and ownership of life insurance policies must be tended to. Contracts of sale, loan agreements, and mortgages held or taken against property must be properly executed and recorded. Wills and codicils must be changed or drawn so as to reflect the new individual estates. In addition trusts and arrangements for children must also be attended to as part of the will. Consultation with your accountant, insurance agent, and personal attorney may be necessary in order to accomplish these various tasks.

CHAPTER SIXTEEN

DECIDING ON SPOUSAL SUPPORT OR MAINTENANCE

As has already been discused in Chapter 8 there is growing support throughout the country for a concept of spousal maintenance which emphasizes need and the changes which occur in that level of need over a period of time. Whereas the concept of spousal maintenance or alimony used to be one in which the award was for life or till remarriage, the newer concept emphasizes the necessity for both spouses to become self-supporting and self-sufficient. There are many factors that enter into the decisions of how much and how long spousal maintenance should be planned for.

PREPARING FOR YOUR DISCUSSION

1) Reread Chapter 8.
2) Prior to even considering the setting of spousal maintenance you must first determine whether there is in fact a need. You've already put together a monthly budget. Looking at it, you can determine your monthly needs to live in the style to which you've each become accustomed. Your individual monthly total is that level of spending which would support you in the approximate style to which you've been accustomed.
3) The next task is to look at your available income, using the financial statement provided in the Appendix. In calculating income you should use your net take home pay plus any interest or dividends which you might earn on your investment income. In figuring investment income remember to calculate interest on any monies which you which might have received or might be about to receive as a result of the distribution of marital assets. In addition calculate any regular overtime income or any income from second jobs. Lastly, take into account any income which might be generated as a result of the changes about to take place. An example might be rental income generated from the marital home if you are planning to rent out a portion of it, or income generated from employment which is about to start. Do not count child support at this time.

4) The next step is to compare your income with your needs. If your needs are greater than your income then you may be in need of spousal maintenance.

As we've already stated, if incomes between the two spouses are approximately equal then one would not normally expect any spousal maintenance. The situation where one spouse earns significantly more than the other and the spouse with the lower earnings does not have enough income to maintain a reasonable lifestyle, is when it is most likely that spousal maintenance would be needed.

Ideally the spouse with higher earnings can simply supplement the spouse with low earnings, to the point where all of his or her needs will be met. The limitation most likely to apply is when the spouse with the greater income does not earn enough to supply the needs of the spouse needing maintenance. This is where careful planning and careful discussion are crucial.

THE FACTORS INFLUENCING SPOUSAL MAINTENANCE

The first issue in determining spousal maintenance should be the issue of "need". If there is no need for either spouse to be maintained by the other after the divorce, then spousal maintenance should not be a consideration. Need should be determined based on income and on the budgetary needs of the particular lifestyle to which the needy spouse has been accustomed to. In addition, other factors such as health, length of marriage, earnings of the non-needy spouse, and the general ability of the spouse in need to acquire the ability to become self-sufficient.

In addition, the principal of rehabilitation must be taken into consideration. The principal of rehabilitative maintenance assumes that maintenance should last only as long as it takes the spouse being maintained to develop the skills and abilities to become self-sufficient. This principal usually governs the length of time that maintenance will be awarded by the courts and may influence your decision as to how long you will agree to spousal maintenance. In considering the rehabilitative aspect of maintenance you must look at the health of the maintained spouse, the education level, the need for child care, the age and likelihood of becoming self-sufficient in meeting financial needs.

You should consider retirement income and at what point it will start being paid. This should include social security.

In almost all cases spousal maintenance will end upon remarriage of the spouse being maintained.

The following examples may be helpful.

GEORGE AND MIRIAM

George and Miriam were both school teachers and their youngest child, aged twelve, was attending school full-time.

George earned about fifty thousand dollars a year while Miriam, who had taken several years off for child care and had lost seniority, earned an income of approximately thirty five thousand dollars per year.

Discussing the differences between them, George and Miriam reasoned that while their incomes were different the difference was not so great as to warrant spousal maintenance. Miriam felt that her income was sufficient for her to live on especially given the fact that she would have an additional seven or eight thousand dollars investment income and she did not want to feel that she was being "supported" by George. With this in mind George and Miriam agreed to waive all spousal maintenance from each other but Miriam requested and received from George a somewhat larger share of the marital estate as a recompense for the years of seniority which she had lost while taking care of their son.

STAN AND MARIE

Stan and Marie were married seven years and were childless. Stan is an attorney and earned close to one hundred thousand dollars last year. Marie worked as an administrative assistant and was earning twenty three thousand dollars per year. Marie calculated that her earnings would leave her at least ten thousand dollars per year short of her needs. She also felt that in order to become self-sufficient she would require a Bachelors degree. At the time of the divorce Marie had completed one and half years of college and calculated that she could finish her schooling and obtain a Bachelors degree in about six years going at night.

Stan and Marie agreed that Stan would pay Marie spousal maintenance of two hundred dollars per week for a period of six years. In addition Stan agreed to pay Marie's college tuition as long as the credits were required for her Bachelors degree. At the end of the six years Stan's obligation to maintain Marie would end. It was also understood that if Marie remarried prior to the end of the six year period, maintenance would end.

NANCY AND GEORGE

Nancy and George were in their early fifties and had been married twenty five years. Their children were grown and during the marriage Nancy had worked at a few part-time jobs but had not been employed at all for about two years. George was an executive with a small company and earned about fifty five thousand dollars per year.

In discussing the situation it was quite apparent that Nancy would never be able to acquire the skills and background necessary to earn anywhere near the amount that George earned. Due to her age it was unlikely that she could enter the work force in an entry level position and work herself up. Nancy did not want to feel dependent on George but she was unable to maintain herself on her investment income which amounted to only about six thousand dollars a year and was also doubtful that she could get a job which would pay her more than a small wage. At the same time while George earned substantially more than Nancy he did not feel that his income was so great that he could spare very much, especially since he was hoping to retire at age fifty five.

Nancy and George realized that Nancy would probably need maintenance for the rest of her life, or until the social security and pension money started to come in. Nancy had calculated her needs and realized that even if she planned on earning one hundred dollars a week, that money plus her investment income would still leave her about ten thousand dollars short of the amount necessary to maintain her.

George recognized his responsibility and agreed to pay Nancy two hundred dollars per week maintenance until she reached age sixty two, at which time social security would start for her. It was agreed that whatever money Nancy derived from social security would be deducted dollar for dollar from any payment which George was required to make as maintenance. Since the expectation was that Nancy would get more than eight hundred dollars a month in social security, George's spousal maintenance obligation effectively ended when Nancy reached age sixty two.

In addition George and Nancy agreed that if Nancy earned more than the five thousand dollars per year that she felt capable of earning, George's maintenance obligation would be reduced by fifty cents for every dollar over five thousand per year that Nancy earned. This gave Nancy the incentive to earn more money if she could and also gave George some benefit from her increased earnings. Unfortunately George recognized that he could not retire at fifty five as he had planned unless he was willing to maintain Nancy out of his own capital and pension provisions.

PAUL AND JOAN

Paul and Joan were married for twenty years and their youngest child was fifteen years old. Joan was a registered nurse and earned about forty thousand dollars per year. Paul had been an airline mechanic, but was presently unable to work because of an injury received on the job. In fact, he was not sure whether he would ever be able to work full-time again. He was getting a disability payment of one hundred and eighty dollars a week and these payments would continue until he could again enter the job market. From the income and need analysis ratio it appeared that Paul would be at least one hundred and fifty dollars a week short of the amount needed to support him in a style to which he was accustomed. Joan was faced with the prospect of having to pay spousal maintenance to Paul. This was a situation which she had never anticipated probably because she had always thought of spousal maintenance as being paid by "the man". Paul also had never expected this situation and was reluctant to ask for maintenance. However, after some soul searching it became evident that Paul would need maintenance from Joan in the amount of one hundred and fifty dollars per week and this was agreed to. Furthermore, since Paul's disability was essentially an unknown, the term of maintenance had to be left flexible. Paul and Joan agreed that maintenance would continue until Paul was physically able to work again and become self-sufficient. It was also agreed that Joan would be obligated to continue maintenance if Paul were to have a relapse due to his injury and be unable to work again. In addition it was agreed that if Paul received a Workman's Compensation award which would increase his income, then Joan's responsibility for maintenance would be decreased on a dollar for dollar basis.

PETER AND MARION

Peter and Marion have been married for twelve years and have no children. Peter is a top executive with a large company and earns income in excess of three hundred thousand dollars a year. Marion has a Masters Degree in business administration but has been unemployed for the last year and a half. Peter and Marion are accustomed to living on a large income and it was estimated by Marion that in order to maintain herself in the style to which she had become accustomed she would need income of at least fifteen hundred dollars per week. The couple also had substantial savings and retirement funds which have been set aside and it was calculated that Marion could earn about thirty five thousand dollars per year in interest from her share of the equitable distribution.

Peter and Marion agreed that Peter would pay Marion forty thousand dollars per year in maintenance for a period of five years and then twenty thousand dollars per year for an additional two years. It was assumed that in this time Marion would be capable of developing a substantial income as she was only thirty seven years old at this time. The fact that she might never be able to earn the same amount as Peter was compensated for by the fact that she was going to have substantial capital as well as substantial retirement funds at some point in the future.

It was understood that Peter's maintenance obligation would end if Marion remarried.

As you can see from the examples, a number of different scenarios are possible with regard to spousal maintenance. Like distribution of assets and custody, spousal maintenance is an area with many possibilities and options, which you might want to explore with an accountant or other advisor. Since it can be a difficult and sometimes painful area to deal with, we strongly recommend that if you cannot reach agreement fairly quickly that you seek the help of a mediator in order to resolve remaining differences.

CHAPTER SEVENTEEN

INSURANCE DECISIONS

As everyone knows, life is full of "insurance policies". Most of us have dealt with auto insurance, homeowners insurance, liability insurance, income protection insurance, vacation insurance etc. Most insurance policies relate to protecting the individual from loss due to unexpected circumstances or legal claims, and each individual must be guided by his or her own needs.

However, several types of insurance may impact on the divorce or separation agreement. The types most frequently dealt with in a separation agreement are health insurance, life insurance, disability insurance, and the single payment annuity.

We've already mentioned single payment annuity policies as an aid to the distribution of pension benefits, and we've covered certain aspects of health and life insurance but it is worth going into greater detail on these as well as disability insurance at this time.

Insurance is a way of protecting against possible future problems. While it is always a gamble when purchasing insurance, there are certain losses which can be so great that it is almost a necessity to protect against them.

DISABILITY INSURANCE

Disability insurance protects against long term or, in some cases, short term disability which prevents the individual from earning a living. As it relates to the divorce or separation agreement, disability insurance may be useful in protecting the income of the spouse responsible for paying child support or spousal maintenance. Since in most instances child support is dependent on the income of the spouse who is paying it, when income ceases as a result of illness or accident, the inability to pay support may leave the children in dire straits. One possible solution to this problem is for the payor spouse to purchase long term disability insurance which would guarantee child support payments. The cost of this insurance may be paid by an employer or it may be paid by either spouse. The cost may also be shared by spouses depending on circumstances.

STAN AND LORI

Stan and Lori have three children aged four, seven, and nine. They both felt that Lori, who had primary physical custody of the children, should stay home with the children at least until the youngest reaches age fourteen and enters high school. This decision greatly limits Lori's ability to work. As a result Lori's income from her part-time job is only seven thousand dollars per year. Stan earns over ninety thousand and agreed to pay child support and maintenance in the amount of six hundred dollars per week.

In discussing the situation Stan and Lori realized that if Stan were to become disabled, his income would be unavailable to pay child support and maintenance. Lori reasoned that if this happened she would be able to find a full-time job and supplement her income adequately. However, they both realized that this would take Lori away from the children and might still leave less money to support the children than they wanted.

Stan and Lori resolved the problem by purchasing a long term disability policy on Stan which would pay six hundred dollars per week to Lori in lieu of child support and maintenance for a period of ten years. Thus if Stan became disabled, the children's support and Lori's ability to stay home with them would be protected.

They also reasoned that college costs could also be supplemented by the disability payment and this was stated in their agreement.

Stan and Lori resolved their situation through the use of disability insurance. If you want to consider this kind of insurance you should contact your insurance agent prior to drawing any agreement, as these policies can be rather complex and costly. Many associations, unions and other organizations offer group disability policies which may be available at lower premiums.

HEALTH INSURANCE

With the rapidly growing cost of health care and the furor which has emerged regarding health insurance, almost no one is unaware of the need and expense of health insurance. Most people are protected under group health insurance policies supplied by an employer. As this book is being written many new proposals are emerging both on state and federal levels regarding health care coverage for all Americans. Obviously, as these plans go into effect whatever is said here with regard to health insurance may change. Before making any decisions on health care it would be wise to consult with an insurance specialist or health care benefits specialist to make sure that you are properly covered.

In general, most people are covered by employer provided health care insurance which covers "the family". In the event that a divorce takes place children remain a part of the family group. Children remain covered by the family health policy regardless of the divorce or marital status of their parents. This is not true for a spouse. When the marriage ends the spouse who is not the named insured on the health policy ceases to be a member of the family and is therefore no longer covered under the family policy provision. Some insurance policies may also specify that a legally separated spouse is not covered by the family policy. Your health policy should be carefully examined to determine whether this applies in your case.

Federal law currently dictates that all group health policies must have a COBRA provision. This means that for an additional premium, a separated or divorced spouse must have the option to continue his or her coverage under the terms of the policy for a period of a time, usually three years. Understand that while the continuance of coverage can be very important especially in a situation involving a pre-existing condition or where treatment is in progress, it may be quite expensive. It would be important for you to carefully ascertain the cost of continuing health insurance under the COBRA provision, and this cost must be factored into your agreement.

Further, you should understand the availability of medicare or medicaid in your jurisdiction. Again, many groups and organizations offer group rates on health care insurance and these possibilities should also be explored.

STAN AND LORI

When Stan and Lori made their decisions with regard to disability insurance, they also carefully considered their health care insurance needs. Stan's employer provided him with a family policy so that the children's coverage would be assured as long as Stan was employed. Stan agreed to cover the children in his family policy for as long as his employment lasted. If he changed jobs, he would make sure that a family policy was available or he would pay for the children's health insurance on his own.

Lori's health insurance was a different matter. Stan's health policy specifically stated that a legally separated or divorced spouse was no longer covered. However, the COBRA provision did allow Lori to continue her coverage under the terms of the policy for three years. The premium for this continuance amounted to two hundred dollars per month and included hospitalization as well as out-patient treatment. Stan agreed to split the cost of the COBRA coverage for a period of three years. Lori felt that by that time she would either look for a job which would provide her some group health benefit or would purchase hospitalization insurance on her own and forego the major medical portion of the insurance which added greatly to its cost.

LIFE INSURANCE

In the divorce or separation agreement life insurance plays a similar role to that played by disability insurance. However, life insurance is much more frequently used and relied upon than is disability insurance. The primary purpose of life insurance is to guarantee the availability of funds for child support, educational costs, or spousal maintenance, in case of the death of the contributing spouse. Life insurance usually pays a lump sum death benefit. In calculating the amount of insurance needed to protect a particular obligation, you must calculate either the lump sum amount needed (as in college tuition) or you must calculate the principal needed to generate the investment income that would be necessary over a period of time (as in child support or maintenance payments).

In many cases life insurance already exists when the divorce or separation agreement is being formulated. If so, it might be adequate to simply agree that insurance already in force should be kept in force for as long as needed. The beneficiary may have to be changed, or the ownership of the policy may have to be transferred. In addition, when children's welfare is being considered you might consider setting up a trust with the proceeds of life insurance going into that trust. Life insurance can be used in many different ways and should be considered when there is a need. Keep in mind that under certain conditions, especially when there is a sizable estate, a will may make the need for life insurance less pressing. Consult a specialist if your situation seems complicated.

STAN AND LORI: COLLEGE COSTS

As we've already discussed Stan and Lori had resolved their health insurance needs as well as their need for protecting child support and maintenance. However, Stan wanted to make sure that his children's college education would be well provided for. He calculated that by the time the three kids reached college age it could cost anywhere from eighty to one hundred and fifty thousand dollars per child for a college education.

Stan presently had in force a one hundred thousand dollar term life insurance policy which was provided by his employer. In order to protect his children's educational needs Stan agreed that he would keep the hundred thousand dollar term policy with the proceeds dedicated to a trust fund in favor of the children. The terms of the trust insured that the main purpose of the trust would be to provide for the children's educational needs. In the event that any monies in the trust were not used to cover educational needs, the proceeds were to be divided equally among the three children when the youngest reached age twenty two. In addition, Stan agreed to purchase another fifty thousand dollar term life insurance policy which would be held in force until the youngest child reached age twenty two. This would also be applied to the educational trust.

Lori realized that she would also be in a bind if something were to happen to Stan. She had some protection for both herself and the children if Stan were to become disabled but disability insurance terminates if Stan were to die. In order to protect her maintenance and insure that she would be able to manage in the case of Stan's death, Lori and Stan agreed that Lori would purchase a life insurance policy on Stan's life with herself as the beneficiary and that she would pay the premium until she decided to terminate the policy.

Stan and Lori used life insurance as well as disability insurance to protect against catastrophic possibilities. Other people have used life insurance to insure other things such as distributive awards in the buyout of business or real estate, or other payments that could not easily be made in case of death.

Before utilizing life insurance, as in the case of other kinds of insurance, you should discuss the matter with your broker in order to be aware of the types of policies which exist.

Some situations which require the use of insurance policies might be rather complex. If you have any doubts or concerns consult with a matrimonial mediator to learn about the options available to you. You might also use the services of an estate planner or financial planner to gain more insight into the options.

CHAPTER EIGHTEEN

MAKING TAX DECISIONS

Your divorce agreement involves money. Anytime there is a transfer of money, or decisions are made with regard to money, those decisions or transfers will most likely have tax implications. A divorce or separation always creates tax consequences for both spouses. Generally, decisions involve benefits for one and burdens to the other. It is very important to have good professional advice from your accountant before finalizing any agreement which could impact your tax liability for the future.

Before finalizing your agreement it is recommended that you do the following:
1) Consult your accountant or tax preparer regarding the tax impact of your agreement.
2) Consult a financial planner or accountant regarding the options available to you in terms of tax planning.
3) Be aware of both federal tax law and state tax law in your jurisdiction.
4) Read the guides on tax preparation that are available from the I.R.S..

I.R.S. publications may be obtained by writing to the I.R.S. or calling 1-800-424-3673. The following is a partial list of publications. (These publications are subject to change).
1) #504-Tax Information for Divorced or Separated Individuals
2) #523-Tax Information on Selling Your Home
3) #525-Taxable and Non-taxable Income
4) #551-Basis of Assets
5) #552-Record Keeping for Individuals and a List of Tax Publications
6) #561-Valuation of Donated Property
7) #929-Tax Rules for Children and Dependents
8) #503-Child and Dependent Care Credit

The tax law is fluid and constantly changing. As this book is being written the laws and I.R.S rulings may be changing in such a way as to affect your agreement. Unless you are constantly keeping abreast of the changes and regulations you cannot possibly be fully aware of all of the ramifications of your agreement on your future tax responsibilities. Therefore, it may be important to consult with an accountant or tax planner before completing the tax impacting sections of your agreement. In general, the tax issues which are most affected by a divorce or separation are deductibility of spousal support, sharing of retirement equity, filing status, property transfers, capital gains, child care deductions, dependent exemptions, and deductions for educational expense.

We cannot do an exhaustive discussion of all of these issues but you should be aware that discussing each of them with your accountant or tax planner can be important.

USING TAX BENEFITS

Over many years of experience we've learned that benefits can often be gained through the prudent use of the provisions in the tax law. However, in most cases it does not work out well to create an agreement in order to take advantage of the laws. It is usually more prudent to start by working out an agreement that suits your purposes regardless of the tax laws, and then to modify the agreement so as to take advantage of whatever tax benefits may be available. The following is the step by step process that we have found most useful.

Step 1: Work out your agreement in its entirety so that you are both satisfied with the terms and arrangements.

Step 2: Discuss your agreement - especially the clauses relevant to distribution of assets, support, and maintenance with your accountant or tax planner.

Step 3: With the help of your accountant or tax planner as well as with the knowledge you've gained through reading the appropriate I.R.S. bulletins, restructure those aspects of your agreement which would create a tax savings and thus a financial benefit.

Step 4: Work out an agreement by which the benefit can be shared between the two of you.

BOB AND PAT

Bob and Pat have completed all of the major decisions in their divorce agreement. Pat was to have primary physical custody of the children and Bob had agreed to pay twenty five percent of his gross income to support the two children. In addition Bob had agreed to pay Pat fifty dollars a week in spousal maintenance for a period of seven years.

Bob earned approximately eighty thousand dollars a year as an executive, while Pat was making six thousand per year in a part-time job. In addition, Pat thought that she might earn some extra money on the side babysitting during the time that her children were not in school. Despite this, Pat felt that she would be short of money and was hoping to convince Bob to pay her additional support. Bob was resisting this suggestion because his projections were that he would be very hard pressed to survive on the amount of money he would have left after paying the support and maintenance agreed upon.

Bob and Pat discussed the agreement with their accountant, and they read the appropriate literature from the I.R.S and found that there were a number of ways that they could save money through taking advantage of the tax regulations.

Bob and Pat's accountant pointed out that while the children were living primarily with Pat she would automatically have them as a deduction on her taxes. He also explained that if the couple decided and so stated in their agreement, Bob could take the children as deductions rather than Pat. It was also explained that while child support is exchanged without a tax impact, i.e. not deductible by Bob nor taxable to Pat, maintenance payments did have a tax impact. Maintenance payments were deductible to Bob and taxable to Pat. They also learned that there was a possibility of a child care deduction and deductions on interest and taxes paid on the mortgage of their home which was going to be in the sole occupancy of Pat. Since Bob was in a high tax bracket wherein approximately forty percent of his income was taken in taxes by the federal and state governments, and Pat was in a very low tax bracket, the couple, with the help of their accountant, figured out that by electing for Bob to take the children as deductions and by restructuring the maintenance agreement so that a larger proportion was called maintenance and a smaller proportion labeled child support, they were able to save Bob approximately three thousand dollars per year in taxes. Further, if Bob paid the mortgage and taxes on the house and still had title to the house he could save an additional one thousand dollars per year in taxes. This added up to a four thousand dollar savings in taxes for Bob if the agreement was restructured. Through this restructuring it was then discovered that Pat would have to pay an additional five hundred dollars per year in taxes thereby ending up with a net savings of thirty five hundred dollars for the two of them. Bob and Pat decided to split the benefit equally. Bob gave Pat an additional fifteen hundred dollars per year in maintenance which then ended up costing Pat another two hundred and fifty dollars in taxes.

Through discussion with their tax planner and a restructuring of the agreement the couple were able to save themselves a considerable amount of money each year thereby allowing Pat to get the additional maintenance that she needed in order to live more comfortably. At the same time Bob ended up with more spendable dollars on his side of the ledger.

When restructuring an agreement in order to take advantage of tax allowances, one should be careful to provide for changes in circumstances.

With this in mind Bob and Pat stated in their agreement that if Pat should remarry, and Bob therefore would be paying no more maintenance, then the child support aspect of the agreement was to be re-opened for modification.

MOVING ON

We've now completed the decision making portion of your divorce process. You've reached agreement on all of the issues. You've written down what it is that you've agreed to in your Memorandum of Agreement, and you've discussed your agreement with the appropriate specialists in accounting, insurance, and possibly law. It now remains for you to translate your Memorandum of Agreement into a complete separation agreement or a stipulation of settlement for your divorce. Many people at this point might decide to seek out an attorney who would be willing to draw up the agreement for the two of you from your Memorandum of Agreement. If you chose to do this you have saved a great deal of time, trauma and money by reaching this point on your own and may consider yourselves both successful and fortunate. However, for those of you who choose to go on by yourselves, you may now proceed to the next step, Drawing Your Agreement.

When the agreement is drawn you might be well advised to seek a legal opinion as to its completeness and appropriateness with regard to any special requirements in your jurisdiction.

STEP IV
DRAWING YOUR AGREEMENT

CHAPTER NINETEEN

WHAT IS AN AGREEMENT?

Now that you have written the agreed upon terms of your matrimonial matter, you can take the Memorandum of Agreement to an attorney or mediator and present the document for the professional to use as the basis for your more formal Separation Agreement or Stipulation of Settlement.

If you do not wish to use a professional to draft the formal agreement, then you can use your Memorandum of Agreement as the basis to prepare, by yourself, the Separation Agreement or the Stipulation of Settlement. The Memorandum of Agreement is the end product of following the recommended steps in this book, which must now be transformed to a more formal agreement.

The agreement that you will sign is commonly referred to by several different names. The agreement can be called a **separation agreement; stipulation of settlement; or a property settlement agreement.** Whichever name is used, you will be signing a contract which will bind you to the terms and conditions contained in the document, with most of the terms not subject to change by a court.

Basic contract law is applicable to the matrimonial field with a few exceptions. Matters concerning the children are subject to modification by the court, as children are wards of the court, and agreements made between parents do not bind the children if such agreements are not in the best interests of the children. Thus, issues such as child support, visitation, college, and special needs will be subject to modification by the court where the facts warrant, and of course, should be subject to negotiation and mediation between the parties where change is warranted.

Issues that are not concerned with the welfare of the children are generally **NOT** subject to modification by the court, as with any contract. The parties will be obligated to comply with the terms of the contract. Contractual obligations of a matrimonial agreement are subject to enforcement in the event that there is non compliance or breach of an obligation.

Some statutes do provide for modification of contractual terms between the parties where one party can show undue hardship or a burden. However, when a contract is signed, it is basically not subject to change, and accordingly you should be aware of each and every term and condition in the contract and be fully prepared to abide by its terms and conditions.

As with any legal contract, a matrimonial contract is a complex document and should be drafted with care in order that the language in the contract reflect the intent of the parties accurately; that there be no misunderstanding, and that there be no "loop holes" by which one party can seek to escape from a contractual obligation.

When an agreement is presented to the court as part of the final divorce papers, if the agreement is fair and reasonable, the terms and conditions of the agreement will not be changed by the court. Thus, the final judgement of divorce will reflect the existence of the agreement and recite that the agreement will be a binding contract between the parties and survive the judgement of divorce.

A copy of a sample matrimonial agreement is included in Table 11 of the Appendix of this book. Following are explanations of some of the most commonly used articles of a typical agreement, together with some commonly used option clauses. After each explanation a sample article or clause is presented.

The material printed in *italics* below are from the complete Stipulation of Settlement, which can be found in the Appendix (Table 11).

When you prepare your Agreement, work from the complete Stipulation of Settlement, in Table 11, and refer for explanation, if needed, to those articles that are set forth with explanations below.

PREAMBLE

The beginning of the agreement should set forth the names and addresses of the parties, names of the children, date of marriage, and dates of birth of the children.

The top of the preamble page will contain what is called a "caption", indicating the title of the case even though you may not be processing your matter to a divorce, but only executing the agreement at the present time. Ultimately when the matter is processed through the court, one party will appear as the plaintiff or the petitioner in the caption, and the other as the defendant or respondent.

As long as you resolve your matter in an amenable manner and both parties execute the agreement, the designation of plaintiff or petitioner, and defendant or respondent, is immaterial.

SUPREME COURT OF THE STATE OF
COUNTY OF _____
————————————————————X

_____,
                    Plaintiff,

    -against-

STIPULATION OF SETTLEMENT

_____,
                    Defendant.
————————————————————X

        STIPULATION OF SETTLEMENT, made and entered into in the County of _____, State of _____,on the ___ day of____, 1992, by and between _____, residing at _____ (hereinafter referred to as the "Wife" and /or "Mother"), and _____, residing at _____ (hereinafter referred to as the "Husband" and/or "Father");

        WITNESSETH:
        WHEREAS, the parties are Husband and Wife and were married on the day of ____, ____, in the County of _____, State of ____, and

        WHEREAS, there is/are _____ child/children born of this marriage, to wit: _____ ; and

        WHEREAS, the parties desire to settle the within action and to settle certain questions relating to their property rights, support and maintenance and the equitable distribution of their marital property in accordance with (name of Statute in your state), and other interests and obligations growing out of the marriage relationship (including custody of their minor children).

        NOW, THEREFORE, in consideration of the premises and mutual covenants and undertakings herein set forth, the parties do covenant and agree as follows:

PROPERTY DISTRIBUTION

The following article is illustrative of a property distribution article. It is essential that all assets acquired during the marriage be referred to in the agreement, with a designation as to which party is going to receive the asset in order that there be no misunderstanding with regard to this issue. It is also advisable to reflect the valuation of the assets so that each party knows the value of that portion of the marital estate that he or she is receiving, and also knows the full value of the marital estate, etc. (These valuations were obtained in Steps II and III of this book. Valuations can be formalized by virtue of engaging experts such as actuaries for pension valuations, real estate appraisers for real estate valuations; or you can agree upon the valuation as long as there is a reasonable basis for the agreed upon value.)

ARTICLE III: DIVISION OF PROPERTY AND ASSETS

All of the furniture, furnishings, household goods and appliances, fixtures and appurtenances, books and works of art, china, crystal, silverware, jewelry, clothing and other items of personal property located in the marital residence located at _____, shall be and are hereby declared to constitute the sole and exclusive property of the ____. There is excepted from the foregoing the items of personal property set forth on the schedule annexed hereto as Schedule "A", which said articles of personal property are, and shall remain, the sole and exclusive property of the ____. Said articles of personal property shall be removed by the ____ at sole cost and expense within thirty (30) days of the execution of this Stipulation of Settlement.

The Husband shall be entitled to sole possession, use and title to the following vehicle (s): 19__, The Husband shall be solely responsible for the maintenance, insurance and loan, if any, with respect to such vehicle, and shall indemnify and hold the Wife harmless from any liability therefrom.

The Wife shall be entitled to sole possession, use and title to the following vehicle (s): 19__. The Wife shall be solely responsible for the maintenance, insurance and loan, if any, with respect to such vehicle, and shall indemnify and hold the Husband harmless from any liability therefrom.

With regard to the Husband's pension with _____,which pension constitutes marital property, and which pension has been valued by ____ by way of report dated the ____ day of ____,19__, the present day value of said pension being _____,said pension shall belong exclusively to the ____, and the ____ hereby waives any claim to said pension.

The marital home located at _____ is marital property and has a fair market value of approximately $____,is subject to a mortgage, leaving an approximate equity of $_____, shall belong exclusively to the Wife, and the Husband waives any claim with reference to said property. The provision for the disposition of the home is more fully set forth hereinafter in this Stipulation of Settlement.

With regard to the Husband's IRA with _____, which IRA constitutes marital property, in the approximate sum of two hundred thousand ($200,000.00) dollars, the Husband agrees to execute the appropriate documents to cause a rollover to the Wife's IRA simultaneously with the execution of this Stipulation of Settlement, of one hundred thousand ($100,000.00) dollars, as and for partial payment of the Wife's interest in the Husband's Corporation as more fully discussed hereinafter in this Article.

With regard to the Wife's 401K with _____, which 401K constitutes marital property, in the approximate sum of fifty thousand ($50,000.00) dollars, said 401K shall belong exclusively to the Wife, and the Husband hereby waives any claim to said monies.

With regard to the parties' profit sharing plan with _____, the parties agree that the Wife shall retain, as her separate property, her portion of the aforesaid profit sharing plan worth approximately twenty-nine thousand ($29,000.00) dollars on deposit at _____, and that the Husband shall retain, as

73

his separate property, his portion of the profit sharing plan worth approximately forty five thousand ($45,000.00) dollars on deposit at _____ . Each party waives any claim to the others share of the aforementioned profit sharing plan.

With regard to the parties' savings, stocks and bonds, more fully described on Schedule "B(1)" hereto, the Wife shall be entitled to nine hundred thousand ($900,000.00) dollars of the total value of one million four hundred thousand ($1,400,000.00) dollars, and the Husband shall be entitled to five hundred thousand ($500,000.00) dollars. The parties agree to divide the aforesaid savings, stocks and bonds as more fully detailed on Schedule "B(2)" hereto.

MARITAL RESIDENCE

The next article concerns the marital residence which I like to treat in a separate article than other assets because of the nature of the asset and the options that are available.

Generally speaking, the custodial parent will be permitted, either through negotiation, mediation, or court decree, to remain in the marital residence with the children until the emancipation of the youngest child. Accordingly the agreement must reflect that the custodial parent has the right to remain in the home and also provide for the contingency as to when the home will be sold, and how the monies will be disbursed.

In addition to the home being sold at the time the youngest child is emancipated, it could also be sold at such time as the custodial parent remarries; or at such time as the custodial parent cohabits in the marital residence for a prolonged period of time with another person; at the option of the custodial parent; or if there was a change in custody from the custodial parent to the other parent prior to emancipation.

There should also be a provision for the disposition of the monies from the sale of the home. The agreement should provide that after the payment of usual and customary closing costs, first mortgage, possible home equity loan, or any other agreed upon jointly incurred marital obligations, that the proceeds be divided either equally, or as agreed upon between the parties.

ARTICLE IV: MARITAL ABODE

NO SALE - ONE PARTY HAVING EXCLUSIVE OCCUPANCY OF MARITAL RESIDENCE

The parties presently are owners, as tenants by the entirety, the marital abode located at _____ (hereinafter referred to as the "home").

The parties agree that the Mother shall have exclusive occupancy of the home until the earliest of the following events: (1) the Mother remarries; (2) the youngest child is emancipated; (3) the Mother's option to TERMINATE her exclusive occupancy; or (4) the Mother no longer has custody of the infant children of the marriage. Upon the occurrence of the earliest of the aforesaid events, the home is to be sold (unless option rights are exercised as hereinafter provided for) and the proceeds divided equally between the parties, subject to adjustments, if any, as more fully set forth hereinafter in this Stipulation of Settlement.

During the period of exclusive occupancy of the home by the Mother, the Mother shall be solely responsible for the timely payment of home mortgage interest and principal, real estate taxes, homeowners insurance, and all other expenses related to the upkeep and maintenance, providing the Husband had complied with his support obligations as provided for in this Agreement, except for major repairs of the home, and shall indemnify and hold the Husband harmless therefrom in all regards.

Inasmuch as the custodial parent will remain in the home, the home will probably become more important to the custodial parent than the non-custodial parent. It is advisable, therefore to provide that the custodial parent have the option to purchase the noncustodial parent's interest in the home at or prior to the time of the sale contingency.

In this way, the custodial parent would be able to remain in the home with or without the children subsequent to emancipation or the occurrence of one of the sale contingencies, while at the same time paying the noncustodial parent his/her financial interest in the home.

The following is a typical option clause:

NO SALE - PARTY OCCUPYING HOME HAVING OPTION TO PURCHASE OTHER PARTIES INTEREST IN HOME

At or prior to such time as the home is to be sold pursuant to the terms of this Stipulation of Settlement, the party having exclusive occupancy shall have the first option to purchase the non-occupying party's interest, and the non-occupying party the second option to purchase the occupying party's interest. The sales price, as provided for herein, with regard to one party purchasing the other party's interest in the home, shall be calculated based upon the fair market value of the home, less the mortgage balance, and any other joint-legally incurred encumbrance, less a deduction of seven (7%) percent for usual and customary brokerage fees, together with any adjustment that may be attributable to either party as provided for in this Stipulation of Settlement.

Some agreements will be reached wherein the parties agree that the home should be sold at the time the agreement is entered into. This provision will permit the custodial parent or perhaps both parents to remain in the home until the home is sold, but provide that the home will be listed for sale at the time of execution of the agreement. This option provision will also provide for how the carrying charges on the home will be paid until the sale and also provide for the disposition of monies at the time of sale.

JOINT SALE - WIFE/HUSBAND RECEIVING EXCLUSIVE OCCUPANCY UNTIL SALE OR BOTH OCCUPYING HOME UNTIL SALE

The parties presently are owners, as tenants by the entirety, of the marital home located at _____ hereinafte referred to as the "home").

The parties agree that the home shall be listed (or has been listed for sale) forthwith, and sold as soon as practically possible for the highest marketable price.

The parties have executed (or agree to execute) a multiple listing agreement simultaneously with the execution of this Stipulation of Settlement.

The parties further agree that the Husband/Wife shall have exclusive occupancy or share of the home until the closing thereof.

Until the closing of title, the Husband/Wife shall be responsible for all expenses for the premises and its maintenance, including but not limited to mortgage, real property taxes, utilities, appropriate insurance, gardening and repairs.

75

Another option with regard to the disposition of the home, is for one party to purchase the other party's interest in the home at or about the time of the execution of the agreement. This provision provides of course for the valuation of the home and the computation of one party's interest in the home, usually the noncustodial parent, with a provision that the other parent, usually the custodial parent, purchase the other's interest in the home within a certain period of time.

In addition to purchasing the other party's interest in the home for cash, there is a possibility of the custodial parent receiving title to the home in exchange for the noncustodial parent receiving the equivalent monetary interest in another marital asset such as a pension; a business; a license; savings or other asset.

This option may require the custodial parent obtaining a mortgage in an amount sufficient to satisfy the existing mortgage on the home, if any, in addition to an amount of money equal to the other party's interest and closing costs. Of course if the person purchasing the other's interest can obtain funds from other sources, then the necessity of securing a new mortgage will be avoided.

There are advantages to both parties by having one party purchase the other party's interest in the home, rather than both continuing to remain co-owners of the property.

The noncustodial parent will receive his or her financial interest in the home in cash many years prior to the time that party would otherwise receive payment, especially if there are young children.

The custodial parent of course would own the home entirely, and any appreciation in equity would belong exclusively to the custodial parent as there would be no sharing of the value of the home at the time of sale.

In addition, the custodial parent would not have to discuss any modifications, changes, alterations, or repairs to the home with the noncustodial parent. The following article is illustrative of this kind of provision.

ONE PARTY CONVEYING INTEREST TO THE OTHER PARTY

The parties presently own, as tenants by the entirety, the marital abode located at (hereinafter referred to as the "home").

The Husband/Wife shall convey his/her interest in the home to the Husband/Wife, and he/she shall become the sole and exclusive owner thereof.

Simultaneously with the execution of this Stipulation of Settlement, the Husband/Wife shall execute a bargain and sale deed with covenants conveying his/her interest in the home to the Husband/Wife. The Husband/Wife shall pay the recording cost of the deed.

The Husband/Wife shall have no further claim to the home, and the Husband/Wife shall be solely responsible for maintaining the home and paying the mortgage on the home and shall indemnify and hold the Husband/Wife harmless therefrom.

The Husband/Wife represents to the other that except for the first mortgage, now a lien upon the home, he/she has not mortgaged, pledged, liened or otherwise encumbered the home, or his/her right, title and interest therein, agrees to indemnify and hold harmless the other with reference to the representation herein, including, but not limited to, reasonable attorney's fees.

In consideration of the Husband/Wife conveying the home as his/her separate property, the parties agree that the Husband/Wife shall be entitled to retain as his/her separate property, the pension and other retirement benefit earned at XYL Corporation.

or

The Husband/Wife shall have 90 days to secure a mortgage and pay to the Husband/Wife fifty thousand ($50,000) dollars representing the Husband/Wife's interest in the marital residence.

RESPONSIBILITY FOR DEBTS

The next article concerns debts. There should be a provision that both parties acknowledge that subsequent to the execution of the agreement that they will no longer charge or incur a debt for which the other party will be responsible, and will hold the other party harmless from such obligation. There should also be a schedule to your agreement listing the existence of marital debts and a designation as to which party will be responsible to pay for the marital debt.

Since you have designated a disposition of all marital assets as discussed in the previous section, and designated which party will be responsible for which debt, there should be no misunderstanding in the agreement with regard to the sharing of assets and liabilities acquired and incurred during the marriage.

ARTICLE V: RESPONSIBILITY FOR DEBTS

The Husband and Wife represent and warrant to each other that they will not, at any time in the future, incur or contract any debts, charges or liabilities whatsoever for which the other or the estate of the other shall or may become liable or answerable. Except as otherwise set forth herein, the Husband agrees to hold the Wife harmless and to indemnify the Wife against the payment of any monies which he shall have been compelled or obliged to make to third parties, for or by reason of any act or omission of his and against any necessary expenses arising therefrom. The Wife agrees to hold the Husband harmless and to indemnify the Husband against the payment of any monies which se shall have been compelled or obliged to make to third parties for or by reason of any act or omission of hers and against any necessary expense arising therefrom.

In the event a party pays a debt or liability which the other party is responsible for pursuant to this Stipulation of Settlement, the party paying shall be entitled to recover the debt or liability paid, with interest of ten (10%) percent per year, as well as counsel fees reasonably incurred in connection with payment of the debt or liability and recovery of the amount so paid, from the party responsible for the debt or liability. Annexed hereto and marked as Schedule " ___ " is a list of marital debts and provision for the repayment of said debts.

CUSTODY AND VISITATION

It is always better practice to provide for a detailed custody and visitation provision in order to eliminate any misunderstandings and to minimize disputes, rather than to use general language such as "the parties will agree upon visitation". The parties can always agree upon visitation, and they can always by agreement modify the written provisions in the formalized agreement. However, if the language in the agreement is vague, and a dispute arises, then the parties might be left with arguments, discord and possibly the need to seek arbitration or court intervention.

As discussed in Chapter Six, custody can take a variety of forms. Custody can be sole, joint, or joint custody with physical residency in one parent.

The thrust of the law today is that both parents retain as many rights as possible to the children. It is generally recognized that parental input, love and guidance from both parents, notwithstanding a divorce, is healthier for the children. You will note in the visitation article that the noncustodial parent has full rights with regard to receiving school information, medical information, psychiatric information: in short, **any** information pertaining to the welfare of the children.

Curtailing the rights of the noncustodial parent is the exception rather than the rule, and there must be a bonafide reason for such curtailment.

ARTICLE VI: CUSTODY, VISITATION AND NOTIFICATION

I have listed several different options for use in your Agreement depending upon the terms of your Agreement. For example, if you have agreed upon sole custody, use the language in Option 1. If you have agreed upon residential custody in one parent, use the language in Option 2. And if have agreed upon joint custody, use the language in Option 3.

If you have selected sole custody or joint custody with residential custody in one parent, the language that follows that designation would be the visitation clauses, which would designate the visitation schedule agreed upon. A standard visitation clause appears in the full Stipulation of Settlement , which you will find in Table 11 of the Appendix. This, of course, can be modified to your particular needs.

If you select Option 3, joint custody, you need to then provide a detail of how the joint custody will work. For example, one month in each parent's home, etc.

OPTION 1: SOLE CUSTODY

Custody of the infant child/children of the parties hereto is hereby conferred upon the Mother (or) Father.

    VISITATION CLAUSES FOLLOW

OPTION 2: JOINT CUSTODY - With Residential Custody in One Parent

The parties shall share joint custody of the child/children with residential custody in the Mother or Father.

    VISITATION CLAUSES FOLLOW

OPTION 3: JOINT CUSTODY

The parties agree that they shall share joint custody of the child/children of the marriage as more particularly detailed hereinafter in this article.

DETAILS OF JOINT CUSTODY AND VISITATION ARRANGEMENTS are given in Table 11, Sample stipulation of Settlement, Article VI: Custody, Visitation and Notification.

CHILD SUPPORT

Child support can be predicated on a "needs" basis; by guidelines or statutory mandates if your state provides same; or can be set by agreement between the parties by "opting out" of the guidelines or standardized formula applicable in your state, providing the opt out agreement is fair and reasonable. Remember, children are not bound by agreements made between the parties, and if the child support provision is not fair and reasonable even though both parties agree to it, a subsequent application to the court by one party may be successful in modifying the child support provision on the grounds that it was not in the best interest of the children.

In addition to the support to be paid by the noncustodial parent to the custodial parent, there are health needs, (medical, dental, etc., deductible and uncovered health expenses), as well as possible child care concerns and college concerns. I will now illustrate a child support provision which is predicated upon the New York State Child Support Standard Act, and thereafter illustrate "opt out" language where the parties agree to set support in an amount other than as provided in the guidelines.

ARTICLE VII: CHILD SUPPORT

The Father represents that his weekly salary is _____. Annexed hereto is a copy of the Father's most recent pay stub.

The Mother represents that her weekly salary is _____. Annexed hereto is a copy of the Mother's most recent pay stub.

The parties represent that they have been advised by their respective attorneys of the provisions of New York Domestic Relation Law 240 (1-b) and Family Court Act 413 ("Child Support Standards Act"). The parties are aware that under the CSSA, for ___ child/children, a non-custodial parent may be required to pay the custodial parent ____(__%) percent of his/her gross income from all sources, including the possibility that various facts may result in additional income being imputed or attributed to the non-custodial parent. The parties have also been informed of the various deductions which can be made from the income before the above percentage is applied. Further, the parties have been advised that in connection with the combined parental income over or under eighty thousand ($80,000.00) dollars, the Court could, in its discretion, consider various factors set forth in the law and fix support which is higher or lower than that resulting from the use of the above percentage. Finally, the parties have also been advised that in addition to such child support, the Court would direct the non-custodial parent to pay pro-rata share of child-care expenses and non-reimbursed medical expenses and may also direct the payment of a discretionary amount for educational expenses.

Accordingly, predicated on the parties' income and the provisions of CSSA, child support will be set at the time of the execution of this Stipulation of Settlement at $____ per week.

OPT OUT CLAUSE

Notwithstanding the foregoing, the parties intend and agree that the child support obligations of the parties be governed by this Stipulation of Settlement. In this Stipulation of Settlement, the provisions for child support have been set in a fair amount based on many considerations, including the parties' respective finances and the other financial provisions of the is Stipulation of Settlement.

Accordingly, the _____agrees to pay to the _____, ____ dollars per week as and for child support for the two infant children of the marriage.

HEALTH CARE

The following clause illustrates a comprehensive health insurance clause together with a broad definition of health care, and a provision to insure reimbursement to the party who advances money for health services and is entitled to insurance reimbursement.

ARTICLE VIII: MEDICAL INSURANCE AND EXPENSE

The Husband agrees to maintain Blue Cross/Blue Shield, Major Medical or equivalent medical coverage and dental insurance as presently exists for the benefit of the child/children until each child attains the age of nineteen (19) years, or in the event said child/children is/are fully enrolled in college or post graduate school, then until such child (ren) completes his or her course of study in said institution.

In the event either parent advances money for medical and health related needs on behalf of any child, then the party who advances the money shall be entitled to receive reimbursement from the health-care provider and both parties agree that they will cooperate in completing and filing any form that may be reasonably required in order to process insurance reimbursement from the health-care provider. Each party agrees that immediately upon receipt of the insurance proceeds, that if said proceeds are due as reimbursement to the other party that they will forthwith remit said funds to the party who advanced said monies.

Any and all health-related expenses of the child/children not covered by any of the aforesaid policies of insurance, shall be the responsibility of the Husband and the Wife, pro-rata to their respective incomes pursuant to CSSA.

Health-related expenses shall include, but not be limited to, medical, dental, orthodontic, psycho-therapeutic, prescription drug expense and the cost of prescription eyeglasses.

The Husband hereby assigns any and all rights he has to receive reimbursement from the insurance carrier for monies paid by the Wife on behalf of the children's health care directly to the Wife, and hereby authorizes the insurance carrier to remit said refund monies directly to the Wife at the address so indicated by the Wife on the insurance claim form.

LIFE INSURANCE

The custodial parent with young children needs and relies upon the support of the other parent to help support the children during their minority.

Thus, the loss of life of the noncustodial parent will result in the loss of substantial income and support. It is therefore necessary and recommended that the noncustodial parent secure a policy of life insurance for the benefit of the children until the emancipation of the youngest child. In this way, the death of the noncustodial parent will result in an insurance policy providing a source of money with which the custodial parent can support the children.

The cheapest kind of insurance for the maximum amount of financial benefit is called **term insurance**. You should consult your insurance broker or perhaps a savings bank regarding the purchase of term life insurance.

When the youngest child is emancipated, the noncustodial parent will no longer have a legal obligation to maintain the policy since it is not necessary to support the children beyond emancipation.

To insure that the noncustodial parent maintains the policy that has been agreed upon, there should be a provision that authorizes the other party to inquire directly from the insurance company, usually once a year, as to the existence of the policy and the payment of the premiums. We want to avoid the situation where the noncustodial parent dies and the custodial parent finds that the insurance policy does not exist.

In the event that the insurance policy has lapsed for nonpayment or some other reason, and the noncustodial parent dies without the benefit of insurance, then the custodial parent will have a claim against the estate of the noncustodial parent to the extent of the insurance obligation that should have been provided for pursuant to the agreement. If the estate is without assets however, such claim will be worthless.

ARTICLE IX: LIFE INSURANCE

The Husband agrees to maintain a life insurance policy in the sum of $^ and to designate the child/children as irrevocable beneficiary/beneficiaries and the Wife as Trustee of the said policy until such time as the child/children are emancipated, at which time the Husband's obligation to maintain said policy shall terminate.

The Husband represents and warrants that said policy is presently in full force and effect and that all premiums have been fully paid to the date hereof.

The Husband agrees to pay, or cause to be paid, all premiums, dues and/or assessment which may become due and owing on said life insurance policy at least fifteen (15) days prior to the end of the grace period for making said payments, and he shall deliver to the Wife prior to the said fifteen (15) day period written proof of payment thereof.

Upon the reasonable request of the Wife (not less often than once each year), the Husband shall provide the Wife documentation showing his full compliance with his obligations under this Article. In addition, the Husband hereby authorizes the Wife to obtain direct confirmation from any insurance carrier and/or any employer of his compliance with the provisions of this Article and agrees that, upon demand, he will execute and deliver to the Wife, without charge, whatever instruments, documents or authorizations which may be necessary or desirable in order that she may obtain direct confirmation of the Husband's compliance with this Article.

If the Husband shall default in the payment of any dues, premiums or assessments on any of such policies of insurance, the Wife shall have the right, but not the obligation, to pay the same. In the event the Wife shall pay any such dues, premiums or assessments, the Husband shall forthwith become indebted to the Wife in the sum or sums so paid, and such sum or sums shall be paid by the Husband to the Wife on the first day of the month immediately following the date os such payment.

If any of such policies of insurance are not in full force and effect at the time of the Husband's death, or if for any reason the Wife does not receive the proceeds thereof to which she is entitled under the provisions of this Article, then, and notwithstanding anything to the contrary contained in this Stipulation of Settlement, the Wife shall have a creditor's claim against the Husband's estate for the difference between the insurance proceeds which she should have received and the insurance proceeds which she actually receives upon the Husband's death.

COLLEGE EDUCATION

The following is a college education clause which defines what is meant by college education; provides for the sharing of costs, and limits the parental obligation to what costs would be at a state university after credits for aid and grants received.

ARTICLE X: COLLEGE EDUCATION

The parties agree that the parties and their child/children shall research all avenues of financial aid in order to utilize same.

The obligation, if any, of the parties, as hereinabove provided, shall continue until the child shall complete his or her college education, provided only that he or she shall pursue the same as a full-time student on a normally continuous basis, but in no event beyond the age of twenty-two (22) years.

The parties shall be credited with any and all sums which the child shall receive, or which shall be applied for the benefit of the child, by way of scholarships, grants in aid or any other benefits received by the child, and may apply the same towards their obligation to pay and provide for the child's college education expenses. Notwithstanding anything herein contained to the contrary, the parties' obligation to pay and provide for the college education expenses of the child/children shall be limited to what would be the cost of such college education expenses during the period of the child's attendance at college, had the child attended the State University at Albany, New York.

College education expenses shall be defined as: tuition, room/board, books and reasonable costs such as travel and activity expenses, including one SAT review course, the cost of the SAT exam , and the cost of four applications to college.

The parties shall be responsible for reasonable college education expenses defined hereinabove on behalf of the infant children of the marriage pro-rata to their respective incomes and providing that each of the parties has the ability to make such pro-rata contributions.

SPOUSAL MAINTENANCE

We have provided two option clauses, one providing for waiver of support from one spouse to the other, with a representation that each party is self-supporting. Following the waiver of support is the waiver of either spouse to require medical insurance or support by way of money for health needs.

The other option provides for the payment of support by one spouse to the other. Support paid by one spouse must be defined in terms of how long and how much. Support can either be lifetime (or until the death or remarriage of either party), or support can be for a certain number of years.

There could also be other contingencies such that support would be terminated upon the recipient spouse co-habitating on a permanent basis with another person; or that support would be decreased when the recipient spouse earns a certain amount of money annually; or that support would be decreased for every dollar that the recipient spouse earns above a certain amount of money.

ARTICLE XI: SUPPORT, MAINTENANCE AND MEDICAL INSURANCE OF SPOUSE

OPTION - WAIVER OF SUPPORT

The parties state that, in no event and under no circumstances, now or in the future, do either of them desire or require the other party to make any payment for his or her support, ordinary or extraordinary, directly or indirectly. The parties declare and acknowledge that each has been and is self-supporting and is capable of earning such sums as are reasonably required to maintain him or her in the standard of living which the parties had during the period that they resided together as Husband and Wife. The continued ability to have such earnings is not, however, a condition of any of the other provisions of this Article and shall not be deemed in any respect to impair the other provisions of this Article.

The Husband acknowledges that he is entitled to medical insurance through his place of employment and requests no contribution now or in the future from the Wife.

The Wife represents that she is entitled to medical insurance through her place of employment and requests no contribution now or in the future from the Husband.

OPTION - PAYMENT OF SUPPORT

The Husband covenants and agrees that he shall pay to the Wife the sum of $ per week as and for her support and maintenance until she remarries, cohabits on a permanent basis with another person; dies, or years from the date of the execution of this Stipulation of Settlement, whichever event shall first occur.

All payments to be made by the Husband to the Wife, as hereinabove provided, shall be by check, or postal money order and, if not given directly, shall be mailed by the Husband to the Wife at her present address or at such other address as she may direct.

The payments required to be made by the Husband to the Wife, as hereinabove provided, shall commence the first Friday immediately following the execution of this Stipulation of Settlement and be paid on each successive Friday thereafter.

The parties have been advised that under Internal Revenue laws maintenance payments are deductible by the Husband and are includable by the Wife in her income and subject to the payment of income taxes.

OPTION: HEALTH INSURANCE

Upon the option of the parties' the Husband agrees, however, that he shall execute all documents necessary to effectuate continuation coverage for a period of three (3) years, as provided for under Public Law 99-272, Title 10 - Private Health Insurance Coverage (also known as COBRA) for the Wife, including without limitation, giving proper notice to his employer or insurance plan administrator, (OPTION) [and the Husband will pay the premiums for the three year period of time, or until the Wife's earlier demise, or remarriage. The Husband shall immediately authorize his employer to provide the Wife with written confirmation that she is covered under the insurance policy. The Husband shall also immediately authorize his employer to furnish the Wife, upon her request, any prescription cards, insurance forms, etc. for her to utilize. At the earliest of the three aforementioned events, the Husband shall no longer be required to pay for medical insurance on behalf of the Wife, and the Wife shall be solely responsible for her medical insurance and her medical expenses.] at the Wife's option, which the wife will exercise in writing, certified mail, return receipt requested, to the Husband at least sixty (60) days prior to the divorce. The Wife, however, shall pay and be responsible for all premiums on said insurance.

STEP V
FILING YOUR DIVORCE

INTRODUCTION

One you have drafted and executed your Agreement, you are legally separated, but not divorced. If you are going to proceed to a divorce immediately after the execution of your Agreement, there is no need to file your Agreement separately from the divorce papers. If you are not going to proceed to a divorce, there may be a requirement in your jurisdiction to file your Agreement with the County Clerk's office or some other such office. You must check your local rules to ascertain whether your Agreement should be filed and if so where.

To secure a divorce, certain documents must be prepared and filed in Court, and ultimately a document is signed by a judge granting the divorce and dissolving the marriage. Only a judge can dissolve a marriage and thus, certain documents must be presented to the Court for signature.

OVERVIEW OF THE DIVORCE PROCESS

The divorce process, referring to paperwork and procedure, is one which is relatively simple where the parties agree upon the divorce and cooperate with one another.

There are two people to a divorce, and there are basically two kinds of documents that must be prepared. There are documents that are prepared on behalf of the Plaintiff or Petitioner, the party who is bringing the divorce proceeding, and papers that are prepared on behalf of the Defendant or Respondent, the person against whom the proceeding is brought.

The Summons and Complaint state the nature of the process, to wit: a divorce proceeding, and the basis upon which the divorce will be secure. These documents are signed by the Plaintiff or Petitioner. The Answer is a document signed by the Defendant or Respondent. In uncontested cases the Answer contains language which basically consents to the divorce.

In addition to the basic documents I've already mentioned, each jurisdiction requires supplemental documents. You need to consult your local Clerk of the Matrimonial Court to ascertain exactly the documents you need.

Finally, a Judgement of Divorce or a Decree dissolving the marriage must be prepared, which is sent to the Court, together with the documents discussed above, and your Agreement will, if fair and reasonable, be accepted and approved by the Court, and incorporated into your final Decree by the Court.

By incorporating your Agreement into the final Decree, it means that what you and your spouse have agreed to will not be changed by the Court, and will survive the judgement of Divorce as a binding contract.

CHAPTER TWENTY

SAMPLE FORMS

Forms that are needed to process your uncontested divorce vary from state to state. In almost all jurisdictions however, the documents that you will need have a commonality in general terms, and serve the same purpose. I will now discuss the nature of the forms in general, what they mean, and provide sample forms used in New York State.

also include any ancillary relief requested such as custody, support, maintenance, property distribution, and counsel fees. The summons should reflect the name of the attorney for the plaintiff/petitioner. If the plaintiff/petitioner is processing the divorce without an attorney, it will reflect the name and address of the plaintiff pro-se (meaning without an attorney).

THE SUMMONS

An action for a divorce must be commenced by the service of a document called a summons or a petition, which when served upon one party, called the defendant or respondent, invokes the jurisdiction of the court and enables the court to render matrimonial relief.

The person serving the summons who commences the matrimonial action is called the **plaintiff** or **petitioner**, and the other party to the marriage who receives the summons is referred to as the **defendant** or **respondent.**

The summons must contain words such as "Action For Divorce", in order to notify the other party as to the nature of the relief requested, and should

THE COMPLAINT

The next document needed, which can be attached to the summons or can be served separately, is called a complaint or petition. The complaint details the basis for the divorce. In no fault states the complaint will recite words such as "divorce based on irreconcilable differences."

In fault states the complaint will recite language reflecting cruel and inhuman treatment, adultery, or any other fault ground.

The following is a typical summons as well as a complaint based on living separate and apart pursuant to a separation agreement, and another complaint based on sexual abandonment for one year, which is a ground for divorce in New York State.

SAMPLE: SUMMONS

SUPREME COURT OF THE STATE OF
COUNTY OF
————————————————————————————-X   Index No.
                                  Plaintiff designates
                                  as the place of trial.
_____
_____ , Plaintiff
                                  The basis of the venue is
                                  SUMMONS WITH NOTICE

-against-
                                  Plaintiff resides at

_____
_____ ,
_____ , Defendant   County of _____
————————————————————————————-X

ACTION FOR A DIVORCE OR A SEPARATION OR, IN THE ALTERNATIVE, SUPPORT PURSUANT TO ARTICLE 4 OF THE FAMILY COURT ACT

TO THE ABOVE NAMED DEFENDANT:

You are hereby summoned to serve a notice of appearance, on the Plaintiff's Attorney within 20 days after the service of this summons, exclusive of the day of service (or within 30 days after the service is complete if the summons is not personally delivered to you within the State of New York); and in case of your failure to appear, judgment will be taken against you by default for the relief demanded in the notice set forth below.

Dated: Attorneys for Plaintiff or
____ , 19__   Plaintiff pro se
Smithtown, New York

NOTICE: The nature of this action is to dissolve the marriage between the parties or, in the alternative, for a separation, on the grounds of ____ or, in the alternative, for support pursuant to Article 4 of the Family Court Act.

The relief sought is,

A judgment of absolute divorce in favor of the plaintiff dissolving the marriage between the parties in this action or, in the alternative, separation Plaintiff from the bed and board of Defendant or, in the alternative, support pursuant to Article 4 of the Family Court Act.

The nature of the ancillary demanded is:

Maintenance for Plaintiff;

Child Support of the unemancipated issue of the marriage;

Exclusive, use, occupancy and ownership of the marital residence of the parties;

Determination of the respective rights of the parties in separate and marital property and an equitable distribution of the marital property;

Alternatively, a distributive award to Plaintiff;

Direction that Defendant maintain or assign appropriate medical insurance coverage for Plaintiff and the children;

Direction that Defendant purchase, maintain or assign appropriate policies of life insurance designating Plaintiff and the unemancipated issue of the marriage as irrevocable beneficiaries thereof;

Custody of the minor children of the parties;

Judgment for necessaries;

Counsel fees, Appraisal fees; and

Such other and further relief as to the Court may seem just and proper.

SAMPLE: COMPLAINT (SEPARATION)

SUPREME COURT OF THE STATE OF
COUNTY OF
————————————————————X

Mary Doe_____,   Plaintiff,

-against-   VERIFIED COMPLAINT

John Doe_____,   Defendant.

————————————————————X

Plaintiff, by attorneys or Plaintiff Pro se complaining of the defendant, alleges as follows:

FIRST: That at the time of the commencement of this action, both the Plaintiff and Defendant were over the age of eighteen (18) years.

SECOND: That at the time of the commencement of this action and for a continuous period of at least one (1) year immediately preceding such commencement, Plaintiff and Defendant resided in the State of New York.

THIRD: That the Plaintiff and Defendant are husband and wife, having been married in the County of ____, State of ____, on the ____ day of ____, 19__. That the marriage was solemnized by a person specified in DRL Sec. 11(1).

FOURTH: That there is one (1) issue of the marriage, to wit: Barbara, born July, 2, 1989

FIFTH: That the Plaintiff has taken, or will take, prior to the entry of final judgement, all steps solely within here power to remove any barrier to the Defendant's remarriage following a divorce.

SIXTH: That no decree of divorce or annulment has been granted to the Plaintiff against the Defendant, or to the Defendant against the Plaintiff by any Court of this State or any other Court in the United States, or in any foreign country, domain, or territory.

SEVENTH: (a) That the Plaintiff and Defendant entered into a written Separation Agreement, which they subscribed and acknowledged on the 1 day of May, 1990 in the form required to entitle a deed to be recorded;

(b) That a Memorandum of Agreement of Separation has been filed in the Office of the Clerk of the County of _____, wherein Plaintiff and/or Defendant reside;

(c) That the parties have lived separate and apart for a period of one (1) or more years after the execution of said Separation Agreement: and

(d) That the Plaintiff has substantially performed all of the terms and conditions of such Separation Agreeement.

WHEREFORE, the Plaintiff demands judgment against the Defendant as follows:

(a) for an absolute divorce dissolving the bonds of matrimony between the parties;

(b) for all relief outlined in the Separation Agreement entered into between the parties on the 1 day of May, 1990; and

(c) for such other and further relief as this Court seems just and proper.

Dated:
___, 19_
Smithtown, New York

                    Yours, etc.
                    Attorney or
                    Plaintiff pro se

SAMPLE: COMPLAINT (SEXUAL ABANDONMENT)

SUPREME COURT OF THE STATE OF
COUNTY OF

————————————————————X

John Doe_____,
                Plaintiff,
     -against-
Mary Doe_____,
                Defendant.

————————————————————X

                VERIFIED COMPLAINT

Plaintiff, by attorneys, _____ or plaintiff pro se complaining of the Defendant, alleges as follows:

FIRST: That at the time of the commencement of this action, both the Plaintiff and Defendant were over the age of eighteen (18) years.

SECOND: That at the time of the commencement of this action and for a continuous period of at least one (1) year immediately preceding such commencement, Plaintiff and Defendant resided in this State of New York.

THIRD: That the Plaintiff and Defendant are husband and wife, having been married in the County of ___, State of __, on the __ day of __, 199_. That the marriage was solemnized by a person specified in DRL Sec. 11(1).

FOURTH: That there are two (2) issue of the marriage, to wit: John, born April 1,1985; and Sue, born August 23,1990.

FIFTH: That the Plaintiff has taken, or will take, prior to the entry of final judgment, all steps solely within his power to remove any barrier to the Defendant's remarriage following a divorce.

SIXTH: That no decree of divorce or annulment has been granted to the Plaintiff against the Defendant, or to the Defendant against the Plaintiff by any Court of this State or any other Court in the United States, or in any foreign country, domain, or territory.

SEVENTH: That at all times throughout the marriage, Plaintiff performed all of his duties and obligations as Defendant's husband.

EIGHTH: That commencing with in or about Dec. 1, 1990, and continuing up until the present time, the Defendant has, without any good or justifiable cause therefor or without any provocation therefor, and without Plaintiff's consent, refused to have sexual relations with the Plaintiff and Defendant has thereby disavowed her marriage to the Plaintiff and abandoned him.

NINTH: Despite Plaintiff's repeated requests to Defendant that she discontinue her refusal to fulfill her marital obligations and to have sexual relations with the Plaintiff, the Defendant has persisted and continued to refuse to fulfill her marital duties and to have sexual relations with the Plaintiff, and such refusal has been willful and intentional on the part of the Defendant, without any just cause or provocation therefor and without Plaintiff's consent.

WHEREFORE, the Plaintiff demands judgment against the Defendant as follows:

(a) for an absolute divorce dissolving the bonds of matrimony between the parties;

(b) for all relief outlined in the Stipulation of Settlement entered into between the parties on the __ day of __, 1992; and

(c) for such other and further relief as this Court seems just and proper.

Dated: Smithtown, New York
       _____ , 1992

                Yours, etc.
                Attorneys for plaintiff or
                Plaintiff pro se

SAMPLE: ANSWER

Where the divorce is on consent between the parties, the defendant will serve a document called an *answer* which will basically neither admit nor deny the allegations in the complaint and consent to the entry of an uncontested divorce. The following is a typical answer in this regard.

SUPREME COURT OF THE STATE OF NEW YORK
COUNTY OF SUFFOLK

————————————————————-X

_Mary Doe_____,

                           Plaintiff,

        -against-   VERIFIED ANSWER

_John Doe_____,

                           Defendant.

————————————————————-X

       The Defendant, as and for his Verified Answer to the Verified Complaint of the Plaintiff herein, respectfully alleges as follows:

       FIRST: That Defendant neither admits nor denies the allegations contained in the Complaint, and consents to this matter being placed on the uncontested matrimonial calendar.

       SECOND: That the Defendant has taken, or will take prior to the entry of final judgment, all steps solely within power to remove any barrier to the Plaintiff's remarriage following a   divorce.

       WHEREFORE, the Defendant consents that the within matter be placed on the uncontested matrimonial calendar.

Dated: Smithtown, New York   Yours, etc
    _____, __92   Attorney or
                                      Defendant pro se

After the preparation and the service of the summons, complaint and answer, the matter is ready to be placed on the calendar in order that the case can be presented to the Judge for the signing of the Judgement of Divorce.

In most jurisdictions, uncontested or consent divorces can be processed by the forwarding of papers to the court without the necessity of a personal appearance of the parties or their attorneys. The summons, complaint, answer and a proposed judgement of divorce, as well as the proposed Qualified Domestic Relations Order (QDRO), if applicable, will be sent by mail or delivered to the matrimonial clerk's at the courthouse. If the documents are in proper order, the Judgement of Divorce and QDRO will be signed by the Judge. The signed documents will be available from your attorney or the county clerk in the county in which you live.

The following is a typical Judgement of Divorce based on living separate and apart for a period of one or more years, which reflects the incorporation by reference of the separation agreement.

SAMPLE: JUDGEMENT OF DIVORCE

At a Trial Term, Part _____ of the
Supreme Court of the State of
    held in and for the County of
    , at   on the _____
day of _____, 19^.

P R E S E N T :

              HON._____
                Justice.

————————————————————————-X

    ___Mary Doe___,

               Plaintiff,   Index No.

     -against-   JUDGMENT OF DIVORCE
    ___John Doe___,

              Defendant.

————————————————————————-X

       The Plaintiff having brought this action for a judgment of absolute divorce by reason of the parties having lived separate and apart for a period of one or more years pursuant to a written agreement of separation entered into between the parties on the __ day of __, 19_, and the Summons bearing the notation "Action For a Divorce", together with a Verified Complaint having been duly served upon the Defendant personally within this State, and the Defendant having appeared and answered pro se, with a Verified Answer and the parties having entered into Separation Agreement dated ___ , 1992, and the defendant having consented that the matter be placed upon the uncontested calendar for divorce by submission or inquest, and the Plaintiff having applied, on due notice to the Defendant, to the Court at a Trial Term thereof for judgment for the relief demanded in the Verified Complaint, and the matter having been set for submission on the __ day of __, 1991; and the Plaintiff having submitted written proof in support of the essential allegations of the Verified Complaint, and such proof having been read and considered by me, I decide and find as stated in the separate FINDINGS OF FACT AND CONCLUSIONS OF LAW of even date herewith.

       NOW, on motion of Plaintiff's attorney for the Plaintiff pro se, it is

       ADJUDGED, that the marriage between _Mary Doe_ Plaintiff, and _John Doe_ Defendant, is dissolved by reason of separation of the parties for a period of one or more years pursuant to a written agreement of separation entered into on the __ day of ___ , ,199_; and it is further

       ORDERED AND ADJUDGED that the Separation Agreement entered into between the parties on the __ day of __ , 1991, a copy of which is attached to and incorporated in this Judgment by reference, shall survive and shall not be merged in this Judgment, and the parties hereby are directed to comply with every legally enforceable term and provision of such Separation Agreement including any provision to submit an appropriate issue to arbitration before a single arbitrator, as if such term or provision were set forth in its entirety herein, and the Court retains jurisdiction of the matter concurrently with the Family Court for the purpose of specifically enforcing such of the provisions of the Separation Agreement as are capable of specific enforcement, to the extent permitted by law, and of making such further judgment with respect to maintenance, support, custody or visitation as it finds appropriate under the circumstances existing at the time application for that purpose is made to it, or both; and it is further

       ORDERED AND ADJUDGED that Plaintiff is authorized to resume the use of her maiden name or other former surname, to wit:

                E N T E R

             Justice Supreme Court

SAMPLE: THE QUALIFIED DOMESTIC RELATIONS ORDER

If the matter involves the sharing of pension benefits by the employed spouse and the nonemployed spouse, referred to as the alternate payee, the way to protect the alternate payee's interest in the pension is to have the court sign a Qualified Domestic Relations Order (QDRO) which is described in detail in Chapter 9 of this book. The following is a typical example of the Qualified Domestic Relations Order.

At a Matrimonial Special Term
of the Supreme Court Part _,
held in and for the County of Suffolk
at the Courthouse thereof,
located at

on the __ day of   , 1992.

P R E S E N T :

HON. _____

_____-X
_____, Plaintiff,   :   Index No.

-against-   DOMESTIC RELATIONS ORDER

_____ , Defendant.
_____-X

This Court having granted a Judgment of Divorce on the __ day of _____, 199_, by the HON. _____, and filed in the Suffolk County Clerk's Office on the __ day of _____,199_, and upon the Stipulation entered into by the parties on the __ day of _____, 199_, and it appearing to the Court as follows:

The parties hereto were formerly husband and wife.

This Order is made pursuant to the Judgment of Divorce granted on the __ day of _____, 199_, and filed in the Suffolk County Clerk's Office on the __ day of _____,   199_, which Judgment of Divorce incorporated but did not merge the provisions of a Stipulation entered into by the parties on the __day of _____, 199_.

The parties hereto were married on the __ day of _____, 199_, and an action for a divorce was commenced on or about the __ day of _____, 199_.

The _____ is hereafter referred to as the "Plan".

The Plaintiff/Defendant, _____, is hereafter referred to as "Participant" in the _____.

The Plaintiff/Defendant, _____, is hereafter referred to as ("Alternate Payee" in the _____ or "Former Spouse" of the Participant) in the _____.

The current and last known mailing address of Participant is _____, and h__ social security number is _____.

The current and last known mailing address of (Alternate Payee/Former Spouse) is _____, and h__ social security number is _____.

This Order pertains to that portion of the Participant's retirement benefits which accumulated during the marriage up to the date of the commencement of the action for divorce, that being _____.

To accommodate the marital property distribution between the parties, it is hereby

ORDERED, that the Plan benefits/Participant's retirement benefits with the _____, to the extent to which (they have/it has) accrued during the marriage (are/is) marital property; and it is further

ORDERED, that the Plan Administrator issue separate checks to the Participant and the (Alternate Payee/Former Spouse) for their respective interests in the Plan at the time the benefits become payable; and it is further

ORDERED, that at such time as the Participant has retired from and is actually receiving a retirement allowance from the Plan, or upon the occurrence of the Participant's Normal Retirement Date, the said Plan, in accordance with the formula devised in the case of Majauskas v. Majauskas is directed to pay to the (Alternate Payee/Former Spouse) from the Participant's retirement allowance, __ (_%) percent of a fraction of the Participant's maximum monthly retirement allowance prior to any option modification; and it is further

ORDERED, that the numerator shall be ___ months and the denominator shall be the total number of months of service credit in the Plan which the Participant has at the time of retirement, or any time after the Participant's Normal Retirement Date that the (Alternate Payee/Former Spouse) chooses to begin collection of benefits if the Participant has not yet retired. The term "retirement allowance" as used herein, shall be deemed to include any annuity, as well as supplemental retirement allowance which is paid by the Plan to the Participant. If the Participant elects to receive an early retirement benefit and receives an early retirement subsidy, the amount payable to the (Alternate Payee/Former Spouse) shall be recalculated so that the (Alternate Payee/Former Spouse) shares in said subsidy. The (Alternate Payee/Former Spouse) may opt to receive any of these benefits in any method allowed by the Plan; and it is further

ORDERED, that the Plan is directed to designate the (Alternate Payee/Former Spouse) as beneficiary of the Plan, as consistent with the Property Settlement Agreement placed on the record, so that in the event the Participant dies, the (Alternate Payee/Former Spouse) shall receive her pro-rata share of any survivor benefits calculated pursuant to the formula hereinabove set forth; and it is further

ORDERED, that nothing contained in the Order shall, in any way, require the Plan to provide any form, type or amount of benefit not otherwise provided for under the Plan, nor shall the Plan be required to provide increased benefits determined on the basis of actuarial value; and it is further

ORDERED, that the Plan shall have no obligation or responsibility as a consequence of this action apart from the specific direction contained in this Order; and it is further

ORDERED, that in the event of change of address of said (Alternate Payee/Former Spouse), she will immediately notify, in writing, _____; and it is further

ORDERED, that this Order shall not require the Plan to pay any benefits to the (Alternate Payee/Former Spouse) which are required to be paid to another (Alternate Payee/Former Spouse) under another Order previously determined by the Plan Administrator to be a Qualified Domestic Relations Order; and it is further

ORDERED, that this Order is to be deemed appropriate to effectuate the division of the retirement benefits earned by _____, pursuant to his participation in the Plan; and it is further

ORDERED, that this Court retain jurisdiction to implement and supervise the payment of retirement benefits as provided herein should either party or the Plan Administrator make such application, and the Court determines such to be appropriate and necessary.

ENTER

J.S.C.

In addition to the basic forms that have been shown above, there may be other miscellaneous forms that are required in your particular jurisdiction and these could vary not only from state to state, but from county to county. Your attorney will know what forms have to be supplied.

If you are processing your divorce without an attorney, then you should visit the clerk of the matrimonial part in the court house in your county and ascertain exactly which forms are needed. Secure copies of the forms if available at the clerk's office or inquire as to where the forms may be obtained.

CHAPTER TWENTY-ONE

APPEARANCE IN COURT

Most matters that are settled by the execution of an agreement do not require a personal appearance in court. The attorneys can prepare divorce papers or can amend divorce papers that were initially prepared for litigation, in view of the now "settled case", and conclude the matter on what we call an uncontested basis. This means that papers will be prepared in the attorney's office, or by yourself if you are not using an attorney, and forwarded to the court for signature by the judge. However, there are certain situations where personal appearances are recommended even though the matter is settled.

For example, if one person is receiving far less than that person is entitled to by way of existing law and/or guidelines, then in order to insure that the agreement will withstand a possible subsequent attack on its validity, and to insure that the person is entering into the agreement freely and voluntarily, it may be recommended that the parties appear in court and be questioned in front of the court as to the voluntary waiver of certain rights and the knowing, voluntary, and willing acceptance of the agreement that is being proffered.

Where for example, one party may be suffering from a form of mental disability which does not require institutionalization, yet leaves the other party and perhaps the attorneys to be concerned, it may be appropriate to have this party appear before the court and be questioned so that the court itself sanctions the agreement.

In short, if there is any question as to the capacity of a party to enter into an agreement, or the fairness of the agreement, it may be recommended to have all parties appear before the court.

Where the matter is settled however, and where there is no question as to the fairness of the agreement and as to the capacity of the parties to understand the nature and concept of the agreement, appearances will not be required in most cases, and the matter can be concluded on papers forwarded to the courts.

CONCLUSION

We have covered everything you need to know in order to proceed with your divorce or separation, and have shown you a process by which you can reach agreement on the issues. You can now complete as much of the process as you want by yourselves, or you can select whatever professional help you need along the way.

The power is in your hands to complete a successful divorce. Although it may seem difficult at times, remember that thousands of other couples have done it, and the effort will be well worth it, both emotionally and financially. Follow the Steps outlined in this book, and the benefits to you and your children will amaze you.

TABLE 1

SPOUSE _____

DATE _____

DIVORCE DECISION WORKSHEET

MY MARRIAGE:

GOOD PARTS

1. _____
2. _____
3. _____
4. _____
5. _____
6. _____
7. _____
8. _____

BAD PARTS

1. _____
2. _____
3. _____
4. _____
5. _____
6. _____
7. _____
8. _____

MY SPOUSE:

GOOD PARTS

1. _____
2. _____
3. _____
4. _____
5. _____
6. _____
7. _____
8. _____

1. _____
2. _____
3. _____
4. _____
5. _____
6. _____
7. _____
8. _____

WHAT I LIKED ABOUT MY SPOUSE WHEN WE GOT MARRIED:

1. _____
2. _____
3. _____
4. _____
5. _____
6. _____

WHAT I'M DISAPPOINTED IN NOW:

1. _____
2. _____
3. _____
4. _____
5. _____
6. _____

RESULTS OF KEEPING MARRIAGE TOGETHER:

POSITIVES

1. _____
2. _____
3. _____
4. _____

NEGATIVES

1. _____
2. _____
3. _____
4. _____

TABLE 1

SPOUSE

DATE

DIVORCE DECISION WORKSHEET

MY MARRIAGE:

GOOD PARTS	BAD PARTS
1. _____	1. _____
2. _____	2. _____
3. _____	3. _____
4. _____	4. _____
5. _____	5. _____
6. _____	6. _____
7. _____	7. _____
8. _____	8. _____

MY SPOUSE:

GOOD PARTS

1. _____	1. _____
2. _____	2. _____
3. _____	3. _____
4. _____	4. _____
5. _____	5. _____
6. _____	6. _____
7. _____	7. _____
8. _____	8. _____

WHAT I LIKED ABOUT MY SPOUSE WHEN WE GOT MARRIED:

1. _____
2. _____
3. _____
4. _____
5. _____
6. _____

WHAT I'M DISAPPOINTED IN NOW:

1. _____
2. _____
3. _____
4. _____
5. _____
6. _____

RESULTS OF KEEPING MARRIAGE TOGETHER:

POSITIVES	NEGATIVES
1. _____	1. _____
2. _____	2. _____
3. _____	3. _____
4. _____	4. _____

TABLE 2
STATE PROVISIONS REGARDING DIVORCE

STATE	PROVISION FOR DIVORCE MEDIATION	DISTRIBUTION OF PROPERTY — EQUITABLE	COMMUNITY PROPERTY	FAULT AS A CONSIDERATION	AWARD OF MAINTENANCE/ALIMONY — DISCRETION OF THE COURT	LIMITATIONS OF TIME	GROUNDS FOR DIVORCE — FAULT	NO-FAULT OPTION	NO-FAULT ONLY	AGE OF EMANCIPATION
ALABAMA		X		X	X		X	X		19
ALASKA	X	X			X				X	18
ARIZONA	X		X		X				X	18
ARKANSAS		X		X	X		X			18
CALIFORNIA	X		X		X		X	X		18
COLORADO	X	X			X				X	21
CONN.	X	X		X	X		X	X		18
DELAWARE	X	X			X	X	X	X		18
DIST. OF COL.		X		X			X	X		18
FLORIDA	X			X	X		X	X		18
GEORGIA		X		X	X		X	X		18
HAWAII	X	X		X	X		X	X		18
IDAHO	X	X		X	X		X	X		18
ILLINOIS	X	X			X		X	X		18
INDIANA	X	X			X		X	X		18
IOWA	X	X			X				X	18
KANSAS	X	X		X		X	X	X		18
KENTUCKY	X	X			X				X	18
LOUISIANA			X				X	X		18
MAINE	X	X			X		X	X		18
MARYLAND	X	X		X	X		X	X		18
MASS.	X	X		X	X		X	X		18
MICHIGAN	X	X		X	X				X	18
MINNESOTA	X	X			X				X	18
MISSISSIPPI		TITLE			X		X	X		21
MISSOURI	X	X		X	X				X	18

TABLE 2 (CONT)

STATE PROVISIONS REGARDING DIVORCE

STATE	PROVISION FOR DIVORCE MEDIATION	DISTRIBUTION OF PROPERTY		FAULT AS A CONSIDERATION	AWARD OF MAINTENANCE / ALIMONY		GROUNDS FOR DIVORCE			AGE OF EMANCIPATION
		EQUITABLE	COMMUNITY PROPERTY		DISCRETION OF THE COURT	LIMITATIONS OF TIME	FAULT	NO-FAULT OPTION	NO-FAULT ONLY	
MONTANA	X	X			X					18
NEBRASKA	X	X			X		X	X		19
NEVADA			X		X		X	X		18
NEW HAMP.	X	X		X			X	X		18
NEW JERSEY		X			X		X	X		18
NEW MEXICO	X		X		X		X	X		18
NEW YORK		X		X	X		X			18
N. CAROLINA							X	X		18
N. DAKOTA	X	X		X	X		X	X		18
OHIO	X	X			X		X	X		18
OKLAHOMA	X	X			X		X	X		18
OREGON	X	X			X		X	X		18
PENN.	X	X		X	X		X	X		21
RHODE ISL.	X	X		X	X		X	X		18
S. CAROLINA	X	X			X		X	X		18
S. DAKOTA	X	X		X	X		X			18
TENNESSEE	X	X		X	X		X	X		18
TEXAS			X			X	X	X		18
UTAH	X	X			X		X	X		18
VERMONT		X			X		X	X		18
VIRGINIA	X	X		X	X		X	X		18
WASHINGTON	X		X		X				X	18
W. VIRGINIA		X		X	X		X	X		21
WISCONSIN	X				X				X	18
WYOMING		X	X		X		X	X		19

TABLE 3

PRELIMINARY LIST OF MARITAL ASSETS

ITEM	CHECK IF INFO AVAILABLE ( )	VALUE
A. Bank accounts		
Savings		
Cash on hand		
B. Notes due you		
C. Stocks		
Bonds		
Mutual funds		
D. Real Estate		
Home		
Other		
E. Life Insurance		
F. Business or Professional		
G. Licenses & degrees		
H. Pensions, Annuities		
I. Miscellaneous		
Patents		
Trademarks		
Royalties		
Copyrights		
Other		
J. Automobiles		
1.		
2.		
3.		
K. Personal effects		
Jewelry		
Collectibles		
Other		

TABLE 3

PRELIMINARY LIST OF MARITAL ASSETS

ITEM	CHECK IF INFO AVAILABLE ( )	VALUE
A. Bank accounts		
Savings		
Cash on hand		
B. Notes due you		
C. Stocks		
Bonds		
Mutual funds		
D. Real Estate		
Home		
Other		
E. Life Insurance		
F. Business or Professional		
G. Licenses & degrees		
H. Pensions, Annuities		
I. Miscellaneous		
Patents		
Trademarks		
Royalties		
Copyrights		
Other		
J. Automobiles		
1.		
2.		
3.		
K. Personal effects		
Jewelry		
Collectibles		
Other		

TABLE 4

HOUSEHOLD ITEMS CHECKLIST

SPOUSE

_____

DATE

ITEM	WANT (Y / N)	$ VALUE
Kitchen Table		
Kitchen Chairs		
Kitchen Dishes		
Cooking Utensils, Pots		
Knives		
Dining Room Table		
Dining Room Chairs		
Dishes, China		
Silverware		
Glassware		
Linens		
Buffet		
Living Room Rugs		
Living Room Sofa		
Living Room Chairs		
Television Set		
Coffee Tables		
Stereo		
Art		
Books		
Lamps		
Beds		
Dressers		
Night Tables		
Linens		
Desks		
Chairs		
Chests		
Bookcases		
Air Conditioners		
Sports Equipment		
Electronic Equipment		
Computer		
Golf Clubs		
Bicycles		
Fishing Equipment		
Lawn Mower		
Other		

TABLE 4

HOUSEHOLD ITEMS CHECKLIST

ITEM	WANT (Y / N)	$ VALUE
Kitchen Table		
Kitchen Chairs		
Kitchen Dishes		
Cooking Utensils, Pots		
Knives		
Dining Room Table		
Dining Room Chairs		
Dishes, China		
Silverware		
Glassware		
Linens		
Buffet		
Living Room Rugs		
Living Room Sofa		
Living Room Chairs		
Television Set		
Coffee Tables		
Stereo		
Art		
Books		
Lamps		
Beds		
Dressers		
Night Tables		
Linens		
Desks		
Chairs		
Chests		
Bookcases		
Air Conditioners		
Sports Equipment		
Electronic Equipment		
Computer		
Golf Clubs		
Bicycles		
Fishing Equipment		
Lawn Mower		
Other		

FINANCIAL INFORMATION AND INCOME STATEMENT

ASSETS

Estimate the value of each of the following items of property, and place value in appropriate column on right. If any item is located in a jurisdiction other than in which you live, indicate where such item is located, and, if necessary, give details on a separate sheet.

	Husband	Wife	Joint
A. Bank Accounts, Savings, and Cash on Hand:			
_____	___	___	___
_____	___	___	___
_____	___	___	___
_____	___	___	___
B. Notes, Accounts Receivable (i.e. money owed to you. Indicate by whom payable, amount, and date or dates payable):			
_____	___	___	___
_____	___	___	___
_____	___	___	___
_____	___	___	___

103-1

283 Commack Road • Suite 215 • Commack • New York • 11725 • (516) 499-0205

C.   Stocks, Bonds, Mutual Funds: Husband   Wife   Joint

_____   _____   _____   _____

_____   _____   _____   _____

_____   _____   _____   _____

_____   _____   _____   _____

D.   Real Estate (Home and other):

_____   _____   _____   _____

_____   _____   _____   _____

_____   _____   _____   _____

_____   _____   _____   _____

E.   Life Insurance - Name of
     Company, policy number, face
     value, type (i.e., "term",
     "ordinary life," etc.) Place
     cash value on right:

_____   _____   _____   _____

_____   _____   _____   _____

_____   _____   _____   _____

_____   _____   _____   _____

F.   Business   or   Professional
     Interests.   (Please furnish
     last balancesheet and P&L
     statement, tax return, buy-sell
     agreements,etc.):

_____   _____   _____   _____

_____   _____   _____   _____

_____   _____   _____   _____

_____   _____   _____   _____

	Husband	Wife	Joint

G.   Licenses & Degrees: List any licenses, college degrees, or professional degrees awarded during the marriage. Include the date of award:

_____

_____

_____

_____

H.   Pensions and Tax Deferred annuities: Include all pensions, IRA's, Keoughs, 401Ks, tax deferred annuities, or any other retirement accounts. If value is unknown, leave right hand column blank:

_____

_____

_____

_____

I.   Miscellaneous Property: Patents, trademarks, copyrights, royalties, employee benefits (furnish last statement and descriptive booklet), stock options, etc:

_____

_____

_____

_____

	Husband	Wife	Joint

J.   Automobiles:

K.   Personal Effects, and Tangible Personal Property:

L.   Other:

TOTAL ASSETS

LIABILITIES

A.   Mortgages on Real Estate:

		Husband	Wife	Joint

B.   Notes Payable to Banks and
     Others:

_____   _____   _____   _____

_____   _____   _____   _____

_____   _____   _____   _____

_____   _____   _____   _____

C.   Loans on Insurance Policies:

_____   _____   _____   _____

_____   _____   _____   _____

_____   _____   _____   _____

_____   _____   _____   _____

D.   Credit Card Debt:

_____   _____   _____   _____

_____   _____   _____   _____

_____   _____   _____   _____

_____   _____   _____   _____

E.   Other Debts:

_____   _____   _____   _____

_____   _____   _____   _____

_____   _____   _____   _____

_____   _____   _____   _____

Total Liabilities: _____   _____   _____

Net Worth (Assets minus Liabilities):   _____   _____   _____

Annual Income

	Husband	Wife
Gross Salary	_____	_____
Less:		
Withholding	(_____)	(_____)
FICA	(_____)	(_____)
Other Deductions (Itemize):		
_____	(_____)	(_____)
_____	(_____)	(_____)
_____	(_____)	(_____)
_____	(_____)	(_____)
Net Salary	_____	_____
Dividend Income*	_____	_____
Interest Income*	_____	_____
Income from Trusts*	_____	_____
Rental Income*	_____	_____
Other Income (specify)*	_____	_____
Total Annual Income	_____	_____

Less Deductions for:	Husband	Wife
Estimated Taxes	(_____)	(_____)
Other Deductions for Tax Payments on Income Not Subject to Withholding	(_____)	(_____)
Total Deductions	(_____)	(_____)
Net Annual (take home) Income	_____	_____
Average Monthly Net (take home) Income (1/12th of Annual Figure)	_____	_____

* If this income is received jointly, so indicate ( ) and divide between husband and wife.

LEGAL ECONOMIC EVALUATIONS, INC.

1000 Elwell Court   #203   Palo Alto   CA 94303   (415) 969-7682   Fax (415) 969-0266

Pension Valuation

Attorney/Mediator Information

Name _____

Firm _____

Street _____

City, state & zip code _____

Telephone [   ] _____

Today's date ____/____/____

How did you hear of us? _____

Do you need a fax response?   ❑ Yes ❑ No

Fax [   ] _____

Case Information *(For faster service, please collect the information below and call one of our Economists at (800) 221-6826)*

Pensioner name _____   Gender ❑ M ❑ F Birthdate ____/____/____

Employer _____   Occupation _____

Date entered plan ____/____/____   Still employed? ❑ Yes ❑ No   If no, termination date ____/____/____

Spouse name _____   Birthdate ____/____/____ Date of marriage ____/____/____

Date spouse's interest in pension ends ____/____/____ *(Date of separation, filing, dissolution or trial, as appropriate in your state.)*

If the pensioner is already receiving benefits, how much are they $_____ and when did they begin ____/____/____?

Have you enclosed a copy of the pension plan booklet? ❑ Yes

Have you enclosed the pensioner's most recent benefits statement? ❑ Yes

Is the pensioner employed by a government entity? ❑ Yes ❑ No If yes, please list base pay, overtime and total pay for the last 3 years.

Is there any other recent correspondence regarding pension benefits? ❑ Yes ❑ No If so, please enclose a copy.

Does the pensioner have any life threatening illness? ❑ Yes ❑ No If so, please describe.

_____

_____

_____

_____

In addition to the present value of the pension, do you wish us to show the spouse's net interest based on the ratio of service during marriage to total plan service (also known as the "Time Rule" or "Coverture Percentage")? ❑ Yes ❑ No

Billing ❑ Enclosed is a check for $100 payable to Legal Economic Evaluations, Inc. Please mail remittance and this completed form to the above address. Price subject to change without notice.

Questions? Please call us at (800) 221-6826

Monthly Expense Budget

If you do not anticipate that the children of your present marriage will be living with you, complete only column A. If you anticipate that the children will be living with you, attempt to distribute your estimated monthly needs between columns A and B. Some will be difficult, such as rent. On rent, for example, you may estimate what a residence for yourself alone would cost and list that cost in column A, then estimate the cost for yourself and the children, and list in column B the difference between that cost and the amount listed in column A. Fill out annexed schedules A, B, and C, prior to completion of this form.

ITEMS	A (Yourself)	B (Children)
Set-Asides:		
Emergencies and Future Goals (from Schedule A)	_____	_____
Seasonal Expenses (from Schedule B)	_____	_____
Regular Monthly Expenses:		
Housing Rent	_____	_____
House Payments		
Principal and Interest	_____	_____
Real Estate Taxes	_____	_____
Home Insurance	_____	_____
Other (specify)_____	_780.00_	_____

Utilities:

    Electricity   100.00   _____

    Gas/Heating Oil   _____   _____

    Telephone   100.00   _____

    Water   _____   _____

    Other (specify) Cable   40.00   _____

Installment Debt Payments
(from Schedule C)   _____   _____

           Total of Above   _____   _____

Day-to-Day Expenses: (Estimate per month)

    Food and Dairy:
    At Home   200.00   _____

    Away from Home   100.00   _____

    Clothing: (including working
               clothes)   100.00   _____

    Transportation:

        Gas and Oil   150.00   _____

        Auto Repair & Maintenance   50.00   _____

        Other (bus-taxi-parking, etc.)_____   _____

    Health, Medical and Dental:

        Medical, Dental & Hospital
           Insurance   100.00   _____

        Medical & Health Care
           (not covered by insurance)   25.00   _____

        Dental (not covered
           by insurance)   _____   _____

        Medicines & Drugs   _____   _____

Household Operation & Maintenance:

Repairs _____ _____

Garden or Yard Work ___75.00___ _____

Replacement of Furnishings _____ _____

Dry Cleaning & Laundry ___25.00___ _____

Domestic Help (~~5~~ days at
  $ ~~30~~ per day) ~~100.00~~ _____

Children's Day Care ___100.00___ _____

Other(specify) _____ _____

Education, Self and Children
  (Immediate Needs)

Private School Tuition ___150.00___ _____

College Tuition _____ _____

Books and Fees _____ _____

Other (specify)_____ _____ _____

Variable Monthly Expenses:

Drug/Variety Store Items _____ _____

Books, Magazines, Newspapers _____ _____

Children's Allowances _____ _____

Charities, Gifts,
  Contributions ___25.00___ _____

Dues (Club or Professional
  not included as business
  expenses) _____ _____

Cultural/Recreational _____ _____

Other (specify)_____   _____   _____

_____   _____   _____

Total Day to Day Expenses   _____   _____

Grand Total: (day to day
plus total of regular
monthly expenses)   _____   _____

Emergencies and Future Goals

Schedule A

Type of Fund	Probable Cost	Date Desired	Amount to set aside this year	Amount to set aside per month
Emergency	500.00			
Savings	500.00			
Major Appliances and Equipment				
Home Improvement, Painting, Major Repair				

Education
   Self
   Children				

Auto Replacement				
Debt Retirement (other than installment)				
Investment				
Other (specify):				
TOTALS	$	XXX	$	$

Seasonal Expenses

Schedule B

Expense	Date Needed	Amount Per Year	Per Month
Taxes (Auto Tags, (Ad Valorum)			
Auto Insurance			
Life & Disability Insurance			
Vacation			
Other (specify)			
TOTALS	XXX	$	$

Installment Debt Payments

Schedule C

Name of Creditor	Balance Owed*	Amount of Monthly Payment	Date of Last Payment	Due Date of Next Payment**
Total				
Balance and Monthly Payments				
Total Delinquent Payments				

* Payment times remaining number of payments.

** If payments are delinquent, <u>due date of next payment</u> may be earlier than current date or even the date of last payment.

Monthly Expense Budget

If you do not anticipate that the children of your present marriage will be living with you, complete only column A. If you anticipate that the children will be living with you, attempt to distribute your estimated monthly needs between columns A and B. Some will be difficult, such as rent. On rent, for example, you may estimate what a residence for yourself alone would cost and list that cost in column A, then estimate the cost for yourself and the children, and list in column B the difference between that cost and the amount listed in column A. Fill out annexed schedules A, B, and C, prior to completion of this form.

ITEMS

	A (Yourself)	B (Children)

Set-Asides:

Emergencies and Future Goals
    (from Schedule A)   _____   _____

Seasonal Expenses
    (from Schedule B)   _____   _____

Regular Monthly Expenses:

Housing
    Rent   _____   _____

    House Payments

        Principal and Interest _____   _____

        Real Estate Taxes   _____   _____

        Home Insurance   _____   _____

        Other (specify)_____   _____   _____

Utilities:

    Electricity   _____   _____

    Gas/Heating Oil   _____   _____

    Telephone   _____   _____

    Water   _____   _____

    Other (specify)_____ _____   _____

Installment Debt Payments
(from Schedule C)   _____   _____

        Total of Above   _____   _____

Day-to-Day Expenses: (Estimate per month)

Food and Dairy:
At Home   _____   _____

    Away from Home   _____   _____

Clothing: (including working
          clothes)   _____   _____

Transportation:

    Gas and Oil   _____   _____

    Auto Repair & Maintenance _____   _____

    Other (bus-taxi-parking, etc.)_____   _____

Health, Medical and Dental:

    Medical, Dental & Hospital
       Insurance   _____   _____

    Medical & Health Care
    (not covered by insurance) _____   _____

    Dental (not covered
      by insurance)   _____   _____

    Medicines & Drugs   _____   _____

Household Operation & Maintenance:

    Repairs   _____   _____

    Garden or Yard Work   _____   _____

    Replacement of Furnishings   _____   _____

    Dry Cleaning & Laundry   _____   _____

    Domestic Help (__ days at
      $_____ per day)   _____   _____

    Children's Day Care   _____   _____

    Other(specify)   _____   _____

Education, Self and Children
(Immediate Needs)

Private School Tuition   _____   _____

    College Tuition   _____   _____

    Books and Fees   _____   _____

    Other (specify)_____   _____   _____

Variable Monthly Expenses:

    Drug/Variety Store Items   _____   _____

    Books, Magazines, Newspapers   _____   _____

    Children's Allowances   _____   _____

    Charities, Gifts,
     Contributions   _____   _____

    Dues (Club or Professional
     not included as business
     expenses)   _____   _____

    Cultural/Recreational   _____   _____

Other (specify)_____   _____   _____

_____   _____   _____

Total Day to Day Expenses   _____   _____

Grand Total: (day to day
plus total of regular
monthly expenses)   _____   _____

Emergencies and Future Goals

Schedule A

Type of Fund	Probable Cost	Date Desired	Amount to set aside this year	Amount to set aside per month
Emergency				
Savings				
Major Appliances and Equipment				
Home Improvement, Painting, Major Repair				
Education Self Children				
Auto Replacement				
Debt Retirement (other than installment)				
Investment				
Other (specify):				
TOTALS	$	XXX	$	$

Seasonal Expenses

Schedule B

Expense	Date Needed	Amount Per Year	Per Month
Taxes (Auto Tags, (Ad Valorum)			.
Auto Insurance			
Life & Disability Insurance			
Vacation			
Other (specify)			
TOTALS	XXX	$	$

Installment Debt Payments

Schedule C

Name of Creditor	Balance Owed*	Amount of Monthly Payment	Date of Last Payment	Due Date of Next Payment**
Total				
Balance and Monthly Payments				
Total Delinquent Payments				

* Payment times remaining number of payments.

** If payments are delinquent, <u>due date of next payment</u> may be earlier than current date or even the date of last payment.

MEMORANDUM OF AGREEMENT

Name _____ Date _____

Address _____

_____

Children & Ages: _____

_____

_____

_____

Married _____ years   Date of Marriage _____

Employment, Income & SS#: _____

_____
Husband

_____

_____
Wife

Action Requested _____

Grounds for Action _____ Plaintiff_____

106- 1

LISTING OF MARITAL ASSETS

A.   **Real Estate**   **Title**   **Approx. Value**   **Mortgage**

1.   **Marital Home**

_____   _____   _____   _____

_____   _____   _____   _____

2._____   _____   _____   _____

_____   _____   _____   _____

3._____   _____   _____   _____

_____   _____   _____   _____

B.   **Savings**

Institution   Title   Amount

1._____   _____   _____

2._____   _____   _____

3._____   _____   _____

4._____   _____   _____

5._____   _____   _____

C.   **Life Insurance**

Company & Policy Type   Insured   Owner   Face Value   Cash Value

1._____   _____   _____   _____   _____

2._____   _____   _____   _____   _____

3._____   _____   _____   _____   _____

4._____   _____   _____   _____   _____

5._____   _____   _____   _____   _____

6._____   _____   _____   _____   _____

D.   **C.D.'s**

Institution   Title   Amount

1._____   _____   _____

2._____   _____   _____

3._____   _____   _____

4._____   _____   _____

5._____   _____   _____

6._____   _____   _____

E.   **Pension & Tax Deferred Annuities**

Type of Pension   Company   Title   Value

1._____   _____   _____   _____

2._____   _____   _____   _____

3._____   _____   _____   _____

4._____   _____   _____   _____

5._____   _____   _____   _____

6._____   _____   _____   _____

F.   **Checking Accounts**

Institution   Title   Amount

1._____   _____   _____

2._____   _____   _____

3._____   _____   _____

4._____   _____   _____

5._____   _____   _____

G. Cash on Hand

Location   Amount

1._____   _____

2._____   _____

H. Stocks and Bonds

Brokerage Account or Company   Title   Amount

1._____   _____   _____

2._____   _____   _____

3._____   _____   _____

4._____   _____   _____

5._____   _____   _____

Separate list if needed on separate sheet

I. Collectibles

Item   Value

1._____   _____

2._____   _____

3._____   _____

4._____   _____

5._____   _____

J. Jewelry

Item   Title   Value

1._____   _____   _____

2._____   _____   _____

3._____   _____   _____

4._____   _____   _____

106- 4

K.   **Mortgages** (owed to you)

Property   <u>Title</u>   <u>Amount</u>

1._____   _____   _____

2._____   _____   _____

3._____   _____   _____

L.   **Notes** (owed to you)

<u>From Whom</u>   <u>Title</u>   <u>Amount</u>

1._____   _____   _____

2._____   _____   _____

3._____   _____   _____

M.   **Leases** (held by you)

<u>Property</u>   <u>Title</u>   <u>Value</u>

1._____   _____   _____

2._____   _____   _____

N.   **Professional degrees or licenses**

<u>Type</u>   <u>Holder</u>   <u>When Acquired</u>   <u>Value</u>

1._____   _____   _____   _____

2._____   _____   _____   _____

3._____   _____   _____   _____

O.   **Businesses, private corps., partnerships, etc.**

<u>Name</u>   <u>Title</u>   <u>Value</u>

1._____   _____   _____

2._____   _____   _____

3._____   _____   _____

106-5

P.   **Automobiles**

Make & Year   Title   Value

1._____   _____   _____

2._____   _____   _____

3._____   _____   _____

Q.   **Personal Property**

_____

_____

_____

_____

_____

R.   **Contents of Home**

_____

_____

_____

_____

_____

S.   **Other**   Title   Value

1._____   _____   _____

2._____   _____   _____

3._____   _____   _____

T. Non-marital or separate assets (gifts, inheritances, etc.)

	Title	Value
1._____	_____	_____
2._____	_____	_____
3._____	_____	_____
4._____	_____	_____

LIABILITIES

A. Auto Loans

Creditor	Title	Amount	How Payable
1._____	_____	_____	_____
2._____	_____	_____	_____
3._____	_____	_____	_____

B. Mortgages

Property	Title	Amount	How Payable
1._____	_____	_____	_____
2._____	_____	_____	_____
3._____	_____	_____	_____

C. Bank Loans

Institution	Title	Amount	How Payable
1._____	_____	_____	_____
2._____	_____	_____	_____
3._____	_____	_____	_____

D.   **Credit Cards**

Card   Holder   Amount

1._____   _____   _____

2._____   _____   _____

3._____   _____   _____

4._____   _____   _____

5._____   _____   _____

6._____   _____   _____

E.   **Notes**

Creditor   Title   Amount   How Payable

1._____   _____   _____   _____

2._____   _____   _____   _____

3._____   _____   _____   _____

F.   **Other**

Creditor

1._____   _____   _____   _____

2._____   _____   _____   _____

3._____   _____   _____   _____

ASSET & DEBIT TABLES

A.   <u>Assets</u>

	<u>Wife</u>	<u>Husband</u>	<u>Joint</u>
Real Estate	_____	_____	_____
Savings	_____	_____	_____
Life Insurance	_____	_____	_____
C.D.'s	_____	_____	_____
Checking Accounts	_____	_____	_____
Cash on Hand	_____	_____	_____
Stocks & Bonds	_____	_____	_____
Collectibles	_____	_____	_____
Jewelry	_____	_____	_____
Mortgages	_____	_____	_____
Notes	_____	_____	_____
Leases	_____	_____	_____
Degrees & Licenses	_____	_____	_____
Businesses	_____	_____	_____
Autos	_____	_____	_____
Personal Property	_____	_____	_____
Contents of Home	_____	_____	_____
Other	_____	_____	_____
*Sub-Total	*_____	*_____	*_____
Pensions & Annuities (Tax Deferred)	_____	_____	_____
*Grand Total	*_____	*_____	*_____

B.   **Liabilities**   <u>Wife</u>   <u>Husband</u>   <u>Joint</u>

Auto Loans   _____   _____   _____

Bank Loans   _____   _____   _____

Credit Cards   _____   _____   _____

Notes   _____   _____   _____

Other   _____   _____   _____

     *Sub-Total   *_____   _____   _____

Mortgages   _____   _____   _____

     *Grand Total   *_____   *_____   *_____

Assets - Grand Total   _____

Liabilities - Grand Total   _____

Net Worth   _____

DIVISION OF PROPERTY OTHER THAN HOME

_____

_____

_____

_____

_____

_____

_____

_____

_____

_____

MARITAL ABODE

_____

_____

_____

_____

_____

_____

_____

_____

_____

RESPONSIBILITY FOR DEBTS

_____

_____

_____

_____

_____

_____

_____

_____

_____

_____

PARENTING, VISITATION & LEGAL CUSTODY

Parenting: _____

_____

_____

_____

_____

_____

_____

_____

_____

_____

_____

Visitation: _____

_____

_____

_____

_____

_____

_____

_____

_____

_____

Change of Residence: _____

_____

_____

_____

_____

_____

_____

Legal Custody: _____

_____

_____

_____

_____

Special Considerations: _____

_____

_____

_____

_____

CHILD SUPPORT

Amount _____

How Paid _____

How Arrived At _____

_____

_____

_____

_____

Special Considerations: _____

_____

_____

_____

_____

Medical Insurance: _____

_____

_____

_____

_____

_____

College: _____

_____

_____

_____

CONFLICT RESOLUTION

_____

_____

_____

_____

SPOUSAL MAINTENANCE

_____

_____

_____

_____

Amount _____

How Payable _____

Duration _____

Special Considerations: _____

_____

_____

_____

_____

Medical Insurance: _____

_____

_____

_____

_____

INCOME TAXES

_____

_____

_____

LIFE INSURANCE

_____

_____

_____

_____

SPECIAL CONSIDERATIONS

_____

_____

_____

_____

Signature	Date

Signature	Date

TABLE 9

SCHEDULE 1

YOUR REGULAR ACTIVITIES

MON	TUE	WED	THUR	FRI	SAT	SUN

WRITE IN YOUR ACTIVITIES AND THEIR TIMES. INCLUDE WORK, CLUBS, ORGANIZATIONS, RELIGIOUS OR VOLUNTEER ACTIVITIES ETC.

TABLE 9

SCHEDULE 1

YOUR REGULAR ACTIVITIES

MON	TUE	WED	THUR	FRI	SAT	SUN

WRITE IN YOUR ACTIVITIES AND THEIR TIMES. INCLUDE WORK, CLUBS, ORGANIZATIONS, RELIGIOUS OR VOLUNTEER ACTIVITIES ETC.

SPOUSE

DATE

TABLE 9

SCHEDULE 2

TIME YOU HAVE AVAILABLE TO BE WITH YOUR CHILREN

MON	TUE	WED	THUR	FRI	SAT	SUN

WRITE IN THE BLOCKS THE TIME YOU HAVE AVAILABLE
TO BE WITH YOUR CHILDREN

SPOUSE _____

DATE _____

TABLE 9

SCHEDULE 2

TIME YOU HAVE AVAILABLE TO BE WITH YOUR CHILREN

MON	TUE	WED	THUR	FRI	SAT	SUN

WRITE IN THE BLOCKS THE TIME YOU HAVE AVAILABLE
TO BE WITH YOUR CHILDREN

TABLE 9
SCHEDULE 3

SPOUSE _____

SPECIAL DAYS AND HOLIDAYS

DATE _____

OCCASION	DATE	IMPORTANT TO BE WITH KIDS		DECISION:	
		Y	N	MOTHER	FATHER
NEW YEAR'S DAY	JAN 1				
MARTIN LUTHER KING DAY					
PURIM					
LINCOLN'S BIRTHDAY					
WASHINGTON'S BIRTHDAY					
ASH WEDNESDAY					
VALENTINE'S DAY	FEB 14				
ST. PATRICK'S DAY	MAR 17				
PALM SUNDAY					
PASSOVER					
GOOD FRIDAY					
EASTER SUNDAY					
MOTHER'S DAY					
MEMORIAL DAY					
FATHER'S DAY					
GRADUATION/END OF SCHOOL					
INDEPENDENCE DAY					
LABOR DAY					
ROSH HASHANAH					
YOM KIPPUR					
COLUMBUS DAY					
HALLOWEEN	OCT 31				
VETERANS DAY					
THANKSGIVING DAY					
HANUKKAH					
CHRISTMAS	DEC 25				
NEW YEAR'S EVE	DEC 31				
YOUR BIRTHDAY					
CHILDREN'S BIRTHDAYS					
GRANDPARENTS' BIRTHDAYS					
SCHOOL CONCERTS					
SPORTS EVENTS					
RECITALS					
WEDDINGS					
OTHERS					

TABLE 9
SCHEDULE 3

SPOUSE

DATE

SPECIAL DAYS AND HOLIDAYS

OCCASION	DATE	IMPORTANT TO BE WITH KIDS		DECISION:	
		Y	N	MOTHER	FATHER
NEW YEAR'S DAY	JAN 1				
MARTIN LUTHER KING DAY					
PURIM					
LINCOLN'S BIRTHDAY					
WASHINGTON'S BIRTHDAY					
ASH WEDNESDAY					
VALENTINE'S DAY	FEB 14				
ST. PATRICK'S DAY	MAR 17				
PALM SUNDAY					
PASSOVER					
GOOD FRIDAY					
EASTER SUNDAY					
MOTHER'S DAY					
MEMORIAL DAY					
FATHER'S DAY					
GRADUATION/END OF SCHOOL					
INDEPENDENCE DAY					
LABOR DAY					
ROSH HASHANAH					
YOM KIPPUR					
COLUMBUS DAY					
HALLOWEEN	OCT 31				
VETERANS DAY					
THANKSGIVING DAY					
HANUKKAH					
CHRISTMAS	DEC 25				
NEW YEAR'S EVE	DEC 31				
YOUR BIRTHDAY					
CHILDREN'S BIRTHDAYS					
GRANDPARENTS' BIRTHDAYS					
SCHOOL CONCERTS					
SPORTS EVENTS					
RECITALS					
WEDDINGS					
OTHERS					

TABLE 9
SCHEDULE 4

DATES OF VACATIONS AND LONG HOLIDAYS

SPOUSE

DATE

	YOUR VACATIONS	CHILDREN'S VACATIONS
WINTER		
MID-TERM		
SPRING		
SUMMER		

**LOOK UP DATES OF YOUR VACATIONS & SCHOOL HOLIDAYS
FOR THE COMING YEAR AND ENTER ABOVE.**

TABLE 9
SCHEDULE 4

DATES OF VACATIONS AND LONG HOLIDAYS

	YOUR VACATIONS	CHILDREN'S VACATIONS
WINTER		
MID-TERM		
SPRING		
SUMMER		

**LOOK UP DATES OF YOUR VACATIONS & SCHOOL HOLIDAYS
FOR THE COMING YEAR AND ENTER ABOVE.**

TABLE 9
SCHEDULE 5

SIGNIFICANT OTHERS IN CHILDREN'S LIVES

PERSON	RELATIONSHIP	WHEN TO SEE THEM

INCLUDE GRANDPARENTS, AUNTS, UNCLES, COUSINS, FRIENDS
AND OTHERS AND WHEN THEY USUALLY SEE THEM.

TABLE 9
SCHEDULE 5

SIGNIFICANT OTHERS IN CHILDREN'S LIVES

PERSON	RELATIONSHIP	WHEN TO SEE THEM

INCLUDE GRANDPARENTS, AUNTS, UNCLES, COUSINS, FRIENDS
AND OTHERS AND WHEN THEY USUALLY SEE THEM.

TABLE 10
(Page 1 of 3)

SPOUSE _____

DATE _____

WANT LIST OF MARITAL ASSETS & LIABILITIES

ASSETS WANTED	VALUE
A. BANK ACCOUNTS	$ _____
_____	_____
_____	_____
_____	_____
B. NOTES & ACCOUNTS RECEIVABLE	_____
_____	_____
_____	_____
_____	_____
C. STOCKS, BONDS, MUTUAL FUNDS	_____
_____	_____
_____	_____
_____	_____
_____	_____
_____	_____
D. REAL ESTATE	_____
_____	_____
_____	_____
_____	_____
E. LIFE INSURANCE	_____
_____	_____
_____	_____
F. BUSINESS OR PROFESSIONAL PRACTICE	_____
_____	_____
TOTAL VALUE (This Page)	$ _____

TABLE 10
(Page 1 of 3)

SPOUSE _____

DATE _____

WANT LIST OF MARITAL ASSETS & LIABILITIES

ASSETS WANTED	VALUE
A. BANK ACCOUNTS _____	$ _____
_____	_____
_____	_____
_____	_____
B. NOTES & ACCOUNTS RECEIVABLE _____	$ _____
_____	_____
_____	_____
_____	_____
C. STOCKS, BONDS, MUTUAL FUNDS _____	_____
_____	_____
_____	_____
_____	_____
_____	_____
_____	_____
D. REAL ESTATE _____	_____
_____	_____
_____	_____
_____	_____
E. LIFE INSURANCE _____	_____
_____	_____
_____	_____
_____	_____
F. BUSINESS OR PROFESSIONAL PRACTICE _____	_____
_____	_____
TOTAL VALUE (This Page) _____	$ _____

TABLE 10
(Page 2 of 3)

SPOUSE
_____

DATE
_____

WANT LIST OF MARITAL ASSETS & LIABILITIES

ASSETS WANTED (cont)	VALUE
G. LICENSES & DEGREES	$ ____
_____	____
_____	____
_____	____
_____	____
H. PENSIONS. ETC.	____
_____	____
_____	____
_____	____
_____	____
I. MISCELLANEOUS (Patents, Trademarks etc.)	____
_____	____
_____	____
_____	____
J. AUTOMOBILES	____
_____	____
_____	____
K. PERSONAL PROPERTY (Jewelry, etc.)	____
_____	____
_____	____

Attach separate pages for additional items.

L. HOUSEHOLD ITEMS

_____

Attach separate pages for list.

VALUE OF ASSETS WANTED	$ ____
VALUE OF ASSETS WANTED (from page 1)	____
TOTAL VALUE OF ASSETS WANTED	____

119

TABLE 10
(Page 2 of 3)

SPOUSE
_____

DATE
_____

WANT LIST OF MARITAL ASSETS & LIABILITIES

ASSETS WANTED (cont)	VALUE

G. LICENSES & DEGREES _____ $ _____

_____ _____

_____ _____

_____ _____

_____ _____

H. PENSIONS. ETC. _____ _____

_____ _____

_____ _____

_____ _____

I. MISCELLANEOUS (Patents, Trademarks etc.) _____

_____ _____

_____ _____

_____ _____

J. AUTOMOBILES _____ _____

_____ _____

_____ _____

K. PERSONAL PROPERTY (Jewelry, etc.) _____

_____ _____

_____ _____

_____ _____

Attach separate pages for additional items.

L. HOUSEHOLD ITEMS

_____ _____

Attach separate pages for list.

VALUE OF ASSETS WANTED	$ _____
VALUE OF ASSETS WANTED (from page 1)	_____
TOTAL VALUE OF ASSETS WANTED	_____

TABLE 10
(Page 3 of 3)

SPOUSE _____

DATE _____

WANT LIST OF MARITAL ASSETS & LIABILITIES

LIABILITIES	VALUE
A. MORTGAGES ON REAL ESTATE _____	$ _____
_____	_____
_____	_____
_____	_____
B. NOTES PAYABLE TO BANKS _____	_____
_____	_____
_____	_____
C. LOANS ON INSURANCE POLICIES _____	_____
_____	_____
_____	_____
_____	_____
_____	_____
D. CREDIT CARD DEBT _____	_____
_____	_____
_____	_____
E. OTHER _____	_____
_____	_____
_____	_____
_____	_____
_____	_____
_____	_____
TOTAL LIABILITIES	**$ _____**
NET VALUE OF ASSETS MINUS LIABILITIES	_____

TABLE 10
(Page 3 of 3)

SPOUSE _____

DATE _____

WANT LIST OF MARITAL ASSETS & LIABILITIES

LIABILITIES	VALUE
A. MORTGAGES ON REAL ESTATE	$
B. NOTES PAYABLE TO BANKS	
C. LOANS ON INSURANCE POLICIES	
D. CREDIT CARD DEBT	
E. OTHER	
TOTAL LIABILITIES	$
NET VALUE OF ASSETS MINUS LIABILITIES	

---X

,

                            Plaintiff,   ***STIPULATION OF SETTLEMENT***

      -against-

,

                          Defendant.

---X

       STIPULATION OF SETTLEMENT, made and entered into in the County of Suffolk, State of New York, on the   day of   ,
199 , by and between   , residing at
(hereinafter referred to as the "Wife" and/or "Mother"), and
        , residing at   (hereinafter referred to as
the "Husband" and/or "Father");

       ***W I T N E S S E T H*:**

       WHEREAS, the parties are Husband and Wife and were married on the   day of   ,   , in the County of   ,
State of   ; and

       WHEREAS, there is/are child/children born of this marriage, to wit: ; and

       WHEREAS, the parties desire to settle the within action and to settle certain questions relating to their property rights,

- 1 -

support and maintenance and the equitable distribution of their marital property in accordance with D.R.L. Section 236(B), and other interests and obligations growing out of the marriage relationship (including custody of their minor child/children).

NOW, THEREFORE, in consideration of the premises and mutual covenants and undertakings herein set forth, the parties do covenant and agree as follows:

ARTICLE I: ACTION FOR DIVORCE

The Husband/Wife has instituted an Action for Divorce by service of a Summons and Verified Complaint on the Husband/Wife personally, on the   day of   ,   , alleging   as grounds for divorce.

The Husband/Wife acknowledges service of said Summons and Verified Complaint. The Husband/Wife has interposed an Answer dated   , responding to the Husband's/Wife's Verified Complaint, neither admitting nor denying the allegations contained therein, and consenting to permitting the Husband/Wife to proceed on his/her Verified Complaint for a Judgment of Divorce, and to place this matter on the uncontested matrimonial calendar.

The parties agree that this Stipulation of Settlement shall be incorporated in any Judgment of Divorce granted by a Court of competent jurisdiction, and shall survive the said Judgment of Divorce, but not merge therein, **(OPTION WHERE THERE ARE CHILDREN) except for the provisions of this Stipulation of Settlement pertaining to the obligation of the parties to provide or contribute to child support and/or visitation, which provisions shall become merged therein.**

The parties agree and represent to each other that both parties deem the terms of this Stipulation Settlement as being fair and reasonable at the time of the making of this Stipulation of Settlement and, further, that the parties represent to each other that the terms of this Stipulation of Settlement are not

- 3 -

unconscionable at the present time, and will not be unconscionable at the time the uncontested Judgment of Divorce to be entered herein is to be presented to the Court for settlement and entry.

ARTICLE II: SEPARATE RESIDENCE

The parties hereto shall have the right to live separate and apart from each other and to reside from time to time at such place or places as each of the parties may see fit, and to contract, carry on and engage in any employment, business or trade which either deems fit, free from control, restraint or interference, direct or indirect, by the other in all respects as if such parties were single and unmarried.

ARTICLE III: DIVISION OF PROPERTY AND ASSETS

All of the furniture, furnishings, household goods and appliances, fixtures and appurtenances, books and works of art, china, crystal, silverware, jewelry, clothing and other items of personal property located in the marital residence located at

shall be and are hereby declared to constitute the sole and exclusive property of the Husband/Wife. There is excepted from the foregoing the items of personal property set forth on the schedule annexed hereto as Schedule " ", which said articles of personal property are, and shall remain, the sole and exclusive property of the Husband/Wife. Said articles of personal property shall be removed by the Husband's/Wife's at his/her sole cost and expense within thirty (30) days of the execution of this Stipulation of Settlement.

The Husband shall be entitled to sole possession, use and title to the following vehicle(s): 19   . The Husband shall be solely responsible for the maintenance, insurance and loan, if any, with respect to such vehicle, and shall indemnify and hold the Wife harmless from any liability therefrom.

The Wife shall be entitled to sole possession, use and title to the following vehicle(s): 19   . The Wife shall be solely responsible for the maintenance, insurance and loan, if any, with respect to such vehicle, and shall indemnify and hold the Husband harmless from any liability therefrom.

With regard to the Husband's/Wife's pension with

- 6 -

123- 6

, which pension constitutes marital property, and which pension has been valued by   by way of report dated the   day of   , 1992, the present day value of said pension being   , said pension shall belong exclusively to the Husband/Wife, and the Husband/Wife hereby waives any claim to said pension.

With regard to the Husband's/Wife's 401K plan on deposit at the   , Account #   , which 401K constitutes marital property, in the approximate sum of   , same shall belong exclusively to the Husband/Wife, and the Husband/Wife hereby waives any claim to said monies.

With regard to the parties' profit sharing plan with   , the parties agree that the Husband/Wife shall retain, as his/her separate property, his/her portion of the aforesaid profit sharing plan worth approximately   on deposit at   , and that the Husband/Wife shall retain, as his/her separate property, his/her portion of the profit sharing plan worth approximately   on deposit at   . Each party waives any claim to the others share of the aforementioned profit sharing plan.

With regard to the Husband's/Wife's IRA with   , which IRA constitutes marital property, and which IRA is presently worth approximately   , said IRA shall belong exclusively to the Husband/Wife, and the Husband/Wife hereby waives any claim to said IRA.

With regard to the parties' savings, stocks and bonds,

- 7 -

more fully described on Schedule " " hereto, the Husband/Wife shall be entitled to   of the total value of   , and the Husband/Wife shall be entitled to   . The parties agree to divide the aforesaid savings, stocks and bonds as more fully detailed on Schedule " " hereto and agree to execute the appropriate documents to effectuate the division of said property at the time of execution of this Stipulation of Settlement.

The parties own, as marital property, a fifty (50%) percent interest in an improved parcel of land located at   . The Husband/Wife shall be entitled to retain the aforesaid interest in the said premises as his/her separate property, and the Husband/Wife waives any claim thereto. The parties' agree that the value of the said property is approximately   and is not subject to any encumbrance.

The parties acknowledge that the Husband/Wife is a   percent shareholder in   (hereinafter referred to as the "Corporation"). The parties agree that the Husband's/Wife's interest in the Husband's/Wife's shares in the Corporation will be satisfied by the payment to the Husband/Wife of the following monies and property:

(a)   , payable by way of a distributive award to be paid by the Husband/Wife to the Husband/Wife in the form of   per year for a period of   years, all payments to be without interest; the first payment due on the anniversary date of the execution of this Stipulation of Settlement and annually thereafter; and

- 8 -

(b)   The Husband/Wife conveying his/her interest in the marital residence to the Husband/Wife pursuant to Article   hereof.

The Husband/Wife has engaged the services of
to value the Husband's/Wife's Corporation, and notwithstanding said valuation, the Husband/Wife agrees to accept as and for his/her interest in the Husband's/Wife's shares of stock the above set forth monies and property (a and b).

Accordingly, the Husband's/Wife's shares of stock in the Corporation shall be his/her separate property and the Husband/Wife waives any claim thereto.

The parties agree that the Husband/Wife shall be personally liable for the payments due the Husband/Wife by way of a distributive award as provided for herein, notwithstanding a bankruptcy or insolvency proceeding concerning the Corporation.

The marital home located at   is marital property and has a fair market value of approximately $, is subject to a mortgage of approximately $.   The provision for the disposition of the home is more fully set forth hereinafter in this Stipulation of Settlement.

The parties represent that the above set forth assets represent the totality of marital assets acquired during the marriage, and/or subject to Equitable Distribution, and in the event any asset(s) not disclosed in this Stipulation of Settlement is/are discovered subsequent to the execution of the Stipulation of Settlement, which asset(s) would have constituted marital asset(s) had same been disclosed prior to the execution of this Stipulation

- 9 -

of Settlement, then, in that event, said asset(s) shall remain subject to equitable distribution and each party shall be entitled to fifty (50%) percent of any such asset(s) not disclosed herein.

Except as otherwise hereinabove or hereafter provided, each of the parties shall hereafter own, have and enjoy, independently of any claim or right of the other party, all items of real or personal property (tangible or intangible) now or hereafter in his or her name, and now or hereafter in his or her possession, with full power to dispose of same as fully and effectually as though he or she were unmarried.

ARTICLE IV: MARITAL ABODE

OPTION: ONE PARTY CONVEYING INTEREST TO THE OTHER PARTY

The parties presently own, as tenants by the entirety, the marital abode located at   (hereinafter referred to as the "home".)

The Husband/Wife shall convey his/her interest in the home to the Husband/Wife, and he/she shall become the sole and exclusive owner thereof.

Simultaneously with the execution of this Stipulation of Settlement, the Husband/Wife shall execute a bargain and sale deed with covenants conveying his/her interest in the home to the Husband/Wife. The Husband/Wife shall pay the recording cost of the deed.

The Husband/Wife shall have no further claim to the home, and the Husband/Wife shall be solely responsible for maintaining the home and paying the mortgage on the home (providing the Husband/Wife is not in default with regard to his/her support obligation as set forth in this Stipulation of Settlement), and shall indemnify and hold the Husband/Wife harmless therefrom.

OPTION:

The Husband/Wife shall vacate the marital residence within fourteen (14) days of execution of this Stipulation of Settlement and shall remove all the personalty set forth in Schedule " " thereof.

The Husband/Wife acknowledges that he/she has previously vacated the home, has removed his/her personal belongings prior to

the signing of this Stipulation of Settlement, and that the Husband/Wife has exclusive occupancy of same.

The parties each warrant and represent to the other that except for the first mortgage, now a lien upon the home, neither party has mortgaged, pledged, liened or otherwise encumbered the home, or his or her right, title and interest therein, and each party agrees to indemnify and hold harmless the other with reference to the representation herein, including, but not limited to, reasonable attorney's fees.

The parties acknowledge that a search of the County Clerk's records with reference to ascertaining the existence of a lien against the property has been recommended by counsel, and the parties agree that such search shall be conducted by a reputable abstract or title company and that the fee for same in the approximate sum of   dollars shall be paid prior to the performance of the search. In addition, the parties acknowledge that they have been advised that the cost of preparing a new deed is   dollars and the cost of recording the new deed is approximately   , and that said fees shall be paid at the time of execution of the new deed.

OPTION:

The Wife/Husband acknowledges that a search of the County Clerk's records with reference to ascertaining the existence of a lien against the property has been recommended by counsel and the Wife/Husband has declined to have such search conducted.

OPTION:

- 12 -

123-12

JOINT SALE - WIFE/HUSBAND RECEIVING EXCLUSIVE OCCUPANCY UNTIL SALE OR BOTH OCCUPYING HOME UNTIL SALE

The parties presently are owners, as tenants by the entirety, of the marital home located at (hereinafter referred to as the "home").

The parties agree that the home shall be listed or has been listed for sale forthwith, and sold as soon as practically possible for the highest marketable price.

The parties have executed or agree to execute a multiple listing agreement simultaneously with the execution of this Stipulation of Settlement.

The parties further agree that the Husband/Wife shall have exclusive occupancy of the home until the closing thereof.

OPTION:

The Wife/Husband, however, shall be permitted to enter the home upon reasonable notice to the Wife's/Husband's counsel, and by agreement between Husband's/Wife's counsel and Husband/Wife's counsel, in order to inventory property which will become the separate property of the Husband/Wife.

Until the closing of title, the Husband/Wife shall be responsible for all expenses for the premises and its maintenance, including but not limited to mortgage, real property taxes, utilities, appropriate insurance, gardening and repairs.

OPTION:

During the period of exclusive occupancy, the

- 13 -

Husband/Wife shall also be responsible for all arrears, if any, that are outstanding with reference to the mortgage, late charges, counsel fees, penalties, interest, and any and all other charges as a result of his non-payment of the mortgage, all of the foregoing sometimes hereinafter collectively referred to as the "arrears". The Husband/Wife agrees that the arrears shall be satisfied at the time of the closing from his/her share of the net proceeds from the sale of the marital dwelling.

The parties each warrant and represent to the other that except for the first mortgage, now a lien upon the home, neither party has mortgaged, pledged, liened or otherwise encumbered the home, or his or her right, title and interest therein, and each party agrees to indemnify and hold harmless the other with reference to the representation herein, including, but not limited to, reasonable attorney's fees.

The Husband/Wife shall have exclusive occupancy of the home until the closing thereof.

OR

OPTION:

NO SALE - ONE PARTY HAVING EXCLUSIVE OCCUPANCY OF MARITAL RESIDENCE

The parties presently are owners, as tenants by the entirety, the marital abode located at   (hereinafter referred to as the "home").

The parties agree that the Husband/Wife shall have exclusive occupancy of the home until the earliest of the following events: (1) the Husband/Wife remarries; (2) the Wife establishes

- 14 -

123-14

a permanent residence with another man, pursuant to Domestic Relations Law 248; (3) the youngest child reaches the age of twenty-one (21) years or twenty-two (22) years, if such child is enrolled as a full-time, fully matriculated student in college; (4) the Husband's/Wife's option to TERMINATE his/her exclusive occupancy; or (5) the Husband/Wife no longer has custody of the infant children of the marriage. Upon the occurrence of the earliest of the aforesaid events, the home is to be sold (unless option rights are exercised as hereinafter provided for) and the proceeds divided equally between the parties, subject to adjustments, if any, as more fully set forth hereinafter in this Stipulation of Settlement.

During the period of exclusive occupancy of the home by the Husband/Wife, the Husband/Wife shall be solely responsible for the timely payment of home mortgage interest and principal, real estate taxes, homeowners insurance, and all other expenses related to the upkeep and maintenance, except for major repairs of the home, and shall indemnify and hold the Husband/Wife harmless therefrom in all regards.

The parties further agree that they will both be equally responsible for all major repairs which may be needed in connection with the home. A major repair shall be defined as one in excess of two hundred ($200.00) dollars. Prior to incurring any expense for a major repair, the party occupying the home shall submit to the other party, in writing, a written estimate detailing the work to be performed. The non-occupying party must be consulted with

- 15 -

before the work is commenced and the non-occupying party must consent to the work being done, said consent shall not be unreasonably withheld. In the event the other party does not approve said proposal and the parties cannot otherwise agree, either party shall be entitled to submit the claim to arbitration for a final determination. **OPTION:** The non-occupying party further agrees that if the occupying party is unable to pay his/her share of the repairs referred to in this paragraph, he/she will pay the entire cost of the repair, and be reimbursed at the sale of the marital residence from the occupying party's net proceeds, for the amount advanced by the non-occupying party for his/her share of said repairs.

At such time as the home is to be sold pursuant to the terms of this Stipulation of Settlement, the party having exclusive occupancy shall have the first option to purchase the non-occupying party's interest, and the non-occupying party the second option to purchase the occupying party's interest. The sales price, as provided for herein, with regard to one party purchasing the other party's interest in the home, shall be calculated based upon the fair market value of the home, less the mortgage balance, and any other joint-legally incurred encumbrance, less a deduction of seven (7%) percent for usual and customary brokerage fees, together with any adjustment that may be attributable to either party as provided for in this Stipulation of Settlement.

The party occupying the home shall have the first option to purchase the non-occupying party's interest in the home as

previously set forth hereinabove in this Stipulation of Settlement.

The Wife/Husband shall have twenty (20) days to notify the Husband/Wife in writing (certified mail, return receipt requested), of her/his desire to exercise her/his option to purchase the Wife's/Husband's interest. The said twenty (20) day period shall commence from the time of the occurrence of an event which requires the sale of the marital home. The Wife/Husband shall have ninety (90) days after her/his notification of intent to purchase the Wife's/Husband's interest to consummate the purchase of the Wife's/Husband's interest in the home.

In the event the Wife/Husband does not so notify the Husband/Wife of her/his intention to exercise her/his option as provided for herein, or notifies the Husband/Wife that she/he does not elect to exercise her/his option, and/or in the event the Wife/Husband is not able to consummate the purchase of the Wife's/Husband's interests as provided for herein, then the Husband/Wife shall be entitled to exercise his/her option.

The Husband/Wife shall notify the Wife/Husband of his/her intention to exercise his/her option to purchase the Wife's/Husband's interest in the home within twenty (20) days of the expiration of the twenty (20) day period the Husband/Wife has to exercise his/her option as provided for hereinabove; or within twenty (20) days after notification that the Wife/Husband does not intend to exercise her/his option to purchase the Husband's/Wife's interest; or within twenty (20) days after the expiration of the ninety (90) day period and the failure of the Husband/Wife to

- 17 -

consummate the purchase as provided for herein.

Payment of the purchasing party's obligation with regard to the purchase shall be made in cash, bank check or certified check.

If the occupying/non-occupying party does not exercise the aforesaid option, the purchase price is to be mutually agreed or determined as set forth below in the event the parties cannot so agree.

In the event that the Husband and the Wife cannot agree upon the price or any terms and conditions of the sale or with respect to any problems concerning brokerage of said sale, then, in that event, the sales price and broker shall be determined as set forth below.

Each party shall obtain an appraisal from an appraiser on the recommended list of the Long Island Board of Realtors and the parties shall be bound by the average of the two (2) appraisals. The appraiser shall also select the broker and the parties shall execute the usual and customary Multiple Listing Agreement. The parties shall share in the cost of the appraiser's fee.

The sales price shall be adjusted from time-to-time as agreed upon by the parties, or, in the event the parties cannot so agree, then as determined by the appraisers selected by the parties.

Each party agrees to be responsible for his or her respective share of the related income tax liability, if any, predicated on each party's respective share of the proceeds

- 18 -

resulting from the sale of the home, and each party agrees to hold harmless and indemnify the other party with regard to such tax obligation.

The parties agree to sell the home to the first bona fide purchaser accepting the listing price, or within ten (10%) percent of the listing price. The parties shall cooperate fully in actively showing the house and cooperate with any brokers in executing whatever documents may be needed to effectuate the sale. The premises shall be available at reasonable times for inspection by brokers and by prospective purchasers. Both parties shall cooperate and use efforts reasonably calculated to produce the best sales price then available in the market.

The parties shall share equally in the net proceeds of the sale, which shall be defined as the gross purchase price, less broker's commissions, costs of satisfying any existing mortgage(s), termite expenses, if any, agreed estimate of repairs or allowance therefor to the purchaser, and any other similar expenses incidental to the sale of the premises and closing of title. Each party shall be responsible for his or her own legal fees involved in connection with such sale.

Immediately upon execution of this Stipulation of Settlement, the parties' survivorship interests in the home as tenants by the entirety shall terminate and be converted into a tenancy in common. Upon the death of either party, his or her interest shall pass not to the other party but as part of the deceased party's estate. The parties intend that this Stipulation

- 19 -

of Settlement constitutes a written instrument satisfying the requirements of General Obligations Law Sec. 3-309.

The Husband/Wife will continue to be responsible for the costs of maintaining the home during the period that it is on the market, even if he/she should move out of it, and the period of exclusive occupancy will be deemed to continue until the home is sold.

ARTICLE V: RESPONSIBILITY FOR DEBTS

The Husband and Wife represent and warrant to each other that they will not, at any time in the future, incur or contract any debts, charges or liabilities whatsoever for which the other or the estate of the other shall or may become liable or answerable. Except as otherwise set forth herein, the Husband agrees to hold the Wife harmless and to indemnify the Wife against the payment of any monies which he shall have been compelled or obliged to make to third parties, for or by reason of any act or omission of his and against any necessary expenses arising therefrom. The Wife agrees to hold the Husband harmless and to indemnify the Husband against the payment of any monies which she shall have been compelled or obliged to make to third parties for or by reason of any act or omission of hers and against any necessary expense arising therefrom.

In the event a party pays a debt or liability which the other party is responsible for pursuant to this Stipulation of Settlement, the party paying shall be entitled to recover the debt or liability paid, with interest of ten (10%) percent per year, as well as counsel fees reasonably incurred in connection with payment of the debt or liability and recovery of the amount so paid, from the party responsible for the debt or liability. (OPTION:) Annexed hereto and marked as Schedule " " is a list of marital debts and provision for the repayment of said debts. (OPTION:) The parties represent to each other that there are no

- 21 -

outstanding marital obligations which either has incurred for which the other party may be liable.

ARTICLE VI: CUSTODY, VISITATION AND NOTIFICATION

Recital: A.   The "Passover-Easter Period", "President's Birthday Period" and the "Christmas Period" are respectively defined as the period from the close of the regular school session respectively, of the school at which the child/children is/are or may be attending, to the recommencement of the next regular session.

B.   "Civil Holidays" shall be defined as the period from the close of the regular school session of the school at which the child/children is/are or may be attending, to the recommencement of the next regular session.

C.   The "Summer Period" is defined as the period from the closing of the Spring semester of the school of the child/children to the opening of the school of the child/children in the Fall semester.

D.   "Mother's Day", "Father's Day", "Mother's Birthday" and "Father's Birthday" shall take precedence over any other regular scheduled visitation period as provided for in this Stipulation of Settlement.

E.   "Civil-Religious Holiday" periods shall take precedence over any other regular scheduled visitation as provided for in this Stipulation of Settlement, except for those periods set forth in "D" hereinabove.

Custody of the infant child/children of the parties hereto is hereby conferred upon the Mother/Father.

- 23 -

<u>OPTION:</u>

The parties shall share joint custody of the child/children with residential custody in the Mother/Father.

<u>OPTION:</u>

Reasonable access between parents and children shall not be denied.

The Father/Mother shall have the following minimum visitation rights:

(i)   The Father/Mother shall have alternate weekend visitation from 5:00 p.m. on Friday until 6:00 p.m. on Sunday. If the day preceding such weekend or the day following such weekend shall be a legal holiday or a day on which the child/children is/are not required to attend school, then such weekend shall be deemed to include such preceding or following day. The Husband/Wife shall give the Wife/Husband at least three (3) days prior oral notice of his/her intention <u>not</u> to exercise his/her visitation rights on any such weekend.

(ii)   One (1) afternoon per week, from 3:30 p.m. until 7:00 p.m., subject to a least twenty-four (24) hours notice to the Father/Mother of the intended visitation. The Father/Mother agrees that during such visitation period that he/she will provide dinner for the child/children.

(iii)   The parties agree to abide by the following alternate holiday visitation schedule with regard to holidays. Any holidays not specifically set forth herein will also be alternated.

<u>MOTHER</u>   <u>FATHER</u>

- *24* -

Mother's Day - every year	Father's Day - every year
Mother's birthday - every year	Father's birthday - every year
Child's/Children's birthday - three (3) hours every year	Child's/Children's birthday - three (3) hours every year
Easter/Passover - odd	Easter/Passover - even
Memorial Day - even	Memorial Day - odd
July Fourth - odd	July Fourth - even
Labor Day - even	Labor Day - odd
Rosh Hashanah - odd	Rosh Hashanah - even
Yom Kippur - even	Yom Kippur - odd
Thanksgiving - odd	Thanksgiving - even
Friday after Thanksgiving - even	Friday after Thanksgiving - odd
Veteran's Day - odd	Veteran's Day - even
Christmas Eve - even	Christmas Eve - odd
Christmas Day - odd	Christmas Day - even
Christmas week - even	Christmas week - odd
New Year's Day - odd	New Year's Day - even
Martin Luther King Day - even	Martin Luther King Day - odd
President's week - odd	President's week - even

(iv)   Two (2) weeks during the summer school visitation, to be taken consecutively or separately at the Father's/Mother's option, provided that the Father/Mother gives at least thirty (30) days prior written notice of the weeks selected by him/her, it being understood that the Mother and Father shall endeavor in good faith to arrange these visitation periods bearing in mind the requirements of the Mother and Father and the planned

activities of the children. It is understood and agreed that the Father/Mother shall be entitled to have the children for the same amount of summer vacation as the Father/Mother. If the Father's/Mother's vacation takes place out of the state, then the Father's/Mother's visitation will be suspended during said vacation period. If the Father/Mother remains at home for vacation purposes, however, the Father's/Mother's visitation shall not be suspended;

(v) Unlimited telephone visitation during reasonable hours.

The Father/Mother shall call for the child/children at the commencement of any visitation period, at the residence of the child/children, and the Father/Mother shall return the child/children to the Father/Mother at said residence at the end of such visitation period. The Father/Mother shall call for the child/children within one (1) hour of the designated time, as above set forth in this Article, unless other arrangements have been made between the Mother and Father. If other arrangements have not been made between the Mother and the Father, the Father/Mother shall be deemed to have waived his/her visitation rights to said period.

The Father and the Mother shall promptly inform each other with respect to any illness or accident of the child/children, and in the event that any such illness or accident causes the child/children to be confined to bed or home (whether of the Mother or Father) for more than forty-eight (48) hours, such other parent shall be entitled to visit the child/children at

reasonable times and for reasonable periods.

The Father and the Mother, at all times, shall inform each other with respect to the residence of the child/children and the residence of each other and any removal of the residence of the child/children.

The Father and the Mother, at all times, shall inform each other with respect to the physical whereabouts and location of the child/children.

All the visitation periods of the Father/Mother are and shall be optional, in all instances, with the Father/Mother.

Each parent shall be entitled to complete and full information from any pediatrician, general physician, dentist, consultants or specialists attending the child/children for any reason whatsoever, and to have copies of any reports given by them, or any of them to a parent.

Each parent shall be entitled to complete and full information from any teacher or school giving instruction to the child/children or to which the child/children may attend, and to have copies of a report given by them or any of them to a parent.

The parents agree to cooperate, and shall cooperate with respect to the child/children so as, in a maximum degree, to advance the child's/children's health, emotional and physical well-being, and to give and afford the child/children affection of both parents and a sense of security. Neither parent will, directly or indirectly, influence the child/children so as to prejudice the child/children against the other parent. The parents will endeavor

- 27 -

to guide the child/children so as to promote the affectionate relationship between the child/children and the Father and the child/children and the Mother.

OPTION:

The parties mutually will determine all matters relating to the health, education and general welfare of the child/children. In matters of day-to-day affairs, the Father/Mother shall have the final decision.

The parties will cooperate with each other in carrying out the provisions of this Stipulation of Settlement for the child's/children's best interests. Whenever it seems necessary to adjust or vary or increase the time allotted to either party or otherwise take action in regard to the child/children, each of the parties will act for the best interests of the child/children. Every reasonable effort will be exerted to maintain full access and unhampered contact between the child/children and the respective parties. Neither party shall do anything which may estrange the other from the child/children or injure the opinion of the child/children as to the other party or which may hamper the free and natural development of the love of the child/children to the other party.

The child/children shall continue to be known by the name of the children as set forth in the Recitals to this Stipulation of Settlement, and by no other name during minority, and the name of the child/children shall not be changed from said name, and the child/children shall be enrolled in all schools and camps under

- 28 -

said name. The child/children shall be raised in no other religion other than the   religion.

In the event of the death of the Father/Mother, the Father/Mother is to have the sole and exclusive custody of the child/children. In that event, the custody of the infant child/children reverts to the Father/Mother. Then, in that event, the Father's/Mother's obligation to pay child support shall terminate.

The child/children shall not be enrolled in any boarding school, private or religious, without the written consent of the Father, which consent will not be unreasonably withheld.

Each party shall be previously consulted (unless such consultation is prevented by emergency) with respect to any hospitalization of the child/children.

OPTION:

In view of the Father's/Mother's desire to maintain a loving and ongoing relationship with his/her child/children, and in order to insure that the Father/Mother will be able to visit with his child/children in accordance with the schedule of visitation as provided for herein, the Father/Mother agrees that he/she will not relocate the child/children's residence more than forty (40) miles from the present location, to-wit:

- 29 -

ARTICLE VII: CHILD SUPPORT

The parties represent that they have been advised by their respective attorneys of the provisions of New York Domestic Relations Law 240 (1-b) and Family Court Act 413 ("Child Support Standards Act") and amendments thereto, hereinafter collectively referred to as "CSSA". The parties are aware that under the CSSA, for   child/children, a non-custodial parent may be required to pay the custodial parent   (%) percent of his/her gross income from all sources, including the possibility that various facts may result in additional income being imputed or attributed to the non-custodial parent. The parties have also been informed of the various deductions which can be made from the income before the above percentage is applied. Further, the parties have been advised that in connection with the combined parental income over or under eighty thousand ($80,000.00) dollars, the Court could, in its discretion, consider various factors set forth in the law and fix support which is higher or lower than that resulting from the use of the above percentage. Finally, the parties have also been advised that in addition to such child support, the Court would direct the non-custodial parent to pay pro-rata share of child-care expenses and unreimbursed medical expenses and may also direct the payment of a discretionary amount for educational expenses.

The Father represents that his weekly salary is
Annexed hereto is a copy of the Father's most recent paystub.

The Mother represents that her weekly salary is
Annexed hereto is a copy of the Mother's most recent paystub.

Accordingly, predicated on the parties' income and the
provisions of CSSA, child support for the   ( ) unemancipated
child/children of the marriage will be set at the time of the
execution of this Stipulation of Settlement at   per week.

The parties further acknowledge that it is their desire
that the child/children attend college and agree to share the cost
of college education pro-rata to their respective incomes as more
fully set forth in Article   hereinafter.

The payments required to be made by the Father/Mother to
the Father/Mother, as hereinabove provided, shall commence the
first Friday immediately following the execution of this
Stipulation of Settlement and be paid on each successive Friday
thereafter.

The computation of child support at all times hereinafter
will be in accordance with CSSA and amendments or any successor
statute.

In addition, the Father/Mother shall be responsible for
the child's/children's health insurance and uninsured health care
pro-rata with the Father's/Mother's income pursuant to CSSA, as
more fully detailed in Article hereof.

OPTION:

Notwithstanding the foregoing, the parties intend and
agree that the child support obligations of the parties be governed
by this Stipulation of Settlement.   In this Stipulation of

- 31 -

Settlement, the provisions for child support have been set in a fair amount based on many considerations, including the parties' respective finances and the other financial provisions of this Stipulation of Settlement.

THE CUSTODIAL PARENT HEREBY WAIVES HIS/HER RIGHT TO SEEK CHILD SUPPORT UNDER THE CSSA FROM THE MOTHER/FATHER NOW AND FOREVER.

THE PARTIES HAVE BEEN ADVISED THAT THE WAIVER OF THE RIGHT TO COLLECT CHILD SUPPORT IS AGAINST THE PUBLIC POLICY OF THE STATE OF NEW YORK AND MAY BE UNENFORCEABLE. ACCORDINGLY, THE PARTIES AGREE THAT IN THE EVENT THE FATHER/MOTHER BREACHES THIS PROVISION AND SEEKS TO COLLECT CHILD SUPPORT, THEN, IN THAT EVENT, THE MOTHER'S/FATHER'S WAIVER TO MAINTENANCE IN THIS ACTION SHALL BE DEEMED OF NO FORCE AND EFFECT AND THE FATHER/MOTHER SHALL HAVE THE RIGHT TO SEEK MAINTENANCE.

CONTINUE FOR ALL STIPULATIONS OF SETTLEMENT:

ADD FOLLOWING PARAGRAPH ONLY IF THERE IS ONE ATTORNEY:

Both parties represent that they have received a copy of the Child Support Standards Chart promulgated by the Commissioner of Social Services pursuant to Subdivision 2 of Section 111-i of New York's Social Service Law, a copy of which is annexed hereto as Schedule " ".

All payments to be paid by the Father/Mother to the Father/Mother, as hereinabove provided, shall be by check, bank check or postal money order and, if not given directly, shall be mailed by the Father/Mother to the Father/Mother at his/her present

address or at such other address as he/she may direct.

All payments made by the Father/Mother to the Father/Mother on behalf of the child/children shall be applied by his/her according to his/her sole judgment and discretion, and nothing herein shall be deemed to obligate his/her to render an accounting to the Father/Mother, at any time, or for any reason, or to indicate to him/her how monies received by him/her have been applied.

Any payments voluntarily made by the Father/Mother to the Father/Mother, at any time, for the support and maintenance of the child/children in excess of the sums hereinabove required to be paid by the Father/Mother to the Father/Mother shall not alter or affect the Father's/Mother's legal obligation hereunder nor be deemed to create any precedent for the future. Further, such excess payments shall not be construed as any proof or indication of the Father's/Mother's ability to make increased payments to the Father/Mother or of the need or necessity for such increased payments.

The payments to be made by the Father/Mother to the Father/Mother on behalf of the child/children, as hereinabove provided, shall not be reduced during those periods when the child/children is/are visiting with the Father/Mother; nor shall the Father/Mother have the right to deduct from such payments any monies paid or expended by the Father/Mother for clothing, sporting goods, entertainment or other items purchased on behalf of the child/children, whether during the period that the child/children

- 33 -

are with him/her or otherwise.

The Father/Mother shall claim the issue of the marriage as a dependent/dependents on his/her Federal, State and local income tax return, and the Father/Mother agrees to execute any documents required by the taxing authorities in order to enable the Mother/Father to claim the child/children on his/her tax return.

OPTION:

In the event the Father/Mother shall fail to pay child support as provided for in this Stipulation of Settlement, then the Father/Mother shall not be entitled to claim the child/children as dependents as provided for herein.

With respect to a child, an Emancipation Event shall occur or be deemed to have occurred upon the earliest happening of any of the following:

(i) attaining the age of twenty-one (21) years or twenty-two (22) years if that child is enrolled as a full-time matriculated student in college, only if and so long as the child pursues college education with reasonable diligence and on a normally continuous basis.

(ii) marriage (even though such a marriage may be void or voidable and despite any annulment of it);

(iii) permanent residence away from the residence of the Mother. A residence at boarding school, camp or college is not to be deemed a residence away from the residence of the Father/Mother, and, hence, such a residence at boarding school,

- 34 -

camp or college is not an Emancipation Event;

   (iv)   death of the child or the Father/Mother;

   (v)   entry into the armed forces of the United States (provided that the Emancipation Event shall be deemed terminated and nullified upon discharge from such forces and, thereafter, the period shall be the applicable period as if such an Emancipation Event by reason of the entry had not occurred);

   (vi)   engaging in full-time employment upon and after the attaining by a child of eighteen (18) years of age, except and provided that (1) by engaging by a child in partial employment shall not be deemed an Emancipation Event; and (2) engaging by a child in full-time employment during vacation and summer periods shall not be deemed an Emancipation Event. Such an Emancipation Event shall be deemed terminated and nullified upon cessation by a child for any reason from full-time employment, and the period, if any, from such a termination until the soonest of any other Emancipation Event shall, for all purposes under this Stipulation of Settlement, be deemed a period prior to the occurrence of an Emancipation Event.

ARTICLE VIII: MEDICAL INSURANCE AND EXPENSE

The Husband/Wife agrees to maintain Blue Cross/Blue Shield, Major Medical or equivalent medical coverage and dental insurance as presently exists for the benefit of the child/children until each child attains the age of nineteen (19) years, or in the event said child/children is/are fully enrolled in college or post graduate school, then until such child completes his or her course of study in said institution.

OPTION:

The Husband/Wife agrees to take full advantage of any health related insurance benefit offered by any present and/or future employer (even if employee contribution is required) in order to provide maximum coverage for child/children.

In the event either parent advances money for medical and health related needs on behalf of any child, then the party who advances the money shall be entitled to receive reimbursement from the health-care provider and both parties agree that they will cooperate in completing and filing any form that may be reasonably required in order to process insurance reimbursement from the health-care provider. Each party agrees that immediately upon receipt of the insurance proceeds, that if said proceeds are due as reimbursement to the other party that they will forthwith remit said funds to the party who advanced said monies.

Any and all health-related expenses of the child/children not covered by any of the aforesaid policies of insurance, shall be

- 36 -

123-36

the responsibility of the Husband and the Wife, pro-rata to their respective incomes pursuant to CSSA.

Health-related expenses shall include, but not be limited to, medical, dental, orthodontic, psycho-therapeutic, prescription drug expense and the cost of prescription eyeglasses.

The parties agree that prior to incurring any extraordinary health related expense, except in emergency situations, that they will consult each other with respect to this matter and if agreement cannot be reached, they will submit the matter to a court of competent jurisdiction.

The Husband/Wife hereby assigns any and all rights he/she has to receive reimbursement from the insurance carrier for monies paid by the Husband/Wife on behalf of the child's/children's health care directly to the Husband/Wife, and hereby authorizes the insurance carrier to remit said refund monies directly to the Husband/Wife at the address so indicted by the Husband/Wife on the insurance claim form.

In the event of the Husband's/Wife's failure to so provide hospitalization and major medical insurance for the benefit of the child/children, he/she shall promptly pay, and forever save, hold harmless and indemnify the Husband/Wife on account of all charges reasonably and necessarily incurred by his/her on behalf of the child/children prior to the child's/children's emancipation for the child's/children's health care needs.

- 37 -

ARTICLE IX: COLLEGE EDUCATION

The parties agree that the parties and their child/children shall research all avenues of financial aid in order to utilize same.

The obligation, if any, of the parties, as hereinabove provided, shall continue until the child shall complete his or her college education, provided only that he or she shall pursue the same as a full-time student on a normally continuous basis, but in no event beyond the age of twenty-two (22) years.

The parties shall be credited with any and all sums which the child shall receive, or which shall be applied for the benefit of the child, by way of scholarships, grants in aid or any other benefits received by the child, and may apply the same towards their obligation to pay and provide for the child's college education expenses. Notwithstanding anything herein contained to the contrary, the parties' obligation to pay and provide for the college education expenses of the child/children shall be limited to what would be the cost of such college education expenses during the period of the child's attendance at college, had the child attended the State University at Albany in New York State.

College education expenses shall be defined as: tuition, room/board, books and reasonable costs such as travel and activity expenses, one (1) S.A.T. review course, the cost of the S.A.T. examination and the cost of four (4) applications to college.

- 38 -

OPTION:

The issue of college education will be preserved for future negotiation or court application.

The parties shall be responsible for reasonable college education expenses defined hereinabove on behalf of the infant children of the marriage pro-rata to their respective incomes and providing that each of the parties has the ability to make such pro-rata contributions.

ARTICLE X: SUPPORT, MAINTENANCE AND MEDICAL INSURANCE OF SPOUSE

The parties state that, in no event and under no circumstances, now or in the future, do either of them desire or require the other party to make any payment for his or her support, ordinary or extraordinary, directly or indirectly. The parties declare and acknowledge that each has been and is self-supporting and is capable of earning such sums as are reasonably required to maintain him or her in the standard of living which the parties had during the period that they resided together as Husband and Wife. The continued ability to have such earnings is not, however, a condition of any of the other provisions of this Article and shall not be deemed in any respect to impair the other provisions of this Article.

The Wife acknowledges that she is fully employed as a and presently earns $ per year.

The Husband acknowledges that he is fully employed as a and presently earns $ per year.

The Husband acknowledges that he is entitled to medical insurance through his place of employment and requests no contribution now or in the future from the Wife.

OPTION:

The Wife represents that she is entitled to medical insurance through her place of employment and requests no contribution now or in the future from the Husband.

OPTION:

- 40 -

The Husband/Wife acknowledges that he/she will be solely responsible to procure and maintain medical insurance for himself/herself.

OPTION:

The Husband covenants and agrees that he shall pay to the Wife the sum of $ per week as and for her support and maintenance until she remarries, lives with another man on a permanent basis, dies, or   years from the date of the execution of this Stipulation of Settlement, whichever event shall first occur.

All payments to be paid by the Husband to the Wife, as hereinabove provided, shall be by check, bank check or postal money order and, if not given directly, shall be mailed by the Husband to the Wife at her present address or at such other address as she may direct.

The payments required to be made by the Husband to the Wife, as hereinabove provided, shall commence the first Friday immediately following the execution of this Stipulation of Settlement and be paid on each successive Friday thereafter.

The parties have been advised that under Internal Revenue laws maintenance payments are deductible by the Husband and are includable by the Wife in her income and subject to the payment of incomes taxes.

OPTION:

Upon the parties' divorce, the Husband agrees, however, that he shall execute all documents necessary to effectuate

- 41 -

continuation coverage for a period of three (3) years, as provided for under Public Law 99-272, Title 10 - Private Health Insurance Coverage (also known as COBRA) for the Wife, including, without limitation, giving proper notice to his employer or insurance plan administrator, (OPTION) [and that the Husband will pay the premiums for the three-year period of time, or until the Wife's earlier demise, or remarriage. The Husband shall immediately authorize his employer to provide the Wife with written confirmation that she is covered under the insurance policy. The Husband shall also immediately authorize his employer to furnish the Wife, upon her request, any prescription cards, insurance forms, etc. for her to utilize. At the earliest of the three (3) aforesaid events, the Husband shall no longer be required to pay for medical insurance on behalf of the Wife, and the Wife shall be solely responsible for her medical insurance and for medical expenses.] at the Wife's option, which the Wife will exercise in writing, certified mail, return receipt requested, to the Husband at least sixty (60) days prior to the divorce. The Wife, however, shall pay and be responsible for all premiums on said insurance.

ARTICLE XI: INCOME TAXES

The parties have heretofore filed certain joint income tax returns (Federal and State).

The parties represent and warrant to each other that to the best of his or her knowledge, all Federal, State and local income taxes on all joint returns heretofore filed by the parties have been paid; that no interest or penalties are due with respect thereto; that no tax deficiency proceedings are pending or threatened against them and that no audit is pending with respect to any such return.

If there is any deficiency assessment on any of the aforesaid returns, each party shall give to the other immediate notice thereof in writing.

Each party hereby indemnifies and holds the other harmless from any claim, damage or expense arising out of any such deficiency assessment on any joint return heretofore or hereafter filed, except to the extent that any such claim or liability is attributable to the incorrect reporting by the other spouse of his or her income or deduction or to separate income of the other party not reflected in such return (in whole or in part), which claim shall be paid by the party responsible for such omission or incorrect information.

If, in connection with any joint income tax returns heretofore or hereafter filed by the parties there is a refund, the amount ultimately refunded shall be shared by the parties pro rata

to their respective incomes.

OPTION:

The parties agree to file joint tax returns for the year 1991 and equally share in any refund that may be due them.

If, in connection with any joint income tax returns heretofore or hereafter filed by the parties there is a deficiency assessment, the amount ultimately determined to be due thereon, including penalties and interest, shall be paid by the parties pro rata to their respective incomes at the time of the assessment, unless and to the extent that the same has been caused by the failure or neglect of the other party in disclosing any income which should have been included in said returns or to the extent that any deduction solely allocable to his/her income is disallowed, and to the Husband/Wife, to the extent that the same has not been caused by any such failure or neglect of the Husband/Wife, hereby indemnifies and agrees to save the Husband/Wife harmless against any such assessment, penalty or interest and expenses including, without limitation, attorneys and accountants fees in connection therewith. Each party agrees to cooperate fully with the other in the event of any audit or examination of the said joint tax returns by a taxing authority and agrees to furnish to the party being examined or his or her designees, promptly and without charge therefore, such papers, records, documents, authorizations and information as may be reasonably appropriate in the connection with said audit or examination.

- 44 -

ARTICLE XII: LIFE INSURANCE

The Husband/Wife agrees to maintain a life insurance policy in the sum of $ and to designate the child/children as irrevocable beneficiary/beneficiaries and the Husband/Wife as Trustee of the said policy until such time as the child/children are emancipated, at which time the Husband's/Wife's obligation to maintain said policy shall terminate.

The Husband/Wife represents and warrants that said policy is presently in full force and effect and that all premiums have been fully paid to the date hereof.

The Husband/Wife agrees to pay, or cause to be paid, all premiums, dues and/or assessment which may become due and owing on said life insurance policy at least fifteen (15) days prior to the end of the grace period for making said payments, and he/she shall deliver to the Husband/Wife prior to the said fifteen (15) day period written proof of payment thereof.

Upon the reasonable request of the Husband/Wife (not less often than once each year), the Husband/Wife shall provide the Husband/Wife documentation showing his/her full compliance with his/her obligations under this Article. In addition, the Husband/Wife hereby authorizes the Husband/Wife to obtain direct confirmation from any insurance carrier and/or any employer of his/her compliance with the provisions of this Article and agrees that, upon demand, he/she will execute and deliver to the Husband/Wife, without charge, whatever instruments, documents or

authorizations which may be necessary or desirable in order that he/she may obtain direct confirmation of the Husband's/Wife's compliance with this Article.

If the Husband/Wife shall default in the payment of any dues, premiums or assessments on any of such policies of insurance, the Husband/Wife shall have the right, but not the obligation, to pay the same. In the event the Husband/Wife shall pay any such dues, premiums or assessments, the Husband/Wife shall forthwith become indebted to the Husband/Wife in the sum or sums so paid, and such sum or sums shall be paid by the Husband/Wife to the Husband/Wife on the first day of the month immediately following the date of such payment.

If any of such policies of insurance are not in full force and effect at the time of the Husband's/Wife's death, or if for any reason the Husband/Wife does not receive the proceeds thereof to which he/she is entitled under the provisions of this Article, then, and notwithstanding anything to the contrary contained in this Stipulation of Settlement, the Husband/Wife shall have a creditor's claim against the Husband's/Wife's estate for the difference between the insurance proceeds which he/she should have received and the insurance proceeds which he/she actually receives upon the Husband's/Wife's death.

ARTICLE XIII: LEGAL REPRESENTATION

The Husband/Wife acknowledges that (s)he has been represented in the negotiation and preparation of the within Stipulation of Settlement by   . The Husband/Wife acknowledges that (s)he has been represented by   . Both parties represent that they are familiar with the terms of this Stipulation of Settlement and that they are acceptable to them. Each party agrees to pay any and all reasonable attorney's fees incurred by the other to enforce the terms of this Stipulation of Settlement in the event that the other party breaches the same.

OPTION: The Husband/Wife agrees to contribute the sum of $ towards the Husband's/Wife's counsel fees.

OPTION: Each party agrees to pay their respective attorneys at the time of execution of this Stipulation of Settlement.

ARTICLE XIV: NO MOLESTATION

Neither party shall, in any way, molest, disturb or trouble the other or interfere with the peace and comfort of the other or compel or seek to compel the other to associate, cohabit or dwell with him or her by any action or proceeding for the restoration of conjugal rights or by any means whatsoever.

ARTICLE XV: SEPARATE OWNERSHIP

Each party shall own, free of any claim or right of the other, all of the items of property, real, personal and mixed, of any kind, nature or description and wheresoever situate, which are now owned by him or her, or which are now in his or her name, or to which he or she or may be beneficially entitled or which may hereafter belong to or come to him or her with full power to him or to her to dispose of the same as fully and effectually in all respects and for all purposes as if he or she were unmarried, except as to those specific properties herein expressly provided for.

ARTICLE XVI: IMPLEMENTATION

Each party will, whenever requested by the other party, make, execute, acknowledge and deliver any instruments which are necessary to effectuate the provisions of this Stipulation of Settlement. Each party, in the event of the death of the other party, whether such party dies testate or intestate, will, whenever requested by the executors, administrators, or other legal representatives of the other party, execute, acknowledge or deliver any instrument which, in the opinion of said executors, administrators and other legal representatives are necessary to effectuate the waiver of his or her right of election against the Last Will and Testament of the other, courtesy and other rights to take as distributee, heir or next-of-kin and the like herein referred to.

ARTICLE XVII: MUTUAL RELEASE AND DISCHARGE OF CLAIMS

Subject to the provisions of this Stipulation of Settlement, each party hereto has remised, released and forever discharged and, by these presents, does for himself or herself or his or her heirs, legal representatives, executors, administrators and assigns, remise, release and forever discharge the other of and from all cause or causes of action, claims, rights or demands whatsoever in law or equity which either of the parties hereto ever had or now has against the other, except those arising out of this Stipulation of Settlement, and by any and all cause or causes of action for absolute divorce (non-financial aspects).

ARTICLE XVIII: MUTUAL RELEASE AND DISCHARGE OF CLAIMS IN ESTATES

The parties hereto each hereby waive, renounce, grant, remise and release to the other, forever, for all purposes whatsoever, all rights in the property, and equitable distribution or distributive award of marital property, all rights and interest which he or she may now have or hereafter acquire in the real or personal property or estate of the other wheresoever situate and whether acquired before or subsequent to the marriage of the parties or before or subsequent to the date of this Stipulation of Settlement, by reason of his or her inheritance of descent or by virtue of any decedent or state law or any statute or custom, or arising out of the marital relations, or for any other reason whatsoever, and each party hereby expressly waives and releases any right of election under the New York Estate, Powers and Trusts Law or any successor statute thereto, or any other law of any and all states, territories and jurisdiction, to take against the Last Will and Testament or codicils thereto of the other whatsoever, whether heretofore or hereafter executed, including, but not limited to, any right to elect to take, as against the same, the intestate share to which he or she would otherwise be entitled, and each party hereby renounces any and all right to administration of the estate of the other party, and further waives any right to be or become the legal representative of the other's estate. Each party hereby revokes any and all testamentary dispositions heretofore made by either party in favor of the other and each party further

- 52 -

renounces any such disposition or special bequest under any Last Will and Testament heretofore executed by the other.

Except as this Stipulation of Settlement otherwise provides, each of the parties shall have the right to dispose of his or her property, by Last Will and Testament, or otherwise as if he or she were unmarried and in case either party shall die intestate, the estate of such party, whether real, personal or mixed, shall belong to the person or persons who would have been entitled thereto if the surviving party had predeceased the other party and had died unmarried.

ARTICLE XIX: WAIVER AND RELEASE

The parties intend this Stipulation of Settlement to constitute an agreement pursuant to Domestic Relations Law, Section 236(B)(3). They intend this Stipulation of Settlement and its provisions to be in lieu of each of their respective rights, pursuant to all aspects of Domestic Relations Law, Section 236(B). Accordingly, except to the extent provided in this Stipulation of Settlement, the parties mutually waive their rights and release each other from any claims for maintenance, the pension of the other party, distribution of marital property, distributive awards, special relief or claims regarding separate property or increase in the value thereof, except as otherwise set forth herein.

The parties intend that their real and personal property division, as provided in this Stipulation of Settlement, shall be final and irrevocable. Unless the parties execute a formal amendment to this Stipulation of Settlement, in writing, it is their intention that the Wife's separate property shall forever remain hers and the Husband's separate property shall forever remain his notwithstanding (i) the reconciliation of the parties; (ii) the rescission or termination of this Stipulation of Settlement; or (iii) a remarriage of the parties, in the event they are divorced.

That each party is convinced that he or she knows the nature, extent and value of the other party's property and business interests. In the event the parties have not exchanged Statements

- 54 -

of Net Worth, the parties represent that the assets set forth in this Stipulation of Settlement represent the total assets of the parties, and in the event of the discovery of any asset owned by either of the parties subsequent to the execution of this Stipulation of Settlement, then such asset shall be subject to equitable distribution, notwithstanding the execution of this Stipulation of Settlement and the entry of a final Judgment of Divorce.

That the parties are aware of their rights to compel discovery and inspection of the other's books and records, business and personal; and of their right to have accountants, appraisers and further investigation into the other's business and property. That each party has elected not to take any further steps, themselves or through others, in connection with discovery, inspection, investigation, appraisal or evaluation of the other's business or property.

ARTICLE XX: ENTIRE UNDERSTANDING

This Stipulation of Settlement is entire and complete and except for the question of entitlement of each party to a divorce (non-financial issues), embodies all understandings and agreements between the parties; and no representations, agreements, promises, undertakings or warranties of any kind or nature have been made to the other to induce the making of this Stipulation of Settlement, except as are expressly set forth in this Stipulation of Settlement or any other document executed simultaneously herewith, and neither of the parties shall assert to the contrary that there is any other prior agreement, oral or written, existing between them. The parties acknowledge that each has had a full and complete opportunity with respect to obtaining any and all financial information of the other, and each is satisfied that this Stipulation of Settlement, and all of the terms and provisions hereof, is fair and equitable. Each party is also aware of the risks attendant to litigation. Each party expressly denies relying on any belief held by virtue of any alleged nondisclosure by the other, as a condition or as consideration for entering into this Stipulation of Settlement. The parties acknowledge that they are entering into this Stipulation of Settlement freely and voluntarily; that they have ascertained and weighed, to their complete satisfaction, all of the facts and circumstances likely to influence their judgment; that they have had the opportunity to obtain legal advice independently of each other; and that they are

aware of their respective legal rights and each understands the provisions hereof, and specifically of their rights under the existing laws of the State of New York as effective on and after July 19, 1980, concerning marital property, separate property, and other financial matters; that all the provisions hereof, as well as all questions pertaining thereto, have been fully and satisfactorily explained to them; that they have given due consideration to such provisions and questions; and that they clearly understand and assent to all the provisions hereof, and that this Stipulation of Settlement constitutes a fair and adequate settlement.

ARTICLE XXI: FULL DISCLOSURE

Both legal and practical effects of this Stipulation of Settlement in each and every respect and the financial status of the parties has been fully explained to both parties, and they both acknowledge that it is a fair and equitable agreement and is not the result of any fraud, duress or undue influence exercised by either party, and they further agree that this Stipulation of Settlement contains the entire understanding of the parties. There are no representations, warranties, promises, covenants or undertakings other than those expressly set forth herein.

ARTICLE XXII: INDEPENDENT COVENANTS

Each of the respective rights and obligations of the parties hereunder shall be deemed independent and may be enforced independently, irrespective of any of the other rights and obligations set forth herein.

ARTICLE XXIII: DEFAULT IN PAYMENTS OR OTHER OBLIGATIONS

In the event that either party defaults with respect to any payment of support or with respect to any other obligation under this Stipulation of Settlement, and said default is not remedied within ten (10) days after the sending of a written notice by registered mail to the defaulting party specifying said default, the defaulting party agrees to indemnify the other party against, and to reimburse him or her for any and all costs, expenses and reasonable attorney's fees resulting from or made necessary by the bringing of any suit or other proceeding or the defense thereof, or to enforce any of the terms or conditions of this Stipulation of Settlement to be performed or complied with by the defaulting party pursuant to this Stipulation of Settlement, provided such suit or other proceeding results in a judgment, decree or order in favor of the other party.

For the purpose of this Stipulation of Settlement, it is understood and agreed that in the event that a suit or other proceeding shall be instituted to enforce any of the terms, covenants or conditions of this Stipulation of Settlement, and after the institution of such action or proceeding, and before judgment is or can be entered, the defaulting party shall comply with such terms or conditions of this Stipulation of Settlement, then in that event, the suit, motion or proceeding so instituted shall be deemed to have resulted in a judgment, decree or order in favor of the non-defaulting party for the purpose of recovering

- 60 -

reasonable expenses including counsel fees.

ARTICLE XXIV: SOLEMNIZATION OF MARRIAGE

The parties acknowledge that the marriage was solemnized by a person designated in Section 11 (1) of the Domestic Relations Law and will take all steps solely within each of their power to remove any barrier to the remarriage of the other.

ARTICLE XXV: APPLICABILITY

All the provisions of this Stipulation of Settlement shall be binding upon the respective heirs, next-of-kin, executors, administrators and assigns.

- 63 -

ARTICLE XXVI: LEGAL INTERPRETATION

This Stipulation of Settlement shall be construed in accordance with the laws of the State of New York, entirely independent of the forum where it may come up for construction or enforcement. If a court of competent jurisdiction at any time holds that a portion of this Stipulation of Settlement is invalid, the remainder shall not be affected thereby and shall continue in full force and effect.

ARTICLE XXVII: RECONCILIATION AND MARITAL DECREES

Both parties agree, stipulate and consent that no judgment, order or decree in any action for divorce or separation, whether brought in the State of New York, or in any other state or country having jurisdiction of the parties hereto, shall make any provision for maintenance or affect the property rights of either party inconsistent with the provisions of this Stipulation of Settlement, But, if any provision be made in any judgment, order or decree which is inconsistent with the provisions of this Stipulation of Settlement, or imposes a different or greater obligation on either of the parties hereto than provided in this Stipulation of Settlement, the provisions of this Stipulation of Settlement shall take precedence and shall be the primary obligation of both of the parties hereto. It is further agreed that upon the trial of any action which may hereafter be instituted by either of the parties against the other for an absolute divorce in any court of competent jurisdiction, the party instituting the action shall read the provisions of this Stipulation of Settlement relating to custody, child support, visitation and maintenance into the record of such action as a Stipulation of Settlement between the parties as to the question of custody, child support, visitation and maintenance, such a provision specifically reciting in words or substance "ORDERED AND ADJUDGED, that the Stipulation of Settlement entered into between the parties, a copy of which is attached to and incorporated in this judgment by reference, shall

survive and shall not be merged therein **(OPTION:)** except for **the provisions of the Stipulation of Settlement that pertain to the obligation of the parties to contribute to child support and/or visitation which provisions shall become merged therein,** and the parties are hereby directed to comply with every legally enforceable term and provision of such Stipulation of Settlement, including any provision to submit an appropriate issue to arbitration before a single arbitrator, and the court retains jurisdiction of the matter concurrently with the Family Court for the purpose of specifically enforcing such of the provisions of that Stipulation of Settlement as are capable of specific enforcement, to the extent permitted by law, and of making such further judgment with respect to custody, child support, visitation and maintenance as it finds appropriate under the circumstances existing at the time application for that purpose is made to it, or both."

This Stipulation of Settlement shall not become void or terminated in the event the parties engage in marital relations, but shall become void and/or terminated only upon the execution of a document declaring said agreement to be void and/or terminated, and signed and acknowledged by both of the parties hereto.

ARTICLE XXVIII: ACKNOWLEDGMENT

The parties hereto acknowledge that they have both read this Stipulation of Settlement in its entirety prior to signing same.

IN WITNESS WHEREOF, the parties have hereunto set their hands and seals the day and year first written above.

_____

_____

STATE OF)
               ss.
COUNTY OF)

On this   day of   , 19   , before me personally came   to me known, and known to me to be the individual described in, and who executed the foregoing instrument, and she duly acknowledged to me that she executed the same.

_____
                                        Notary Public

STATE OF)
               ss.
COUNTY OF)

On this   day of   , 19   , before me personally came   to me known, and known to me to be the individual described in, and who executed the foregoing instrument, and he duly acknowledged to me that he executed the same.

_____
                                        Notary Public

NOTES

NOTES

NOTES

NOTES